COMPLETE
MathSmart

Contents

Level 1 – Basic Skills

Level 2 – Further Your Understanding

Dear Parent or Guardian,

Thank you for choosing our book to help sharpen your child's math skills. Our primary goal is to provide a learning experience that is both fun and rewarding. This aim has guided the development of the series in a few key ways.

Our *Complete MathSmart* series has been designed to help children achieve mathematical excellence. Each grade has 3 levels. In level 1, your child learns all the basic math concepts necessary for success in his or her grade. Key concepts are accompanied by helpful three-part introductions: "Read This" explains the concept, "Example" demonstrates the concept, and "Try It" lets your child put the concept to use. In level 2, and to a greater extent in level 3, these concepts are worked into relatable problem-solving questions. These offer a greater challenge and point children to the every-day usefulness of math skills.

Fun activities, lively illustrations, and real-world scenarios throughout the book help bring the concepts to life and engage your child. Additionally, the QR codes in the book link to motion graphics that explain key ideas in a fun and active way. After your child has completed the core content, they will find two assessment tests. These will test your child's general ability to apply the concepts learned, and prepare them for standardized testing. Finally, your child can use the answer key in the back of the book to improve by comparing his or her results and methods.

With the help of these features, we hope to provide an enriching learning experience for your child. We would love to hear your feedback, and encourage you to share any stories of how *Complete MathSmart* has helped your child improve his or her math skills and gain confidence in the classroom.

Your Partner in Education,
Popular Book Company (Canada) Limited

LEVEL 1
BASIC SKILLS

1 Exponents

• understanding exponents

Exponential notation is a simplified way of expressing repeated multiplication. A number written in this form is also called a power.

Example Identify the power, base, and exponent.

$$3^5$$

power = 3^5 base = 3 exponent = 5

Try It

$$4^3$$

power = ☐

base = ☐

exponent = ☐

Identify the base and exponent for each power.

	base	exponent
① 2^3	_____	_____
② 7^4	_____	_____
③ 5^2	_____	_____
④ 3^4	_____	_____
⑤ 10^6	_____	_____

Hints

The base of a power is the number being repeatedly multiplied.

The exponent is the number of times the base is multiplied.

e.g.   4 to the power of 3

$4\overset{3}{}$ ←— exponent
←— base

$4 \times 4 \times 4$ ←— 4 being multiplied
3 times

Write each multiplication sentence as a power. Then do the matching. Write the letters.

⑥

A _____ = $4 \times 4 \times 4 \times 4 \times 4 \times 4$ ◯ 5 to the power of 4

B _____ = $3 \times 3 \times 3 \times 3 \times 3 \times 3$ ◯ 6 to the fourth power

C _____ = $6 \times 6 \times 6 \times 6$ ◯ 8 to the power of 5

D _____ = $5 \times 5 \times 5 \times 5$ ◯ 3 to the sixth power

E _____ = $2 \times 2 \times 2 \times 2 \times 2 \times 2 \times 2$ ◯ 4 to the power of 6

F _____ = $8 \times 8 \times 8 \times 8 \times 8$ ◯ 2 to the seventh power

Write each multiplication sentence as a product of powers or vice versa.

It is common practice to write a product of powers in order from the power with the smallest base to the one with the greatest base.

e.g. $2 \times 2 \times 5 \times 5 \times 3 \times 3 \times 3$

$= \underline{2^2 \times 3^3 \times 5^2}$

starting with 2, the smallest base

⑦ $2 \times 2 \times 2 \times 3 \times 3 =$ _____ × _____

⑧ $4 \times 4 \times 5 \times 5 \times 5 \times 5 =$ _____

⑨ $3 \times 3 \times 3 \times 3 \times 4 \times 4 \times 4 =$ _____

⑩ $7 \times 7 \times 2 \times 2 \times 2 \times 2 \times 2 =$ _____

⑪ $5 \times 5 \times 3 \times 3 \times 3 \times 4 \times 4 =$ _____

⑫ $2 \times 2 \times 2 \times 7 \times 7 \times 5 \times 5 \times 5 \times 5 =$ _____

⑬ $3^3 \times 4^4 =$ _____

⑭ $5^2 \times 7^3 =$ _____

⑮ $2^4 \times 3^2 \times 5^3 =$ _____

⑯ $3^2 \times 4^5 \times 8^2 =$ _____

Evaluate.

Hints

Any number raised to the power of 1 is the number itself.

e.g. $99^1 = 99$

Any number raised to the power of 0 is 1.

e.g. $99^0 = 1$

⑰ $2^2 =$ _____

⑱ $3^3 =$ _____

⑲ $6^2 =$ _____

⑳ $2^4 =$ _____

㉑ $8^2 =$ _____

㉒ $9^2 =$ _____

㉓ $7^1 =$ _____

㉔ $5^1 =$ _____

㉕ $8^0 =$ _____

㉖ $4^0 =$ _____

㉗ $2^3 \times 3^2 =$ _____

㉘ $2^4 \times 5^2 =$ _____

㉙ $4^1 \times 5^2 =$ _____

㉚ $3^5 \times 10^0 =$ _____

㉛ $3^4 \times 4^0 \times 5^1 =$ _____

㉜ $2^6 \times 3^2 \times 7^0 =$ _____

㉝ $4^2 \times 5^1 \times 8^3 =$ _____

㉞ $2^5 \times 3^3 \times 5^2 =$ _____

Fill in the blanks with the correct base or exponent.

㉟ $3^{\square} = 81$

㊱ $64 = \square^2$

㊲ $1 = 35^{\square}$

㊳ $144 = \square^2$

㊴ $16 = \square^4$

㊵ $48 = 48^{\square}$

㊶ $2^4 = 4^{\square}$

㊷ $3^4 = 9^{\square}$

㊸ $8^2 = \square^6$

㊹ $2^{\square} \times 5^2 = 100$

㊺ $36 = 2^2 \times \square^2$

㊻ $2^{\square} \times 3^{\square} \times 5^{\square} = 90$

Compare the powers and write ">", "<", or "=" in the circles. Then put the powers in order from smallest to greatest.

㊼ a. $6^0 \bigcirc 1$ b. $2^1 \bigcirc 1$

c. $5^3 \bigcirc 1^5$ d. $0^7 \bigcirc 1^0$

e. $3^2 \bigcirc 1^3$ f. $10^0 \bigcirc 10^1$

g. $9^1 \bigcirc 1^9$ h. $12^0 \bigcirc 11^1$

i. $2^4 \bigcirc 2^5$ j. $3^3 \bigcirc 3^4$

k. $6^2 \bigcirc 6^3$ l. $7^2 \bigcirc 7^0$

m. $16^2 \bigcirc 4^4$ n. $8^1 \bigcirc 2^3$

Tips

For powers with the same base, the one with the greater exponent is greater.

e.g. $2^3 > 2^1$ — same base

For powers with the same exponent, the one with the greater base is greater.

e.g. $3^3 > 2^3$ — same exponent

㊽ a. 2^3 6^0 0^3 7^1

b. 1^{10} 10^1 5^2 2^2

_____ < _____ < _____ < _____

_____

c. 3^5 3^4 4^5 4^3

d. 3^5 3^3 5^1 5^3

_____

_____

e. 7^0 2^4 9^1 5^2

f. 2^5 3^4 5^2 4^3

_____

_____

Evaluate the powers of 10. Then write the values in words.

(49) **Powers of 10**

Power	In Numerals	In Words
10^0	1	one
10^1		
10^2		
10^3		
10^4		
10^5		
10^6		

Tips

The value of a power of 10 is equal to 1 followed by a number of zeros equal to the exponent.

e.g. $10^3 = 1000$

exponent = 3   3 zeros

Expand each number using powers of 10. Then write the expanded form in standard form.

Hints

Powers of 10 are special. They can be used to represent numbers in expanded form.

e.g. 237

$= 200 + 30 + 7$

$= 2 \times 100 + 3 \times 10 + 7 \times 1$

$= 2 \times 10^2 + 3 \times 10^1 + 7 \times 10^0$

(50) 324

$= 300 +$ ______ $+$ ______

$= 3 \times 100 +$ ______ $+$ ______

$= 3 \times 10^2 +$ ______ $+$ ______

(51) 5172

$= 5000 +$ ______ $+$ ______ $+$ ______

$= 5 \times 1000 +$ ______ $+$ ______ $+$ ______

$= 5 \times 10^3 +$ ______ $+$ ______ $+$ ______

(52) 813 = ______

(53) 709 = ______

(54) 1240 = ______

(55) 32 001 = ______

(56) 10 500 = ______

(57) $5 \times 10^2 + 4 \times 10^1 + 6 \times 10^0 =$ ______

(58) $9 \times 10^2 + 2 \times 10^0 =$ ______

(59) $7 \times 10^3 + 3 \times 10^1 + 4 \times 10^0 =$ ______

(60) $2 \times 10^3 + 5 \times 10^2 + 3 \times 10^0 =$ ______

(61) $5 \times 10^4 + 3 \times 10^2 + 2 \times 10^1 =$ ______

2 Scientific Notation

• using scientific notation

 Read This

Scientific notation is a way of writing a number as the product of a number between 1 and 10 and a power of 10. It is useful for writing very large or very small numbers.

Example Check the correct scientific notation.

3 900 000

A) 39×10^5

✓ B) 3.9×10^6

↑ between 1 and 10 ↑ power of 10

 Try It

256 000

A) 25.6×10^4

B) 2.56×10^5

Check the scientific notation of each number.

① 27 000 000

A) 270×10^5
B) 2.7×10^7
C) 27×10^6

② 150 000

A) 1.5×10^5
B) 15×10^4
C) 1.5×10^4

③ 621 000

A) 6.21×10^3
B) 621×10^3
C) 6.21×10^5

④ 8 000 000

A) 0.8×10^7
B) 80×10^5
C) 8×10^6

⑤ 78 000 000

A) 7.8×10^7
B) 78×10^6
C) 0.78×10^8

⑥ 206 000 000

A) 2.6×10^7
B) 206×10^6
C) 2.06×10^8

Match each number with the correct scientific notation.

⑦ 23 000 •

2 300 000 •

230 000 •

23 000 000 •

• 2.3×10^5

• 2.3×10^4

• 2.3×10^7

• 2.3×10^6

⑧ 8 300 000 •

83 000 000 •

830 000 •

830 000 000 •

• 8.3×10^5

• 8.3×10^8

• 8.3×10^6

• 8.3×10^7

Write each number in scientific notation or in standard form.

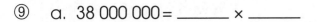

A number in scientific notation is a product of two numbers:

a number between 1 and 10	×	a power of 10

e.g. $130000. = 1.3 \times 10^5$

5 places to the left

⑨   a. $38\ 000\ 000 = \underline{\hspace{1cm}} \times \underline{\hspace{1cm}}$

b. $105\ 000 \quad = \underline{\hspace{2cm}}$

c. $4\ 200\ 000 = \underline{\hspace{2cm}}$

d. $198\ 000 \quad = \underline{\hspace{2cm}}$

e. $2\ 350\ 000 = \underline{\hspace{2cm}}$

f. $4\ 090\ 000 = \underline{\hspace{2cm}}$ g. $3\ 300\ 000 \quad = \underline{\hspace{2cm}}$

h. $81\ 000 \quad = \underline{\hspace{2cm}}$ i. $271\ 000\ 000 = \underline{\hspace{2cm}}$

⑩   a. $4.6 \times 10^3 \quad = \underline{\hspace{2cm}}$ b. $8.5 \times 10^5 \quad = \underline{\hspace{2cm}}$

c. $6.4 \times 10^4 \quad = \underline{\hspace{2cm}}$ d. $9.7 \times 10^4 \quad = \underline{\hspace{2cm}}$

e. $1.06 \times 10^3 = \underline{\hspace{2cm}}$ f. $4.08 \times 10^6 \quad = \underline{\hspace{2cm}}$

g. $6.3 \times 10^6 \quad = \underline{\hspace{2cm}}$ h. $2.07 \times 10^8 \quad = \underline{\hspace{2cm}}$

i. $3.9 \times 10^7 \quad = \underline{\hspace{2cm}}$ j. $4.29 \times 10^7 \quad = \underline{\hspace{2cm}}$

Look at the list of prices for each item. Circle the most expensive one on each list.

⑪

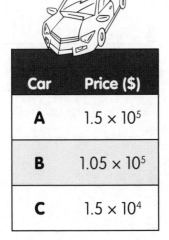

Car	Price ($)
A	1.5×10^5
B	1.05×10^5
C	1.5×10^4

⑫

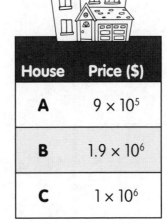

House	Price ($)
A	9×10^5
B	1.9×10^6
C	1×10^6

⑬

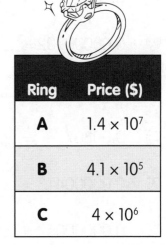

Ring	Price ($)
A	1.4×10^7
B	4.1×10^5
C	4×10^6

Check the scientific notation of each number.

⑭ 0.059

   Ⓐ 59×10^{-3}

   Ⓑ 5.9×10^{-2}

   Ⓒ 0.59×10^{-1}

⑮ 0.000064

   Ⓐ 6.4×10^{-5}

   Ⓑ 64×10^{-6}

   Ⓒ 6.4×10^{-6}

⑯ 0.000901

   Ⓐ 90.1×10^{-5}

   Ⓑ 9.01×10^{-4}

   Ⓒ 9.01×10^{-6}

⑰ 0.0612

   Ⓐ 6.12×10^{-2}

   Ⓑ 61.2×10^{-3}

   Ⓒ 6.12×10^{-4}

⑱ 0.00093

   Ⓐ 9.3×10^{-5}

   Ⓑ 9.3×10^{-3}

   Ⓒ 9.3×10^{-4}

⑲ 0.00000272

   Ⓐ 2.72×10^{-6}

   Ⓑ 2.72×10^{-8}

   Ⓒ 0.272×10^{-5}

Write each number in scientific notation or in standard form.

⑳ 0.0052 = _____

㉑ 0.00013 = _____

㉒ 0.0009 = _____

㉓ 0.00000102 = _____

㉔ 0.00088 = _____

㉕ 0.00307 = _____

㉖ 0.00000413 = _____

㉗ 0.00000052 = _____

㉘ 7.1×10^{-3} = _____

㉙ 1.2×10^{-4} = _____

㉚ 8.5×10^{-5} = _____

㉛ 1.33×10^{-3} = _____

㉜ 9.72×10^{-4} = _____

㉝ 8.06×10^{-6} = _____

㉞ 4.08×10^{-6} = _____

㉟ 2.7×10^{-8} = _____

Fill in the blanks with the measurements in scientific notation.

③⑥   **The Earth and the Moon**

a. Diameter

- Earth: 13 000 km or _____ km

- moon: 3500 km or _____ km

b. Distance

- between Earth and moon: 384 000 km or _____ km

- between Earth and Sun: 149 600 000 km or _____ km

③⑦   **Microscopic Organisms and Cells**

a. Diameter

- a red blood cell: 0.00072 cm or _____ cm

- a bacterium: 0.00005 cm or _____ cm

- a virus: 0.000011 cm or _____ cm

b. The diameter of a white blood cell is about twice that of a red blood cell. Its diameter is about _____ cm.

③⑧   **Electromagnetic Spectrum**

The wavelengths of different waves:

a. radio waves – instant communication

- from 0.001 m or _____ m to more than 100 000 m or _____ m

b. visible light rays – all the colours that we can see

- from 0.00000038 m or _____ m to 0.0000007 m or _____ m

c. x-rays – penetrating radiation

- from 0.000000003 cm or _____ cm to 0.0000003 cm or _____ cm

3 Prime Factorization

• using prime factorization

Read This **Prime factorization is a way of expressing a number as a product of its prime factors.**

Example Find the prime factors of 8 using a factor tree.

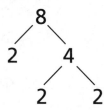

$8 = 2 \times 2 \times 2$

prime numbers

$6 = \underline{\hspace{1cm}} \times \underline{\hspace{1cm}}$

Find the prime factors of the numbers.

①

$4 = \underline{\hspace{2cm}}$

②

$9 = \underline{\hspace{2cm}}$

③ 10

$10 = \underline{\hspace{2cm}}$

④ 14

$14 = \underline{\hspace{2cm}}$

⑤ 15

$15 = \underline{\hspace{2cm}}$

⑥ 21

$21 = \underline{\hspace{2cm}}$

⑦ 25

$25 = \underline{\hspace{2cm}}$

⑧ 35

$35 = \underline{\hspace{2cm}}$

⑨ 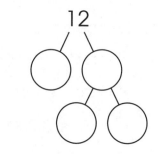 12

$12 = \underline{\hspace{3cm}}$

⑩ 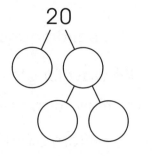 20

$20 = \underline{\hspace{3cm}}$

⑪ 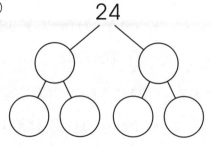 24

$24 = \underline{\hspace{3cm}}$

Write each number as a product of prime factors.
Then find the greatest common factors.

⑫   10 = _____   **GCF**

      15 = _____

⑬   16 = _____   **GCF**

      28 = _____

⑭   18 = _____   **GCF**

      32 = _____

⑮   30 = _____   **GCF**

      40 = _____

⑯   36 = _____   **GCF**   ⑰   15 = _____   **GCF**

      45 = _____   40 = _____

      60 = _____   50 = _____

Hints

Finding the greatest common factor (GCF) of a set of numbers:

❶ Identify their common prime factors.

❷ Multiply the common prime factors.

e.g.   Find the GCF of 12 and 30.

$$12 = 2 \times 2 \times 3$$
$$30 = 2 \times 3 \times 5$$
$$2 \times 3 = 6$$

GCF of 12 and 30: 6

Draw your factor trees here.

Find the least common multiple of each set of numbers using prime factorization.

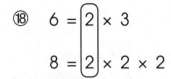

Hints

Finding the least common multiple (LCM) using prime factorization:

❶ Write the prime factors of each number and circle the common ones.

❷ List the prime factors, counting each circled group of factors only once.

❸ Multiply the factors on the list.

e.g. Find the LCM of 4, 6, and 18.

❶ 4 = $\boxed{2}$ × 2
   6 = $\boxed{2}$ × $\boxed{3}$
   18 = $\boxed{2}$ × $\boxed{3}$ × 3

counts as one 2 ↗   ↖ counts as one 3

❷ List: 2, 2, 3, 3

❸ 2 × 2 × 3 × 3 = 36

LCM of 4, 6, and 18: 36

⑱ 6 = $\boxed{2}$ × 3

8 = $\boxed{2}$ × 2 × 2

List: _____ , _____ , _____ , _____

LCM: _____ × _____ × _____ × _____ = _____

⑲ 12 = 2 × 2 × 3

20 = 2 × 2 × 5

List: _____

LCM: _____

⑳ 18 = 2 × 3 × 3

24 = 2 × 2 × 2 × 3

List: _____

LCM: _____

㉑ 18 = 2 × 3 × 3

30 = 2 × 3 × 5

List: _____

LCM: _____

㉒ 8 = 2 × 2 × 2

12 = 2 × 2 × 3

30 = 2 × 3 × 5

List: _____

LCM: _____

㉓ 16 = 2 × 2 × 2 × 2

24 = 2 × 2 × 2 × 3

36 = 2 × 2 × 3 × 3

List: _____

LCM: _____

Write each number as a product of prime factors. Then find the least common multiples.

㉔   20 = _____

       30 = _____

       LCM: _____

㉕   16 = _____

       36 = _____

       LCM: _____

㉖   14 = _____

       28 = _____

       LCM: _____

㉗   25 = _____

       45 = _____

       LCM: _____

㉘   21 = _____

       35 = _____

       LCM: _____

㉙   48 = _____

       60 = _____

       LCM: _____

Find the GCF and LCM for each pair of numbers using prime factorization. Then answer the question.

㉚   100 = _____

       120 = _____

       150 = _____

       180 = _____

       210 = _____

G C F
- 100 and 150: _____
- 100 and 180: _____
- 150 and 210: _____

L C M
- 120 and 180: _____
- 150 and 180: _____
- 180 and 210: _____

㉛   The GCF and LCM of a set of numbers can be found by using prime factorization or by listing out the factors and multiples. Which way do you think is easier? Explain your choice.

_____

_____

_____

Tips

Prime factorization:
$12 = 2 \times 2 \times 3$

_____

Listing out the factors and multiples:

Factors of 12:
1, 2, 3, 4, 6, 12
Multiples of 12:
12, 24, 36, 48…

4 Squares and Square Roots

• using squares and square roots

Squares and square roots are opposite operations.

Example Evaluate.

4^2

$= 4 \times 4$

$= 16$

$\sqrt{16}$

$= \sqrt{4 \times 4}$

$= 4$

Try It

Check the correct answers.

3^2	$\sqrt{9}$
(A) 9	(A) 9
(B) 6	(B) 3
(C) 3	(C) $\sqrt{3}$

Find the first 20 squares and square roots.

First 20 Squares

① 1^2 = _____ 11^2 = _____

2^2 = _____ 12^2 = _____

3^2 = _____ 13^2 = _____

4^2 = _____ 14^2 = _____

5^2 = _____ 15^2 = _____

6^2 = _____ 16^2 = _____

7^2 = _____ 17^2 = _____

8^2 = _____ 18^2 = _____

9^2 = _____ 19^2 = _____

10^2 = _____ 20^2 = _____

First 20 Square Roots

② $\sqrt{1}$ = _____ $\sqrt{121}$ = _____

$\sqrt{4}$ = _____ $\sqrt{144}$ = _____

$\sqrt{9}$ = _____ $\sqrt{169}$ = _____

$\sqrt{16}$ = _____ $\sqrt{196}$ = _____

$\sqrt{25}$ = _____ $\sqrt{225}$ = _____

$\sqrt{36}$ = _____ $\sqrt{256}$ = _____

$\sqrt{49}$ = _____ $\sqrt{289}$ = _____

$\sqrt{64}$ = _____ $\sqrt{324}$ = _____

$\sqrt{81}$ = _____ $\sqrt{361}$ = _____

$\sqrt{100}$ = _____ $\sqrt{400}$ = _____

Determine the ones digit of the squared numbers without using a calculator.

③ $37^2 = 136\underline{\hspace{1em}}$

④ $23^2 = 52\underline{\hspace{1em}}$

⑤ $25^2 = 62\underline{\hspace{1em}}$

⑥ $48^2 = 230\underline{\hspace{1em}}$

⑦ $50^2 = 250\underline{\hspace{1em}}$

⑧ $39^2 = 152\underline{\hspace{1em}}$

⑨ $41^2 = 168\underline{\hspace{1em}}$

⑩ $26^2 = 67\underline{\hspace{1em}}$

⑪ $34^2 = 115\underline{\hspace{1em}}$

⑫ $52^2 = 270\underline{\hspace{1em}}$

⑬ $47^2 = 220\underline{\hspace{1em}}$

⑭ $33^2 = 108\underline{\hspace{1em}}$

Tips

The ones digit of a squared number is the same as the ones digit of the square of its square root's ones digit.

e.g. $3\underline{9}^2 = 152\mathbf{1}$
↑
$9^2 = 8\mathbf{1}$

Check the better estimate of each square root. Then estimate and find the actual answers using a calculator.

⑮ $\sqrt{20}$
Ⓐ 4.5
Ⓑ 5.1

⑯ $\sqrt{40}$
Ⓐ 5.7
Ⓑ 6.3

Tips

To estimate the square root of a number, find its two closest perfect squares first.

e.g. Estimate $\sqrt{30}$.

$\sqrt{30} \approx 5.5$
↑ ↑
between between
$\sqrt{25}$ and $\sqrt{36}$ 5 and 6

⑰ $\sqrt{35}$
Ⓐ 5.9
Ⓑ 6.1

⑱ $\sqrt{45}$
Ⓐ 5.5
Ⓑ 6.7

⑲ $\sqrt{60}$
_____
estimate
_____
actual

⑳ $\sqrt{78}$
_____
estimate
_____
actual

㉑ $\sqrt{119}$
_____
estimate
_____
actual

㉒ $\sqrt{89}$
_____
estimate
_____
actual

㉓ $\sqrt{175}$
_____
estimate
_____
actual

㉔ $\sqrt{240}$
_____
estimate
_____
actual

LEVEL 1 – BASIC SKILLS

Put each group of numbers in order from smallest to greatest.

㉕ 8 $\sqrt{81}$ $\sqrt{49}$ 6

㉖ $\sqrt{110}$ 11 $\sqrt{120}$ 12

_____

_____

㉗ 16^2 $\sqrt{260}$ 130 $\sqrt{169}$

㉘ 12 $\sqrt{150}$ 4^2 $\sqrt{120}$

_____

_____

Find the answers.

㉙ $\sqrt{7^2}$ = _____

㉚ $\sqrt{7}^2$ = _____

㉛ $\sqrt{11^2}$ = _____

㉜ $\sqrt{10}^2$ = _____

㉝ $\sqrt{8}^2$ = _____

㉞ $\sqrt{21^2}$ = _____

㉟ $\sqrt{38^2}$ = _____

㊱ $\sqrt{19}^2$ = _____

㊲ $\sqrt{45}^2$ = _____

㊳ $\sqrt{51^2}$ = _____

㊴ $\sqrt{64^2}$ = _____

㊵ $\sqrt{75}^2$ = _____

Hints

The square root of a number squared is the number itself.

e.g. $\sqrt{5^2}$ = 5
         ↑
     $\sqrt{5 \times 5}$

The square of the square root of a number is the number itself.

e.g. $\sqrt{5}^2$ = 5
         ↑
     $\sqrt{5} \times \sqrt{5}$

Evaluate. Show your work.

㊶ $\sqrt{18 \times 2}$

= $\sqrt{}$

=

㊷ $\sqrt{98 \div 2}$

㊸ $\sqrt{25 \times 4}$

㊹ $\sqrt{96 \div 6}$

Hints

Square roots can be multiplied and divided.

e.g. $\sqrt{4} \times \sqrt{9} = \sqrt{4 \times 9} = \sqrt{36} = 6$

$\sqrt{20} \div \sqrt{5} = \sqrt{20 \div 5} = \sqrt{4} = 2$

㊺ $\sqrt{5} \times \sqrt{20}$

$= \sqrt{\square \times \square}$

$= \sqrt{\square}$

$= \square$

㊻ $\sqrt{2} \times \sqrt{18}$

㊼ $\sqrt{108} \div \sqrt{3}$

㊽ $\sqrt{100} \div \sqrt{4}$

㊾ $\sqrt{147} \div \sqrt{3}$

㊿ $\sqrt{5} \times \sqrt{9 \times 5}$

(51) $(\sqrt{2} \times \sqrt{8})^2$

(52) $\sqrt{200 \div 2} - 10$

Tips

Order of operations:

Brackets

Exponents
(includes square roots)

Division

Multiplication

Addition

Subtraction

(53) $3^2 + \sqrt{9^2}$

(54) $(6 - 1)^2 - \sqrt{9}$

(55) $\sqrt{12 + 4} + 7$

(56) $(2 \times 3)^2 - \sqrt{12 \div 3}$

(57) $3 \times \sqrt{25} - 18 \div \sqrt{4}$

(58) $\sqrt{41}^2 - \sqrt{256}$

(59) $\sqrt{13^2 - 12^2} + 2$

(60) $(\sqrt{64} \div \sqrt{16})^2$

5 Fractions

• multiplying and dividing fractions

Read This **To multiply fractions, multiply their numerators and denominators separately. Then simplify.**

Example Find the product.

$$\frac{1}{2} \times \frac{2}{5}$$

$$= \frac{1 \times 2}{2 \times 5} \quad \leftarrow \text{Multiply numerators.}$$
$$\qquad\qquad \leftarrow \text{Multiply denominators.}$$

$$= \frac{2}{10}$$

$$= \frac{1}{5} \quad \leftarrow \text{in simplest form}$$

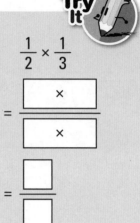

Multiply. Show your work.

① $\frac{1}{3} \times \frac{2}{3}$

② $\frac{3}{4} \times \frac{2}{5}$

③ $\frac{5}{6} \times \frac{2}{5}$

④ $\frac{2}{7} \times \frac{3}{4}$

⑤ $6 \times \frac{7}{12}$

⑥ $\frac{4}{5} \times \frac{3}{4}$

⑦ $2\frac{1}{4} \times \frac{1}{3}$

⑧ $\frac{3}{5} \times 1\frac{1}{6}$

Tips Change all mixed numbers into improper fractions before multiplying.

⑨ $2\frac{3}{4} \times 1\frac{1}{3}$

⑩ $1\frac{1}{5} \times 2\frac{3}{4}$

e.g. $1\frac{2}{3} \times \frac{2}{5}$

$$= \frac{5}{3} \times \frac{2}{5} \quad \leftarrow \text{Converted } 1\frac{2}{3} \text{ into } \frac{5}{3}.$$

$$= \frac{10}{15}$$

$$= \frac{2}{3}$$

Reduce the fractions before multiplying.
Show your work.

⑪ $\dfrac{4}{9} \times \dfrac{3}{8}$

⑫ $\dfrac{9}{10} \times \dfrac{5}{6}$

⑬ $1\dfrac{1}{8} \times \dfrac{2}{15}$

⑭ $2\dfrac{4}{5} \times 1\dfrac{3}{7}$

Tips

Reducing the fractions before multiplying makes the calculation easier.

e.g.

$$\dfrac{2}{3} \times \dfrac{1}{4}$$

$$= \dfrac{{}^1\!\!\!\diagup\!\!2}{3} \times \dfrac{1}{\diagup\!\!4\,_2}$$

$$= \dfrac{1 \times 1}{3 \times 2}$$

$$= \dfrac{1}{6}$$

Multiply. Then match the answers with the letters to see what Jenny says.

⑮ $\dfrac{3}{8} \times \dfrac{2}{5}$ = _____ [m]

⑯ $\dfrac{6}{7} \times \dfrac{1}{3}$ = _____ [i]

⑰ $\dfrac{7}{10} \times 2\dfrac{1}{2}$ = _____ [o]

⑱ $3\dfrac{1}{6} \times 5$ = _____ [r]

⑲ $\dfrac{4}{5} \times 1\dfrac{1}{3}$ = _____ [h]

⑳ $6 \times 1\dfrac{3}{5}$ = _____ [g]

㉑ $1\dfrac{2}{3} \times 2\dfrac{1}{4}$ = _____ [u]

㉒ $\dfrac{4}{5} \times \dfrac{1}{6}$ = _____ [s]

㉓ $2\dfrac{5}{8} \times \dfrac{1}{9}$ = _____ [f]

㉔ $4\dfrac{2}{7} \times 1\dfrac{3}{5}$ = _____ [T]

㉕ $3\dfrac{1}{3} \times 2\dfrac{1}{5}$ = _____ [n]

㉖ $\dfrac{4}{15} \times \dfrac{3}{8}$ = _____ [l]

㉗ $1\dfrac{2}{7} \times 1\dfrac{3}{4}$ = _____ [e]

㉘

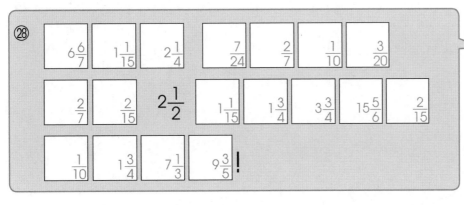

$6\dfrac{6}{7}$	$1\dfrac{1}{15}$	$2\dfrac{1}{4}$	$\dfrac{7}{24}$	$\dfrac{2}{7}$	$\dfrac{1}{10}$	$\dfrac{3}{20}$
$\dfrac{2}{7}$	$\dfrac{2}{15}$	$2\dfrac{1}{2}$	$1\dfrac{1}{15}$	$1\dfrac{3}{4}$	$3\dfrac{3}{4}$	$15\dfrac{5}{6}$	$\dfrac{2}{15}$
$\dfrac{1}{10}$	$1\dfrac{3}{4}$	$7\dfrac{1}{3}$	$9\dfrac{3}{5}$!

Jenny

Write the reciprocals.

㉙ $\frac{2}{5}$ ________

㉚ $\frac{3}{4}$ ________

㉛ $\frac{1}{6}$ ________

㉜ 4 ________

㉝ $\frac{8}{5}$ ________

㉞ $\frac{7}{2}$ ________

㉟ $1\frac{1}{4}$ ________

㊱ $2\frac{1}{5}$ ________

Divide. Show your work.

㊲ $\frac{3}{5} \div \frac{1}{2}$

㊳ $\frac{4}{3} \div \frac{2}{3}$

㊴ $\frac{5}{6} \div 2$

㊵ $4 \div \frac{3}{4}$

㊶ $1\frac{5}{6} \div \frac{1}{2}$

㊷ $2\frac{1}{3} \div 1\frac{1}{4}$

㊸ $5 \div 2\frac{1}{5}$

㊹ $3\frac{1}{3} \div 4$

㊺ $2\frac{1}{8} \div \frac{1}{4}$

Hints

The reciprocal of a fraction has its numerator and denominator swapped.

e.g. $\frac{1}{4}$ ←reciprocal→ $\frac{4}{1}$

Hints

Dividing fractions:

❶ Write mixed numbers as improper fractions.

❷ Change ÷ to × and the divisor to its reciprocal.

❸ Multiply and simplify.

e.g. $2\frac{2}{3} \div \frac{5}{6}$

$= \frac{8}{3} \div \frac{5}{6}$ ← Change mixed numbers to improper fractions.

$= \frac{8}{{}_1\cancel{3}} \times \frac{\cancel{6}^{\,2}}{5}$ ← Change ÷ to × and the divisor to reciprocal.

$= \frac{8 \times 2}{1 \times 5}$ ← Multiply and simplify.

$= \frac{16}{5}$

$= 3\frac{1}{5}$

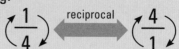

Multiply or divide.

㊻ $3\frac{1}{2} \div 1\frac{1}{4} =$ _____

㊼ $2\frac{1}{2} \times \frac{1}{5} =$ _____

㊽ $\frac{3}{10} \times 2\frac{4}{5} =$ _____

㊾ $6\frac{2}{3} \div 1\frac{1}{4} =$ _____

㊿ $3\frac{3}{5} \div 1\frac{4}{5} =$ _____

51   $1\frac{3}{4} \times \frac{5}{14} =$ _____

52   $7\frac{1}{2} \times \frac{1}{10} =$ _____

53   $3\frac{5}{9} \div 2\frac{2}{3} =$ _____

54   $4\frac{5}{6} \div 2\frac{1}{3} =$ _____

55   $1\frac{3}{8} \times 1\frac{1}{5} =$ _____

Evaluate. Show your work.

56   $(\frac{3}{10} + 1\frac{1}{2}) \times 3\frac{1}{2}$

57   $2\frac{1}{3} \div (4 - 2\frac{1}{4})$

58   $2\frac{1}{2} \times \frac{5}{9} \times \frac{3}{10}$

59   $2\frac{2}{3} \div 1\frac{2}{5} \times 2\frac{2}{5}$

60   $2\frac{3}{4} + 3\frac{1}{5} \div 1\frac{1}{5}$

61   $4\frac{5}{6} \div 2\frac{2}{3} - \frac{3}{4}$

62   $(4\frac{1}{10} + 2\frac{1}{5}) \div (2\frac{1}{15} - \frac{2}{3})$

63   $5\frac{5}{6} \div 2\frac{1}{3} \div 1\frac{1}{4} + 3\frac{1}{2}$

6 Decimals

Read This

Always align the decimal points when doing addition or subtraction, regardless of how many decimal places there are.

Example 4.85 − 1.319 = ?

$$
\begin{array}{r}
4.85\boxed{0} \leftarrow \text{placeholder}\\
-\quad 1.319\\
\hline
\boxed{3.531}
\end{array}
$$

Try It

3.15 + 1.254 = ?

$$
\begin{array}{r}
3.150\\
+\quad 1.254\\
\hline

\end{array}
$$

Find the answers. Show your work.

① 10.25 + 4.151 = _____

② 8.252 − 3.041 = _____

③ 25.114 + 8.203 = _____

④ 15.32 − 9.442 = _____

⑤ 20.349 + 18.23 = _____

⑥ 61.68 − 27.193 = _____

⑦ 4.89 + 11.241 = _____

⑧ 5.94 − 2.114 = _____

⑨ 18.39 − 12.005 = _____

⑩ 3.41 + 2.599 = _____

+ _____

Add or subtract.

⑪ 0.376 + 13.01 = _____

⑫ 10 − 0.194 = _____

⑬ 20.48 + 19.09 = _____

⑭ 31.05 − 7.223 = _____

⑮ 256 − 135.45 = _____

⑯ 34.025 + 6.18 = _____

⑰ 45.188 + 3.95 = _____

⑱ 28.175 − 17.88 = _____

⑲ 30.365 − 4.94 = _____

⑳ 55.49 + 156.7 = _____

㉑ 200.33 + 87.852 = _____

㉒ 240 − 189.37 = _____

㉓ 480 − 176.23 = _____

㉔ 39.99 + 147.25 = _____

Multiply.

㉕
```
    1.8 3
×       3
```

㉖
```
    2 1.2
×     4.8
```

Tips

The number of decimal places in the product is the sum of the decimal places in the question.

e.g.
```
    5 2.0 4   ← 2 decimal places
×       1.7   ← 1 decimal places
    8 8.4 6 8 ← 3 decimal places
```

㉗
```
    3.0 2
×     2 5
```

㉘
```
    3 0.4
×     1.7
```

㉛ 10.425 × 8 = _____

㉜ 0.82 × 6.25 = _____

㉝ 4.85 × 2.4 = _____

㉙
```
    2.3 8
×     2.5
```

㉚
```
    1 5.3 5
×       4.1
```

㉞ 2.9 × 1.88 = _____

㉟ 3.38 × 2.05 = _____

㊱ 10.49 × 3.6 = _____

Divide. Show your work.

㊲ **A** $19.8 \div 4$ = _____

B $10.35 \div 0.5$ = _____

C $16.24 \div 0.08$ = _____

D $1.743 \div 0.7$ = _____

E $6.593 \div 1.9$ = _____

F $5.712 \div 1.02$ = _____

G $1.836 \div 0.34$ = _____

H $1.694 \div 0.28$ = _____

Make sure the divisor in a division question is a whole number.

e.g.

$2.408 \div \boxed{0.4} = ?$

Rewrite.

Change it to a whole number by moving the decimal point 1 place to the right.

$24.08 \div 4 = ?$

$$\begin{array}{r} 6.02 \\ 4\overline{)24.08} \\ \underline{24} \\ 8 \\ \underline{8} \end{array}$$

$2.408 \div 0.4 = \underline{6.02}$

Evaluate. Show your work. Then do the operations with the answers to find the weight of each child.

③⑧ **A** 4.75 + 2.5 × 1.13

B 9.3 ÷ 0.03 − 0.94

C 3.3 × (7.54 − 6.27)

D (3.1 + 7.4) × (2.4 − 1.6)

③⑨ **A** 5.06 + 7.33 − 1.48

B 3.6 × 1.5 ÷ 0.6

C (8 − 2.05) ÷ 1.7

D 2.07 ÷ 0.46 × 7.19

Amy's Weight

C + **B** ÷ **A** − **D**

[ ] + [ ] ÷ [ ] − [ ]

_____ kg

Tom's Weight

D − **A** × **C** − **B**

([ ] − [ ]) × [ ] − [ ]

_____ kg

LEVEL 1 – BASIC SKILLS

7 Percents

• using percents

Read This

To find a part of a set with the given percent, use multiplication.

Example What is 15% of 20?

$20 \times 15\%$

$= 20 \times 0.15$ ← 15% = 0.15

$= 3$

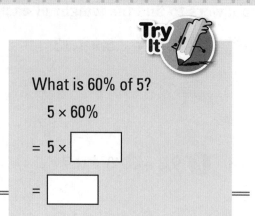

Try It

What is 60% of 5?

$5 \times 60\%$

$= 5 \times \boxed{}$

$= \boxed{}$

Find the answers.

① 50% of 7

② 8% of 25

③ 12% of 50

④ 37.5% of 24

⑤ 0.5% of 200

⑥ 0.4% of 250

Complete each diagram to find how many blocks each child has in total. Then answer the questions.

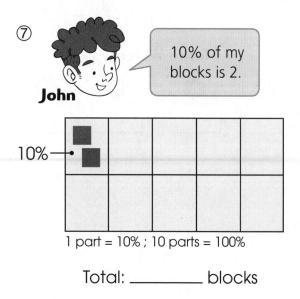

⑦ **John**

10% of my blocks is 2.

10% →

1 part = 10% ; 10 parts = 100%

Total: _____ blocks

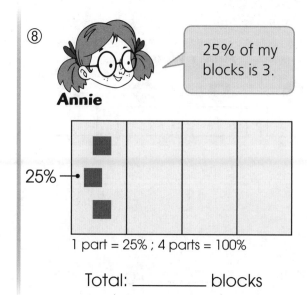

⑧ **Annie**

25% of my blocks is 3.

25% →

1 part = 25% ; 4 parts = 100%

Total: _____ blocks

⑨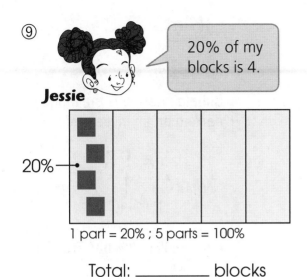

Jessie

20% of my blocks is 4.

20%→

1 part = 20% ; 5 parts = 100%

Total: _____ blocks

⑩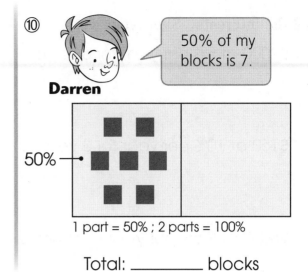

Darren

50% of my blocks is 7.

50%→

1 part = 50% ; 2 parts = 100%

Total: _____ blocks

⑪ How many blocks are there in

a. 25% of John's blocks? _____ blocks

b. 50% of Annie's blocks? _____ blocks

Determine whether each change is an increase or a decrease and fill in the blanks. Then find the change in percent.

⑫ $2500 to $4000

- **increase / decrease** of $_____

- change = $\dfrac{}{2500} \times 100\% =$ _____%

⑬ 120 kg to 90 kg

- _____ of _____ kg

- change = $\dfrac{}{} \times 100\% =$ _____%

Hints

If the new value is greater than the original value, the change in percent is an increase; otherwise, it is a decrease.

Change in percent:

$\dfrac{\text{difference in values}}{\text{original value}} \times 100\%$

⑭ 16°C to 24°C

- _____ of _____°C

- change = $\dfrac{}{} \times 100\%$

= _____%

⑮ 64 people to 72 people

- _____ of _____ people

- change = $\dfrac{}{} \times 100\%$

= _____%

Find the interests. Show your work.

⑯ $2000 at 5% per year for 6 years

⑰ $150 at 10% per year for 3 years

⑱ $5000 at 2.5% per year for 5 years

⑲ $3500 at 4.8% per year for 2 years

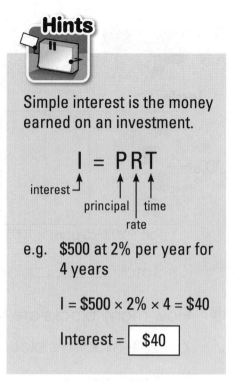

Simple interest is the money earned on an investment.

I = PRT

interest — principal | time | rate

e.g. $500 at 2% per year for 4 years

I = $500 × 2% × 4 = $40

Interest = | $40 |

Ann and Sam have some investment plans to choose from. Complete the table. Then answer the questions.

⑳

	Plan	Principal	Interest Rate	Time (years)	Simple Interest
Ann	A	$5000	2%	4	$5000 × 2% × 4 = _____
Ann	B	$2000	5%	2	
Ann	C	$3000	3%	5	
Sam	A	$3000	5%	2	
Sam	B	$5000	4%	3	
Sam	C	$1000	13.5%	1	

㉑   Which plan yields the most interest for each person? Circle the letters.

㉒   Ann has $5000. She can either invest it all in Plan A, or split it into Plan B and Plan C. In which way will she earn more interest? By how much?

Find the totals. Show your work.

㉓ 20% discount on $80

Amount saved: _____

Sale price: _____

㉔ 13% tax on $50

Tax amount: _____

Total price: _____

㉕ 15% discount on $300

Amount saved: _____

Sale price: _____

㉖ 7% tax on $110

Tax amount: _____

Total price: _____

Hints

A discount is an amount subtracted from a regular price.

e.g. 10% discount on $200

Amount saved:
$200 × 10% = $20

Sale price:
$200 − $20 = $180

A tax is an amount added to a selling price.

e.g. 8% tax on $150

Tax amount:
$150 × 8% = $12

Total price:
$150 + $12 = $162

Look at the regular price of each item. Consider a discount of 10% and a tax rate of 13%. Complete the table. Round each answer to the nearest hundredth.

㉗

	Amount Saved	Sale Price	Tax Amount	Total Price
$18.50	$18.50 × 10% = _____			
$28				
$32.50				
$37.75				

8 Proportions

- solving for unknowns in proportions

A proportion is a mathematical comparison between 2 quantities. It is an equation that shows equivalent ratios.

Example Find the unknown value.

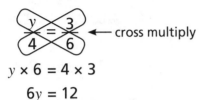 ← cross multiply

$$y \times 6 = 4 \times 3$$
$$6y = 12$$
$$y = 2$$

Try It

$$\frac{n}{3} = \frac{6}{9}$$

$$n \times 9 = 3 \times 6$$

$$9n = 18$$

$$n = \boxed{}$$

Use cross multiplication to find the unknown in each proportion.

① $\dfrac{a}{8} = \dfrac{3}{4}$

② $\dfrac{1}{2} = \dfrac{4}{n}$

③ $\dfrac{v}{3} = \dfrac{12}{9}$

④ $\dfrac{2}{13} = \dfrac{h}{78}$

⑤ $\dfrac{2}{n} = \dfrac{4}{5}$

⑥ $\dfrac{5}{6} = \dfrac{2}{m}$

⑦ $\dfrac{8}{11} = \dfrac{12}{y}$

⑧ $\dfrac{3}{g} = \dfrac{15}{16}$

⑨ $\dfrac{6}{8} = \dfrac{x}{5}$

⑩ $\dfrac{4}{5} = \dfrac{k}{25}$

⑪ $\dfrac{3}{4} = \dfrac{x}{16}$

⑫ $\dfrac{h}{15} = \dfrac{3}{5}$

Write each as a proportion. Then find the unknown.

⑬ 70% of 20 = _____

$$\frac{70}{100} = \frac{x}{20}$$

$$100x = 1400$$

$$x = \boxed{}$$

⑭ 16% of 50 = _____

⑮ 30% of 180 = _____

⑯ 20% of 90 = _____

⑰ 15% of 200 = _____

⑱ 65% of 160 = _____

Check the descriptions that involve direct proportions of the quantities.

Hints

In a direct proportion, as one quantity increases (or decreases), the other one increases (or decreases) at the same rate.

⑲

Ⓐ money earned and number of hours worked

Ⓑ amount of money spent and amount of money saved

Ⓒ distance travelled and gas used

Ⓓ number of apples bought and total cost

Ⓔ number of blocks and total weight

Ⓕ number of construction workers and number of days needed to build a bridge

Ⓖ time spent at the mall and number of books read

Ⓗ amount of water used and cost of water bill

Set up a proportion for each problem. Then solve it.

⑳ 10 apples for $5
8 apples for **?**

㉑ 3 kg of carrots for $4.50
2 kg of carrots for **?**

$_____

_____

㉒ 6 juice boxes for $7.50
8 juice boxes for **?**

㉓ 8 doughnuts for $6.80
12 doughnuts for **?**

_____

_____

Look at the prices and solve the problems. Show your work.

㉔

1 carton for $1.69

3 boxes for $2.10

SALT

2 boxes for 95¢

RAISINS

a. Find the costs.

• 2 boxes of salt   • 3 boxes of raisins

_____   _____

b. Find the quantity for each money amount.

• cartons of milk for $8.45   • boxes of salt for $2.80

_____   _____

Read what Chef Jason says and look at his recipe. Then answer the questions.

㉕

This recipe makes 4 servings.

Chef Jason's Dessert Recipe

- 2 cups of skim milk
- $1\frac{1}{2}$ teaspoons of brown sugar
- 2 cups of vanilla yogourt

- 1 cup of water
- $1\frac{1}{3}$ cups of raisins
- $\frac{1}{4}$ teaspoon of salt

a. How many cups of skim milk are needed to make

- 8 servings?
- 6 servings?

_____ cups

_____

b. How many teaspoons of salt are needed to make

- 12 servings?
- 10 servings?

_____

_____

c. How many servings can be made with

- 9 cups of vanilla yogourt?
- 4 cups of raisins?

_____

_____

d. How many cups of water are needed for

- 3 teaspoons of brown sugar?
- 2 teaspoons of salt?

_____

_____

9 Integers

• using integers

Adding a negative integer is a subtraction.
Subtracting a negative integer is an addition.

Try It

Example Find the answers.

Adding Integers	Subtracting Integers
(+3) + (+5) ← same sign	(+4) − (+2) ← different signs
= 3 + 5 ← add	= 4 − 2 ← subtract
= 8	= 2
(+3) + (-5) ← different signs	(+4) − (-2) ← same sign
= 3 − 5 ← subtract	= 4 + 2 ← add
= -2	= 6

(-5) + (-2) = ?

Ⓐ (-5) + 2

Ⓑ 5 − 2

Ⓒ 5 + 2

Ⓓ (-5) − 2

Rewrite to simplify. Then find the answer.

① (+2) + (-5)

= _____

= _____

② (-9) − (+6)

③ (-2) + (+3)

④ (+5) − (-9)

⑤ (+7) + (-5)

⑥ (-8) + (-3)

⑦ (-6) − (+8)

⑧ (+1) − (-9)

⑨ (-4) − (-5)

⑩ (+7) − (+6)

⑪ (-5) − (+2)

⑫ (+4) + (-7)

Multiply or divide.

⑬ $(+5) \times (+6) =$ _____ ⑭ $(-4) \times (-5) =$ _____

⑮ $(-15) \div (+5) =$ _____ ⑯ $(-20) \div (-2) =$ _____

⑰ $(+18) \div (-3) =$ _____ ⑱ $(-6) \times (+2) =$ _____

⑲ $(+3) \times (-4) =$ _____ ⑳ $(-10) \div (-5) =$ _____

㉑ $(+7) \times (+4) =$ _____ ㉒ $(-16) \div (-4) =$ _____

㉓ $(+21) \div (-3) =$ _____ ㉔ $(-6) \times (+6) =$ _____

㉕ $(+7) \times (+3) =$ _____ ㉖ $(+24) \div (+8) =$ _____

㉗ $(-12) \div (+4) =$ _____ ㉘ $(-5) \times (-7) =$ _____

㉙ $(-11) \times (+3) =$ _____ ㉚ $(-20) \div (-5) =$ _____

㉛ $(-6) \times (-5) =$ _____ ㉜ $(+30) \div (-6) =$ _____

Add signs to complete the number sentences in two ways.

㉝ $(\quad 3) \times (\quad 5) = -15$

   $(\quad 3) \times (\quad 5) = -15$

㉞ $(\quad 20) \div (\quad 4) = +5$

   $(\quad 20) \div (\quad 4) = +5$

㉟ $(\quad 21) \div (\quad 7) = -3$

   $(\quad 21) \div (\quad 7) = -3$

㊱ $(\quad 4) \times (\quad 6) = +24$

   $(\quad 4) \times (\quad 6) = +24$

㊲ $(+5) \quad (\quad 7) = +12$

   $(+5) \quad (\quad 7) = +12$

㊳ $(-2) \quad (\quad 8) = +6$

   $(-2) \quad (\quad 8) = +6$

㊴ $(\quad 9) \times (\quad 2) = -18$

   $(\quad 9) \times (\quad 2) = -18$

㊵ $(\quad 7) \times (\quad 4) = +28$

   $(\quad 7) \times (\quad 4) = +28$

Find the answers.

㊶ (-8) + 7 = _____

㊷ 4 × (-5) = _____

㊸ (-12) – (-3) = _____

㊹ (-9) × (-2) = _____

㊺ (-13) – 5 = _____

㊻ (-7) × (-2) = _____

㊼ 1 + (-6) = _____

㊽ 24 ÷ (-3) = _____

㊾ 25 – (-4) = _____

㊿ (-15) ÷ (-5) = _____

51 (-2) – (-7) = _____

52 (-8) + 6 = _____

Fill in the missing signs.

53 (+18) – (2) = +20

54 (-14) + (12) = -2

55 (-6) × (4) = +24

56 (+18) ÷ (6) = -3

57 (10) + (-8) = -18

58 (15) – (-9) = -6

59 (12) ÷ (+4) = +3

60 (7) × (-5) = +35

61 (5) + (3) = +2

62 (8) – (11) = -3

63 (7) – (6) = +13

64 (4) – (9) = -5

65 (6) × (-8) = -48

66 (-42) ÷ (7) = +6

Circle the missing numbers.

67 (^{2}) + (-36) ÷ (-6) = +31

     -4   +5   +3

68 (-6) × (+4) + (   ) = -27

     +3   -51   -3

69 -2 + (   ) × (-3) = +10

     -4   +4   -2

70 2^2 × (   ) – (-4) = +16

     +3   -5   +5

Evaluate. Show your work.

⑦¹ $10 - 4 \times (-3)$

⑦² $5^2 - (+24) \div (-4)$

⑦³ $19 - (2^2 + 3^2) \times (-2)$

⑦⁴ $(-6) \times (-3) + (-5)^2 \times (-2)$

⑦⁵ $\dfrac{1^2 - 2^2 - 3^2}{(-1) - (-2) - (-3)}$

⑦⁶ $\dfrac{7^2 - 6^0 \times 5^2}{4^0 - 4^1}$

⑦⁷ $\dfrac{(-3) \times (-4) - (-13)}{5^2 \div (-5)}$

⑦⁸ $\dfrac{(-2) \times 3 - (5 \times 2^2)}{(3^2 - 2^0) \div (-2)}$

⑦⁹ $\dfrac{(-6) \div (-3) + (-7)}{(-2)^2 \times (-3)}$

⑧⁰ $\dfrac{5^0 + (-4) - (-7)}{(-3) \times (+4) - 2^2}$

10 Circumferences of Circles

• finding the circumferences of circles

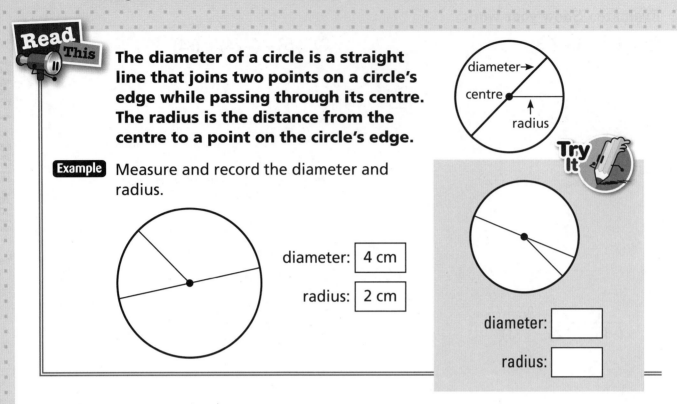

Read This

The diameter of a circle is a straight line that joins two points on a circle's edge while passing through its centre. The radius is the distance from the centre to a point on the circle's edge.

Example Measure and record the diameter and radius.

diameter: 4 cm

radius: 2 cm

Try It

diameter:

radius:

Using the centre of each circle, draw and measure the diameter and radius. Complete the table and fill in the blank.

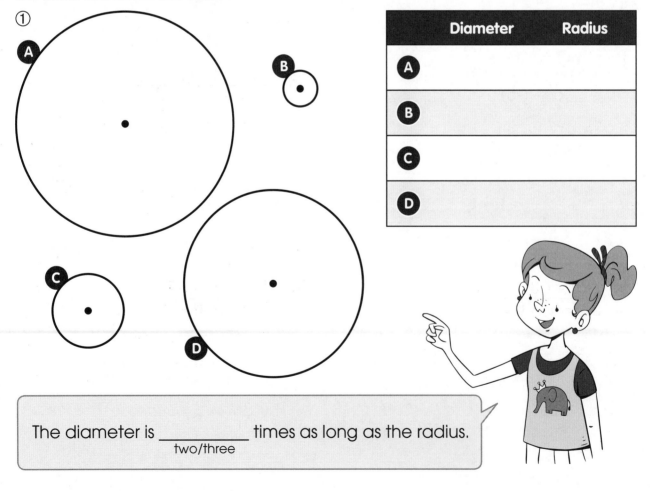

①

	Diameter	Radius
A		
B		
C		
D		

The diameter is _____ times as long as the radius.
two/three

Find the circumference. Consider π as 3.14. Show your work.

②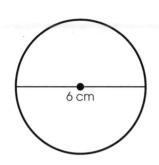

C = _____ × _____

= _____ (cm)

③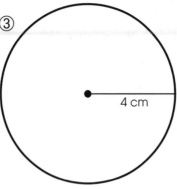

C = _____

= _____

Hints

The circumference of a circle is simply its perimeter. The circumference is directly proportional to the diameter and is related to the constant π.

Circumference of a Circle

$$C = \pi d$$
or
$$C = 2\pi r$$

The "π" symbol is called "pi" (pronounced "pie"). It is an irrational number and is usually considered as 3.14.

④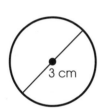

C = _____

= _____

⑤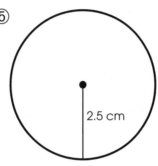

C = _____

= _____

⑥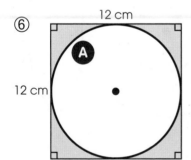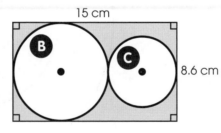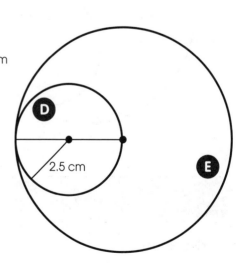

12 cm

15 cm

8.6 cm

12 cm

2.5 cm

Ⓐ C = _____ = _____

Ⓑ C = _____ = _____

Ⓒ C = _____ = _____

Ⓓ C = _____ = _____

Ⓔ C = _____ = _____

Find each circumference using the given measurement.

⑦ diameter: 18 cm   ⑧ radius: 6 m   ⑨ radius: 13 m

⑩ diameter: 15 mm   ⑪ radius: 8.5 cm   ⑫ diameter: 26.5 m

Use a ruler to measure the circles. Complete the table.

⑬

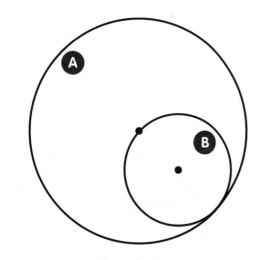
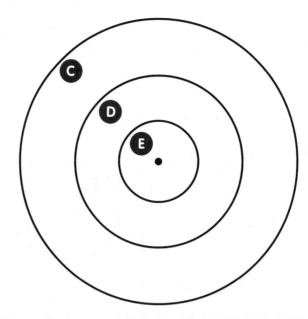

Circle / Measurement	Ⓐ	Ⓑ	Ⓒ	Ⓓ	Ⓔ
diameter					
radius					
circumference					

Find each diameter using the given circumference.

⑭ | C = 12.56 cm

⑮ | C = 31.4 m

Tips

$C = \pi d$

$\dfrac{C}{\pi} = \dfrac{\pi d}{\pi}$

$d = \dfrac{C}{\pi}$ ← value of d

⑯ | C = 78.5 cm

⑰ | C = 18.84 cm

⑱ | C = 17.584 m

Draw circles with the given measurements. Then complete the table.

⑲　Ⓐ radius: 1.7 cm　　Ⓑ radius: 2.5 cm　　Ⓒ diameter: 4 cm

	diameter	radius	circumference
Ⓐ			
Ⓑ			
Ⓒ			

11 Congruence and Similarity

• comparing congruent and similar figures

Read This

Congruent figures are identical in shape and size. Similar figures have the same shape but are not the same size.

Example Measure the shapes. Determine whether they are congruent or similar.

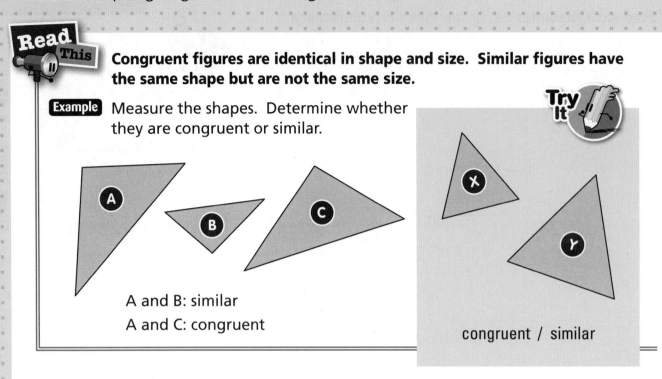

A and B: similar

A and C: congruent

Try It

congruent / similar

Measure and record the angles and side lengths. Determine whether the shapes in each pair are congruent, similar, or neither.

① ②

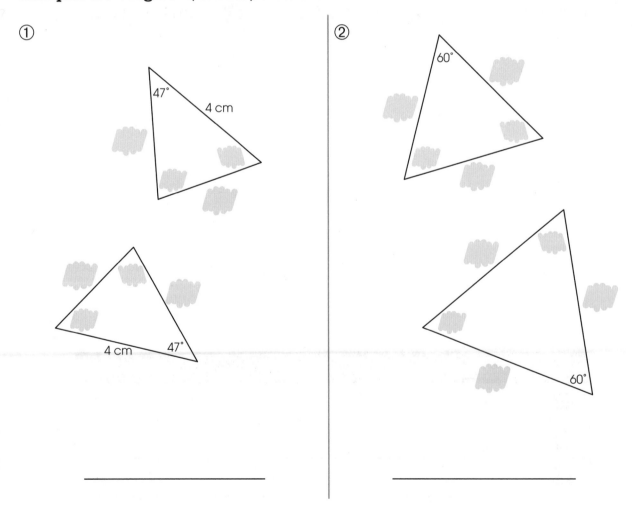

_____ _____

Determine whether the triangles in each pair are similar by finding the ratios of their corresponding sides. Fill in the blanks.

③

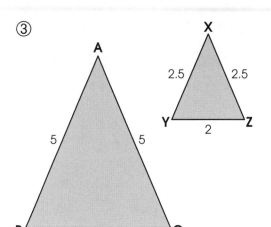

$$\frac{AB}{XY} = \frac{5}{2.5} = \underline{}$$

$$\frac{AC}{XZ} = \frac{5}{2.5} = \underline{}$$

$$\frac{BC}{YZ} = \frac{4}{2} = \underline{}$$

Tips

When shapes are similar, their corresponding angles are equal and their corresponding sides are proportional.

△ABC _____ similar to △XYZ.
　　　　　is/is not

④

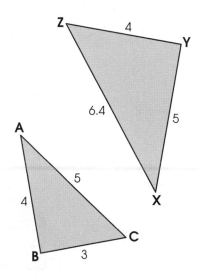

$$\frac{AB}{XY} = \underline{} = \underline{}$$

$$\frac{AC}{XZ} = \underline{}$$

$$\frac{BC}{YZ} = \underline{}$$

△ABC _____ similar to △XYZ.

⑤

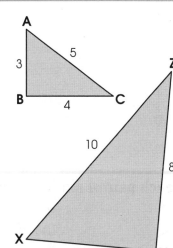

$$\frac{AB}{XY} = \underline{}$$

$$\frac{AC}{XZ} = \underline{}$$

$$\frac{BC}{YZ} = \underline{}$$

△ABC _____ similar to △XYZ.

⑥

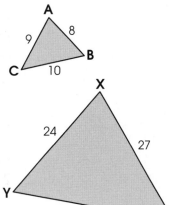

$$\frac{AB}{XY} = \underline{}$$

$$\frac{AC}{XZ} = \underline{}$$

$$\frac{BC}{YZ} = \underline{}$$

△ABC _____ similar to △XYZ.

Using the information about each pair of similar triangles, find the ratio of the corresponding sides. Then find the missing side lengths of each △DEF.

⑦
△ABC is similar to △DEF.

ratio: ___

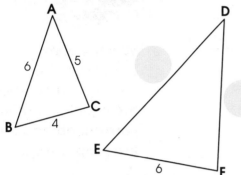

⑧
△XYZ is similar to △DEF.

ratio: ___

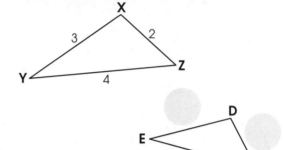

⑨
△MNO is similar to △DEF.

ratio: ___

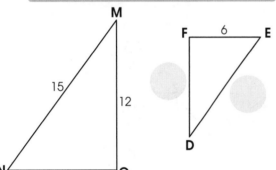

⑩
△PQR is similar to △DEF.

ratio: ___

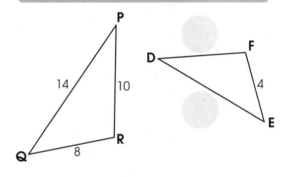

Determine the condition each pair of similar triangles has met.

⑪

Condition _____

Triangles are similar if any one of the conditions below is met.

⑫

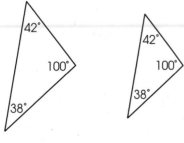

Condition _____

Condition A:
All 3 pairs of corresponding sides are proportional.

Condition B:
All 3 pairs of corresponding angles are the same.

Condition C:
2 pairs of corresponding sides are proportional and the angles they form are equal.

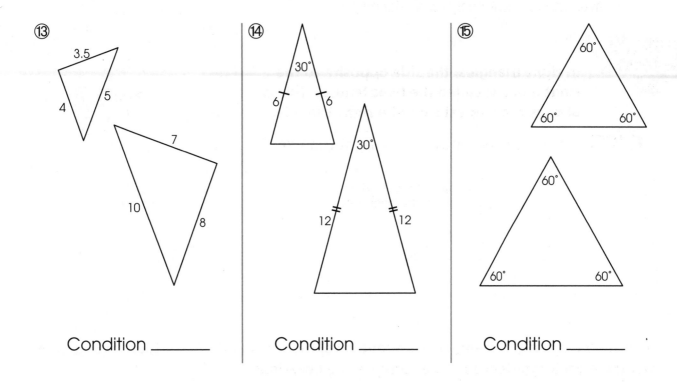

⑬

Condition _____

⑭

Condition _____

⑮

Condition _____

Sketch a triangle that is similar to each one given. Label the corresponding sides and/or angles.

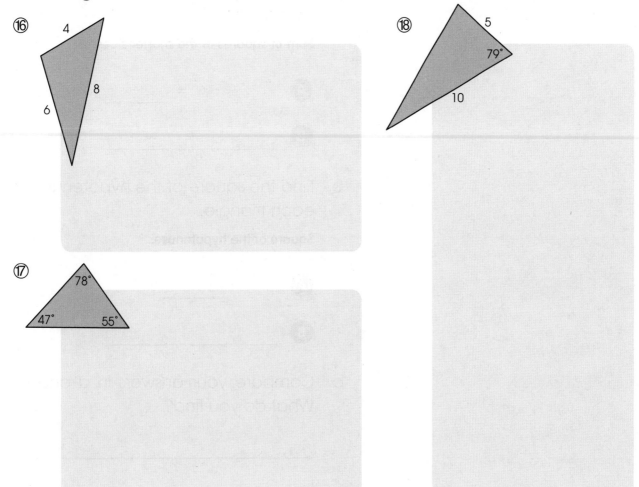

⑯   4   8   6

⑱   5   79°   10

⑰   78°   47°   55°

12 Pythagorean Relationship

• investigating the Pythagorean relationship

In right triangles, the side opposite to the right angle is called the hypotenuse. This is always the longest side of a right triangle.

Example Trace the hypotenuse of the right triangle.

opposite to the right
angle; the longest side

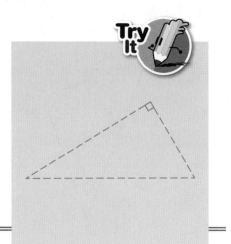

Try It

Identify the two right triangles below and label them A and B. Mark their right angles and trace each hypotenuse. Then answer the questions.

①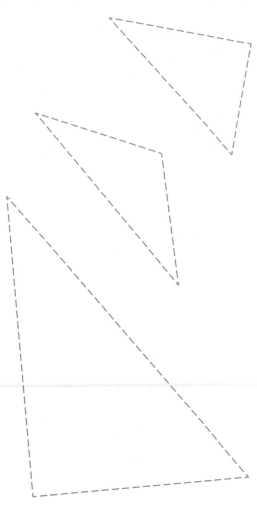

a. For each right triangle, measure and record the sums of the squares of the shorter sides.

Sum of squares of the shorter sides:

(A) $\boxed{}^2 + \boxed{}^2 =$ _____

(B) _____

b. Find the square of the hypotenuse of each triangle.

Square of the hypotenuse:

(A) $\boxed{}^2 =$ _____

(B) _____

c. Compare your answers in a and b. What do you find?

_____

_____

Find the length of each hypotenuse.

②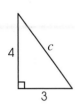

$$3^2 + 4^2 = c^2$$

$$c^2 = $$

$$c = $$

Hints

The **Pythagorean Theorem** states that in any right triangle, the square of the hypotenuse is equal to the sum of the squares of the other two sides.

$$a^2 + b^2 = c^2$$

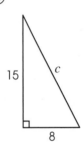

hypotenuse

③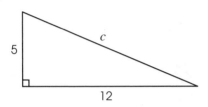

④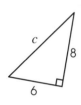

⑤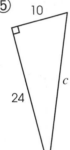

⑥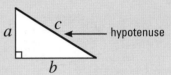

Find the lengths of the unknown sides. Round your answers to the nearest hundredth if necessary.

⑦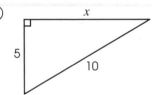

⑧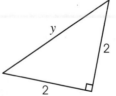

⑨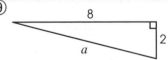

⑩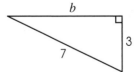

⑪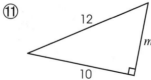

⑫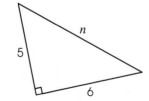

Find the unknown side of each triangle using the Pythagorean relationship. If it cannot be done, explain why. Round to the nearest hundredth.

⑬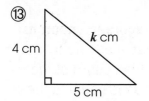

4 cm
k cm
5 cm

⑭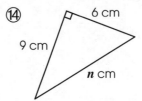

6 cm
9 cm
n cm

⑮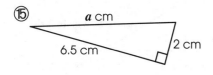

a cm
6.5 cm
2 cm

⑯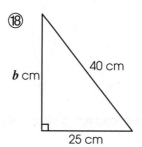

e cm
4 cm
2.5 cm

⑰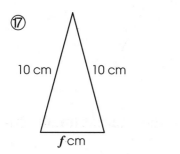

10 cm 10 cm
f cm

⑱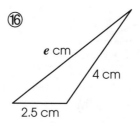

b cm 40 cm
25 cm

⑲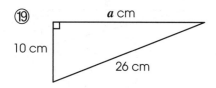

a cm
10 cm
26 cm

⑳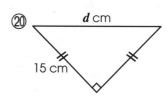

d cm
15 cm

㉑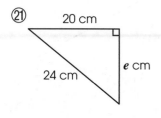

20 cm
24 cm
e cm

㉒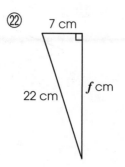

7 cm
22 cm
f cm

Find the unknown side and perimeter of each triangle. Round the answers to the nearest hundredth if necessary.

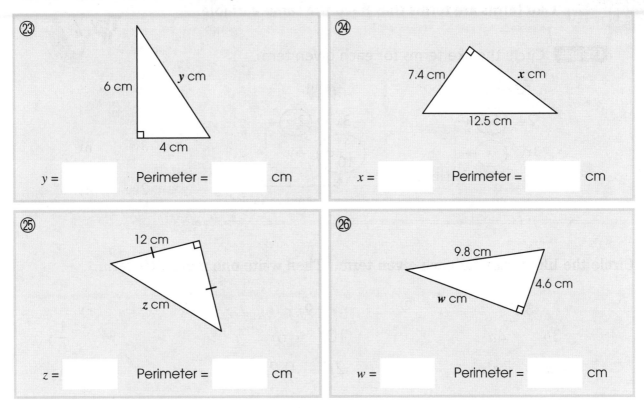

㉓

y cm

6 cm

4 cm

y = ☐   Perimeter = ☐ cm

㉔

7.4 cm   *x* cm

12.5 cm

x = ☐   Perimeter = ☐ cm

㉕

12 cm

z cm

z = ☐   Perimeter = ☐ cm

㉖

9.8 cm

4.6 cm

w cm

w = ☐   Perimeter = ☐ cm

Find the height and area of each isosceles triangle. Round the answers to the nearest hundredth if necessary.

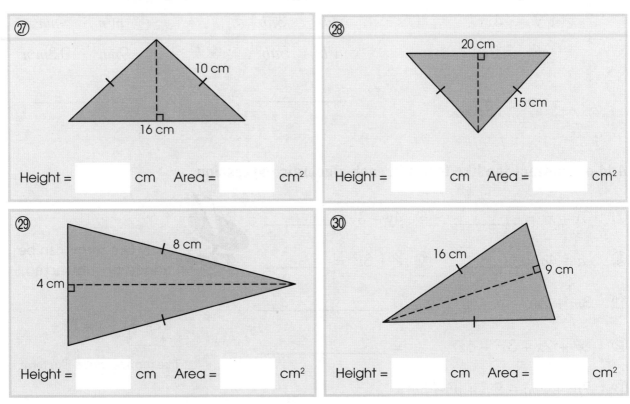

㉗

10 cm

16 cm

Height = ☐ cm   Area = ☐ cm²

㉘

20 cm

15 cm

Height = ☐ cm   Area = ☐ cm²

㉙

8 cm

4 cm

Height = ☐ cm   Area = ☐ cm²

㉚

16 cm

9 cm

Height = ☐ cm   Area = ☐ cm²

13 Algebraic Expressions

• evaluating algebraic expressions

Like terms are terms that have the same variable.

Example Circle the like terms for each given term.

2x

2y (5x)

3xy (-x)

same variable: x

4xy

$3x^2y$ (2xy)

$\frac{1}{10}xy$ 5y

same variable: xy

Try It

6y

8y   6x

2xy   4y

Circle the like terms for each given term. Then write one more like term.

① **3a**

3b   4a

-a   7ab

_____

② **9j**

10i   6j

$2j^2$ 0.2j

_____

③ **-y**

$-y^2$ $\frac{1}{5}y$

4   3y

_____

④ **2xy**

x^2y 4xy

-xy   2x

_____

⑤ **-7ab**

ab   3ab

a^2b^2 $5ab^2$

_____

⑥ **2m²n**

m^2n $-mn^2$

$9mn^2$ $-0.3m^2n$

_____

Add or subtract the like terms in each algebraic expression.

⑦ $3x + x$ = _____

⑧ $4y - 3y$ = _____

⑨ $-a + 4a$ = _____

⑩ $i^2 + 3i^2$ = _____

⑪ $3m + 2m - 4n - n$ = _____

⑫ $-x^2 + 2x + 3x^2 - 6x$ = _____

⑬ $7p^2 + 2pq - 5q^2 + p^2 - 3q^2$ = _____

Tips Only like terms can be added or subtracted.

e.g.

$2x + 3x - y = 5x - y$

like terms   not a like term

Simplify each algebraic expression.

⑭ $4a + 3(a - b)$

   $= 4a +$ _____ $-$ _____

   $=$ _____

⑮ $6(x + y) - 8x$

   $=$ _____ $+$ _____ $- 8x$

   $=$ _____

⑯ $-5(2a - b) - 6b$

⑰ $(7x)(8x^2)$

⑱ $(6x^3)(-x)$

⑲ $(3x)(4x^2) - 2x^3$

⑳ $\dfrac{-21x^4y^6}{7x^3y^4}$

㉑ $\dfrac{5a^4b^8}{15ab^2}$

㉒ $-\dfrac{30a^5b^7}{15a^4b^5} + ab^2$

㉓ $\dfrac{7i^2j^3}{14i^2j^2} - \dfrac{1}{2}j$

㉔ $(5a^2 - 2a + 7) + (3a^2 - 6a - 4)$ _____

㉕ $(3b^3 + 6b^2 - 3b - 14) + (-2b^2 - 3b + 9)$ _____

㉖ $(2n^3 - 8n^2 - 3n + 7) + (n^2 + n - 16)$ _____

㉗ $(4a^2 - 3ab + 6) - (3a^2 - 2ab + 4)$ _____

㉘ $(2m^2 - 3mn + 6n^2) - (mn + 2m^2 - n^2)$ _____

㉙ $(8x^2 + 6x^2y + y^2) - (12x^2 - x^2y)$ _____

Simplify each expression. Then evaluate it with each given value.

㉚ $4n + 6n - 9 - 8n$

    ↳ _____

    a. $n = 8$

    b. $n = -1$

    c. $n = 0.5$

㉛ $3a^2 - 6 + 6a^2$

    ↳ _____

    a. $a = 2$

    b. $a = 0$

    c. $a = -2$

㉜ $5t - 3(t - 2)$

    ↳ _____

    a. $t = 5$

    b. $t = \dfrac{1}{2}$

    c. $t = -5$

Simplify each expression. Then evaluate it with the given values.

㉝ $a = 3 \quad b = -4$

    $4a + 2b - a$

㉞ $c = -1 \quad d = 5$

    $2c + cd - c$

㉟ $e = 0.2 \quad f = -4$

    $5e + 2(e + f)$

㊱ $m = -\dfrac{1}{3} \quad n = \dfrac{2}{3}$

    $-4m + 3n + 2m$

㊲ $p = \dfrac{1}{4} \quad q = \dfrac{2}{5}$

    $5pq - 2p - pq$

㊳ $x = -0.1 \quad y = -9$

    $x^2 + x^2 + 2xy$

㊴ $a = 2 \quad b = 4 \quad c = 6$

    $(-a)(a^2) + 3bc$

㊵ $i = 3 \quad j = 1 \quad k = -2$

    $-\dfrac{i^2j}{i} - (i + k)$

㊶ $d = 1.2 \quad e = \dfrac{1}{2} \quad f = -0.2$

    $4d + (\dfrac{2e^2f}{e})$

Write an algebraic expression to represent the area of each figure. Then simplify the expression and evaluate it.

㊷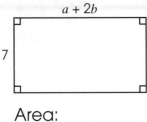

a + 2b

7

Area:

㊸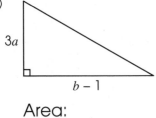

3a

b − 1

Area:

㊹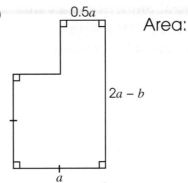

0.5a

2a − b

a

Area:

㊺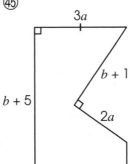

3a

b + 1

b + 5

2a

Area:

㊻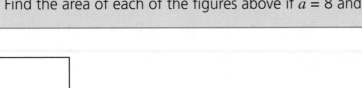

Find the area of each of the figures above if $a = 8$ and $b = 4$.

Area: _____ square units

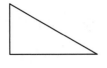

Area: _____ square units

Area: _____ square units

Area: _____ square units

14 Data Analysis

- identifying the type of a data set and determining its measures of central tendency

A measure of central tendency is a value that describes a set of data. Mean, median, and mode are all measures of central tendency.

Example Find the mean, median, and mode.

Data Set

| 13 | 24 | 16 | 19 | 17 | 16 |

Mean: (13 + 24 + 16 + 19 + 17 + 16) ÷ 6 = 17.5

Median: 13   16   (16   17)   19   24   ← in order

(16 + 17) ÷ 2 = 16.5

Mode: 16
— most common

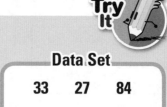

Try It

Data Set

33	27	84
18	56	25
44	41	77

Mean: [　]

Median: [　]

Mode: [　]

Find the mean, median, and mode of each set of data. Complete the table.

①

A

40	19
91	41
38	79
73	65
34	65
44	59

B

60	10
61	86
10	37
75	95
95	60
95	60

C

10	33	91
45	81	62
49	97	63
61	87	72
41	38	16
40	52	16

D

66	16	45
43	30	98
38	22	18
78	21	13
88	73	86
50	41	20

	A	**B**	**C**	**D**
Mean				
Median				
Mode				

Circle "T" for the true statements and "F" for the false ones.

② Two sets of data with the same mean must be identical. T / F

③ It is possible for a set of data to not have a median. T / F

④ It is possible for a set of data to have more than one mode. T / F

⑤ Mean is the best measure of central tendency for all sets of data. T / F

⑥ It is impossible for a set of data to have the same value for the
mean, median, and mode. T / F

LEVEL 1 – BASIC SKILLS

Find the missing values using the given data values and measures of central tendency.

⑦
```
┌──────┐  41
│      │
└──────┘
        ┌──────┐
49      │      │
        └──────┘
42      44
```
Mean: 41.5
Median: 41.5
Mode: 41

⑧
```
┌──────┐  59
│      │
└──────┘
86      42
┌──────┐
│      │  67
└──────┘
```
Mean: 60
Median: 62
Mode: none

⑨
```
        ┌──────┐
59      │      │
        └──────┘
29      27      24
┌──────┐  ┌──────┐
│      │  │      │
└──────┘  └──────┘
```
Mean: 46
Median: 59
Mode: none

⑩
```
28      ┌──────┐
        │      │
        └──────┘
┌──────┐
│      │  95
└──────┘
29      ┌──────┐
        │      │
        └──────┘
36
```
Mean: _____
Median: 84
Mode: 88

⑪
```
┌──────┐  34
│      │
└──────┘
62      19
┌──────┐
│      │  11
└──────┘
34      ┌──────┐
        │      │
        └──────┘
```
Mean: 24.5
Median: _____
Mode: 11

⑫
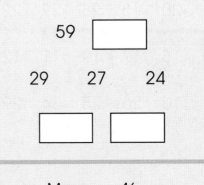
Mean: 52
Median: 49
Mode: _____ , _____
```
84      ┌──────┐  ┌──────┐
        │      │  │      │
        └──────┘  └──────┘
60      77      ┌──────┐
                │      │
                └──────┘
        ┌──────┐
        │      │  53
        └──────┘
```

Read each scenario. Circle the type of data each set is. Then find the answers.

⑬ Some Grade 8 students surveyed their parents to learn about their daily commute distance. The results are shown below.

Commute Distance (km)

35	27	10	20	28	29
19	21	17	35	19	18
25	32	34	11	27	31
20	15	28	29	22	17
15	17	19	11	12	12
10	26	25	34	29	31

a. Circle the correct descriptions of the data.

- **primary / secondary**
- **sample / census**
- **discrete / continuous**

b. Find the mean, median, and mode.

_____   _____   _____
  mean   median   mode

c. Is the mode the best measure of central tendency for this set of data? Explain.

_____

_____

⑭ A farmer measured and recorded the heights of 9 plants on his farm.

Heights of the Plants (m)

0.8	0.8	0.5	0.24	0.7	0.8	0.55	0.6	0.68

a. Circle the correct descriptions.

- **primary / secondary**
- **sample / census**
- **discrete / continuous**

b. Find the mean, median, and mode.

- Mean: _____
- Median: _____
- Mode: _____

c. For each case, determine whether the farmer should use the mean, median, or mode.

- The farmer wants to market his produce as healthy and tall.   _____

- The farmer wants to show a fertilizer company that their fertilizers have not been effective.   _____

Read the graphs. Identify the trends and answer the questions.

⑮

Price of Stock A Over 7 Days

_____ trend

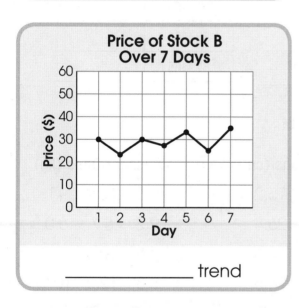

Price of Stock B Over 7 Days

_____ trend

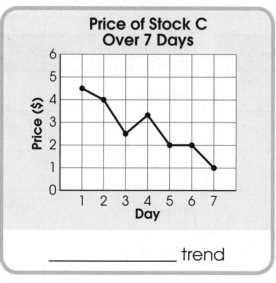

Price of Stock C Over 7 Days

_____ trend

Trends describe the relationship presented in a graph. There are 3 types of trends.

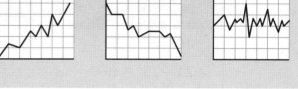

increasing trend   decreasing trend   no trend

a. The sets of data were obtained online. Are they primary or secondary sets of data? Explain.

_____

_____

b. Are they censuses or samples? Explain.

_____

_____

c. If you were a stock broker, what predictions would you make about each stock for Day 8?

• Stock A: _____

_____

• Stock B: _____

_____

• Stock C: _____

_____

15 Graphs

- using frequency tables and choosing the most appropriate graphs

This

A frequency table shows data listed in order with their corresponding frequencies.

Example Complete the frequency table.

Number of Stickers Children Collected

| 25 | 20 | 36 | 18 | 25 | 22 |
| 27 | 29 | 30 | 32 | 34 | 19 |

No. of Stickers	Frequency
16 – 20	3
21 – 25	3
26 – 30	3
31 – 35	2
36 – 40	1

└─ same range in the intervals

Try It

Number of Coins Children Collected

60	59	46	51	54
50	52	48	55	61
47	51	64	48	56

No. of Coins	Frequency
46 – 50	
51 – 55	
56 – 60	
61 – 65	

Complete the frequency table for each set of data.

① **Age of Audience**

6	19	24
18	19	21
23	8	4
18	3	17
20	11	17

Age	Frequency
1 – 5	
6 – 10	
11 – 15	
16 – 20	
21 – 25	

② **Length of Ribbons (cm)**

33.7	30.5	15.2
40.1	10.7	26.4
19.2	25.2	18.3
35.2	4.7	14.5
19.3	9.8	7.3

Length (cm)	Frequency
0 – 9.9	
10 – 19.9	
20 – 29.9	
30 – 39.9	
40 – 49.9	

③ **Weight of Dogs (kg)**

9.8	12.9	11
9.2	5.7	6.0
7.8	10.6	15.0
8.8	12.3	10.9
11.2	6.9	7.5

Weight (kg)	Frequency
5.6 – 7.5	
7.6 – 9.5	
9.6 – 11.5	
11.6 – 13.5	
13.6 – 15.5	

See the three frequency tables made for the same set of data. Check the mistake in each and give a solution.

④

I surveyed 20 families on the number of movies they watched last year. The results are shown below.

Number of Movies Watched									
21	7	15	1	14	5	29	9	14	6
36	29	20	20	10	30	10	22	35	12

a.

No. of Movies	Frequency
0 – 10	7
11 – 25	8
26 – 30	3
31 – 40	2

Mistake:

(A) inconsistent ranges in intervals

(B) intervals not arranged in ascending order

Solution:

_____

_____

b.

No. of Movies	Frequency
0 – 10	7
10 – 20	8
20 – 30	7
30 – 40	3

Mistake:

(A) overlapping end values in intervals

(B) too many intervals

Solution:

_____

_____

c.

No. of Movies	Frequency
1 – 5	2
6 – 10	5
11 – 15	4
16 – 20	2
21 – 25	2
26 – 30	3
31 – 35	1
36 – 40	1

Mistake:

(A) intervals not arranged in order

(B) too many intervals

Solution:

_____

_____

_____

With the given information about each set of data, determine which graph is the most appropriate. Give your reason.

⑤ Description:

a set of data containing the ages of teenagers in two groups: those who were born in Toronto and those who were not

Purpose:

to analyze the differences in the number of teenagers born in and outside Toronto for each age group

Tips Below are the graphs that you can choose from.

- double bar graph
- double line graph
- histogram
- circle graph
- scatter plot

Graph: _____

Reason: _____
_____

⑥ Description: a set of data containing two temperatures measured at different times of each day for a two-week period

Purpose: to find out the temperature trend over the two-week period

Graph: _____

Reason: _____
_____

⑦ Description: a set of data showing the answers of 1000 Canadians on the political party they support

Purpose: to compare the fractions of supporters for each political party

Graph: _____

Reason: _____
_____

⑧ Description: a set of data containing the weights and heights of 100 children

Purpose: to find the correlation between the weight and height of a child

Graph: _____

Reason: _____
_____

Each question contains two graphs that represent the same set of data. Check the graph that helps you find the answer. Then write the answer.

⑨

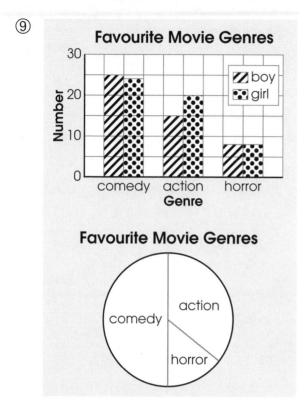

a. Which genre is the most popular?

  ◯ double bar graph; _____

  ◯ circle graph; _____

b. How many more girls prefer action movies than boys?

  ◯ double bar graph; _____

  ◯ circle graph; _____

c. About what percent of children picked comedy as their favourite movie genre?

  ◯ double bar graph; _____

  ◯ circle graph; _____

⑩

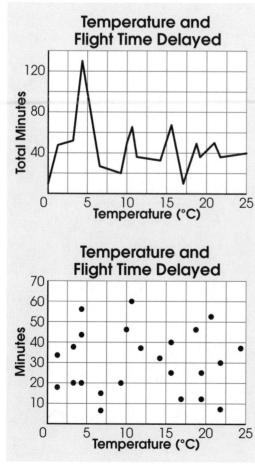

a. Is there a correlation between the temperature and the amount of flight time delayed?

  ◯ line graph; _____

  ◯ scatter plot; _____

b. At what temperature was flight time most delayed?

  ◯ line graph; _____

  ◯ scatter plot; _____

c. Was any delayed time recorded for 15°C?

  ◯ line graph; _____

  ◯ scatter plot; _____

LEVEL 2
FURTHER YOUR UNDERSTANDING

1 Rational Numbers

• understanding rational numbers

Read This

A rational number is any number that can be written as a fraction in which both the numerator and denominator are integers, and the denominator is not 0.

Example Circle the rational number(s).

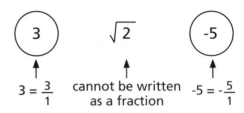

$$\left(3\right) \qquad \sqrt{2} \qquad \left(-5\right)$$

$3 = \frac{3}{1}$ cannot be written as a fraction $-5 = -\frac{5}{1}$

Try It

$$\frac{1}{2} \qquad \frac{6}{0} \qquad \frac{0}{4} \qquad 2^3$$

Write each rational number as a fraction.

①   5 = _____   -4 = _____ $1\frac{4}{5}$ = _____   3.5 = _____

    0 = _____ $\sqrt{4}$ = _____ 3^2 = _____ $\sqrt{25}$ = _____

    $2\frac{1}{2}$ = _____ 1^5 = _____   -5.2 = _____ 3×10^{-1} = _____

Match to sort the rational numbers. Then pair them with the correct fractions.

Hints

Terminating decimals are decimals that end.

e.g.   0.4, 1.92, 8.509

Repeating decimals have digits that repeat infinitely. The repeating digits are indicated by a line over them.

e.g. $1.\overline{3}$, $2.\overline{78}$, $0.1\overline{09}$

② $0.\overline{36}$ •

    $0.\overline{2}$ •   • Terminating Decimal

    0.6 •

    $0.8\overline{3}$ •   • Repeating Decimal

    0.875 •

    0.2 •

$\frac{1}{5}$ _____ $\frac{4}{11}$ _____ $\frac{3}{5}$ _____ $\frac{2}{9}$ _____ $\frac{7}{8}$ _____ $\frac{5}{6}$ _____

Circle the rational number in each pair.

③   -3 $\sqrt{3}$

④ $\dfrac{3}{0}$ $\dfrac{0}{3}$

⑤ $\sqrt{9}$ $\sqrt{8}$

⑥ $0.\overline{3}$ $\sqrt{5}$

⑦ π 1.0881

⑧ $3\dfrac{1}{2}$ $3\sqrt{2}$

⑨ $\sqrt{1}$ $\sqrt{10}$

⑩ $\sqrt{65}$ $\sqrt{64}$

⑪ $2.\overline{72}$ $\dfrac{\sqrt{7}}{2}$

⑫ 3π 1.62

⑬ $\sqrt{7}^{\,2}$ $\sqrt{7}^{\,3}$

⑭ 3×10^{-2} $\dfrac{\pi}{2}$

⑮ $4\sqrt{2}$ 2^4

⑯ $-\sqrt{121}$ $2\sqrt{11}$

⑰ $\sqrt{80}$ $\sqrt{81}$

Write "rational" or "irrational" for each. Then give an example.

⑱

	rational/irrational	example
a. whole numbers	_____	_____
b. zero	_____	_____
c. terminating decimals	_____	_____
d. repeating decimals	_____	_____
e. the product of an integer and π	_____	_____
f. squares of prime numbers	_____	_____
g. square roots of prime numbers	_____	_____
h. integers with integer exponents	_____	_____
i. numbers in scientific notation	_____	_____
j. mixed numbers with integers as numerators and denominators	_____	_____

Look at each pair of numbers. If both numbers are rational, put a check mark.   Then circle the greater number.

⑲
$$0.4 \qquad \frac{4}{7} \qquad \bigcirc$$

⑳
$$\sqrt{11} \qquad 2 \qquad \bigcirc$$

㉑
$$2^3 \qquad 3^2 \qquad \bigcirc$$

㉒
$$0.000025$$
$$\sqrt{125} \qquad \bigcirc$$

㉓
$$2.33$$
$$2.\overline{3} \qquad \bigcirc$$

㉔
$$\sqrt{2}$$
$$1.414 \qquad \bigcirc$$

㉕
$$\sqrt{64}$$
$$8 \times 10^2 \qquad \bigcirc$$

㉖
$$9.42$$
$$3\pi \qquad \bigcirc$$

㉗
$$-\sqrt{9} \qquad -\sqrt{4} \qquad \bigcirc$$

Cross out the irrational number in each set. Then put the rational numbers in order from smallest to greatest.

㉘
$$1.69 \times 10^3 \qquad \sqrt{16.9} \qquad \sqrt{169} \qquad 1.6\overline{9}$$

_____

㉙
$$5^2 \qquad 5.\overline{255} \qquad \sqrt{525} \qquad 5\frac{2}{5}$$

_____

㉚
$$-0.\overline{6} \qquad \frac{\sqrt{3}}{2} \qquad \frac{0.25}{5} \qquad \frac{\sqrt{9}}{4}$$

_____

㉛
$$4.14 \times 10^2 \qquad \sqrt{441} \qquad 44.\overline{1} \qquad \sqrt{414}$$

_____

㉜
$$\sqrt{12 \times 4} \qquad \sqrt{32 + 32} \qquad \sqrt{108 \div 3} \qquad \sqrt{96 - 15}$$

_____

Write "T" for the true statements and "F" for the false ones.

㉝ ☐ All square roots are irrational numbers.

㉞ ☐ All terminating decimals are rational numbers.

㉟ ☐ $\sqrt{2}$ can be written as $\dfrac{\sqrt{2}}{1}$. Therefore, irrational numbers can be written as rational numbers.

㊱ ☐ All fractions that have integers as numerators and denominators are rational numbers.

㊲ ☐ Some repeating decimals are irrational numbers.

㊳ ☐ Irrational numbers are non-terminating decimals that do not have repeating digits.

㊴ ☐ A multiple of an irrational number is also an irrational number.

Evaluate and write whether the answer is a rational (R) or an irrational (IR) number.

㊵ $10^2 - 3 \times 5$

☐

㊶ $1.15 \times 10^3 \div 5$

☐

㊷ $\sqrt{16} \times \sqrt{2}$

☐

㊸ $\sqrt{7}^3 \times \sqrt{5^2} \times 3^0$

☐

㊹ $\sqrt{\dfrac{6^2 + 24}{40 \div (4 - 2)}}$

☐

㊺ $\dfrac{4^2 + 2}{7^2 - 5^2}$

☐

㊻ $\dfrac{\sqrt{30} \times \sqrt{15}}{\sqrt{64} \div \sqrt{32}}$

☐

㊼ $\dfrac{12 - 2^2 \times 3}{\sqrt{36} + 4^2 \times 2}$

☐

㊽ $3\sqrt{2} \times 5\sqrt{3} \div 4\sqrt{6}$

☐

Fractions, Decimals, and Percents

• relating fractions, decimals, and percents

Read This

Some fractions are converted into decimals that have repeating digits. These are repeating decimals. Denote repeating digits by drawing a horizontal line above them.

Example Write the fractions as repeating decimals.

$\frac{1}{3}$ = 0.33333... ← repeating digit: 3

= $0.\overline{3}$ ← Draw a line above the 3.

$\frac{1}{6}$ = 0.16666... ← repeating digit: 6

= $0.1\overline{6}$ ← Draw a line above the 6.

Try It

$\frac{1}{9}$ = 0.1111... = [   ] $\frac{5}{6}$ = 0.83333... = [   ]

Rewrite each repeating decimal. Then do the matching.

① 0.66666... = _____ •

0.06666... = _____ •

0.606060... = _____ •

0.066066... = _____ •

0.006666... = _____ •

• $\frac{1}{15}$

• $\frac{2}{3}$

• $\frac{1}{150}$

• $\frac{20}{33}$

• $\frac{22}{333}$

Tips

Some repeating decimals have more than one repeating digit. Be sure the line drawn is above all the repeating digits.

e.g. 0.2323... ← repeating digits: 23

= $0.\overline{23}$

② 0.454545... = _____ •

0.455555... = _____ •

0.41545454... = _____ •

0.4454545... = _____ •

0.1455555... = _____ •

• $\frac{49}{110}$

• $\frac{457}{1100}$

• $\frac{5}{11}$

• $\frac{131}{900}$

• $\frac{41}{90}$

Convert each repeating decimal into a percent.

③ 0.555... = _____

④ 0.0333... = _____

⑤ 0.2828... = _____

⑥ 0.144144... = _____

⑦ 1.444... = _____

⑧ 5.0888... = _____

⑨ 0.0711... = _____

⑩ 0.00505... = _____

⑪ 0.52434343... = _____

⑫ 0.324983249832... = _____

Tips

To convert a repeating decimal into a percent, move the decimal point 2 places to the right and add "%". Remember to mark any repeating digits.

e.g. $0.\overline{6} = 66.\overline{6}\%$

0.6666...

2 decimal places to the right

Follow the steps to convert each repeating decimal into a fraction.

⑬

$0.\overline{7} =$ _____

Let $x = 0.\overline{7}$ ⎤ the same
$10x = 7.\overline{7}$ ⎦ repeating digit

Subtract $10x = 7.\overline{7}$
$\quad - \quad x = 0.\overline{7}$
_____
$10x - x →$ $9x = 7$ ← $7.\overline{7} - 0.\overline{7}$

$x =$ _____ ← Divide both sides by 9 to isolate x.

Hints

Follow the steps below to convert a repeating decimal into a fraction.

❶ Let x be the decimal.

❷ Multiply the decimal by powers of 10 so that it has the same repeating digits after the decimal point.

❸ Subtract. Then divide to isolate x.

⑭

$0.\overline{18} =$ _____

Let $x = 0.\overline{18}$
$100x = 18.\overline{18}$

Subtract $100x = 18.\overline{18}$
$\quad - \quad x = 0.\overline{18}$
_____

⑮

$0.\overline{23} =$ _____

Let $x = 0.\overline{23}$
$100x = 23.\overline{23}$

Subtract $100x = 23.\overline{23}$
$\quad - \quad x = 0.\overline{23}$
_____

⑯

$0.\overline{45} =$ _____

Let $x = 0.\overline{45}$
$100x = 45.\overline{45}$

Subtract $100x = 45.\overline{45}$
$\quad - \quad x = 0.\overline{45}$
_____

Cross out the one that does not have the same value in each group.

⑰
$$\frac{5}{8}$$
0.58
62.5%
0.625

⑱
0.45
$$\frac{9}{20}$$
0.4$\overline{5}$
45%

⑲
78%
$$\frac{78}{100}$$
$$\frac{49}{50}$$
0.78

⑳
$$1\frac{8}{25}$$
1.32%
1.32
132%

㉑
0.$\overline{1}$
$$\frac{1}{9}$$
0.1
11.$\overline{1}$%

㉒
21.$\overline{1}$%
$$\frac{21}{100}$$
0.2$\overline{1}$
$$\frac{19}{90}$$

㉓
$$\frac{20}{99}$$
0.2$\overline{0}$
0.$\overline{20}$
20.$\overline{20}$%

㉔
$$2\frac{1}{9}$$
2.1$\overline{2}$
$$2\frac{11}{90}$$
212.$\overline{2}$%

Write each number in two other forms.

㉕ $\dfrac{4}{5}$ _____ _____

㉖ 0.4 _____ _____

㉗ 1.75 _____ _____

㉘ 250% _____ _____

㉙ $7\dfrac{3}{5}$ _____ _____

㉚ 0.08 _____ _____

㉛ 0.01 _____ _____

㉜ 0.$\overline{3}$ _____ _____

㉝ 1.$\overline{2}$ _____ _____

㉞ $5\dfrac{2}{15}$ _____ _____

㉟ $\dfrac{1}{90}$ _____ _____

㊱ 8.$\overline{8}$% _____ _____

Convert the decimals into fractions and evaluate. Write the answers in simplest form.

㊲ $0.84 \times 1\dfrac{3}{7} + 1\dfrac{4}{7}$

=

㊳ $9.2 + 4\dfrac{4}{5} \div 0.04$

=

㊴ $2\dfrac{1}{5} - 5.6 \div \dfrac{7}{10}$

=

㊵ $0.2 \div 4 + 2\dfrac{1}{10}$

=

㊶ $\dfrac{3}{4} + 2.5 \div 5$

=

㊷ $\dfrac{4}{5} - \dfrac{1}{5} \times 1.6$

=

Convert the fractions into decimals and evaluate.

㊸ $\dfrac{4}{5} \div 0.8 + 1.7$

=

㊹ $\dfrac{1}{2} + 0.8 \times 1\dfrac{1}{2}$

=

㊺ $3\dfrac{3}{5} \div (0.3 - \dfrac{9}{10})$

=

㊻ $4 \times \dfrac{3}{20} - 5 \times \dfrac{3}{10}$

=

㊼ $(\dfrac{1}{2})^2 + 0.4^2$

=

㊽ $6.5 - 1\dfrac{1}{2} \times 0.6$

=

3 Ratios, Rates, and Proportions

- using ratios, rates, and proportions

To write a ratio in simplest form, divide the terms by their GCF.

Example Write the ratio in simplest form.

$$12{:}18 = 2{:}3$$

The GCF of 12 and 18 is 6.

Try It

15:10 = [ ]   20:24 = [ ]

Write the ratios in simplest form to complete the table. Then answer the questions.

① **Results of the Beach Volleyball Tournament**

Teams		Bolts	Spikers	Movers	Royals
R E S U L T S	wins	9	2	4	3
	losses	3	6	6	3
	ties	3	6	4	6
	games	15	14	14	12
R A T I O S	wins to losses				
	ties to games				
	losses to games				
	wins to losses to ties				
	wins to losses to games				

a. Which team has a higher ratio of wins to losses, the Bolts or the Spikers? _____

b. Which team has a higher ratio of ties to games, the Spikers or the Movers? _____

Find the rates.

② 60 km in 1.5 h

_____ km/h

③ 720 points in 32 games

_____ points/game

④ 6 cups for $7.20

$_____ /cup

⑤ 400 words in 10 min

_____ words/min

⑥ $240 in 6 h

$_____ /h

⑦ 735 pages in 1 week

_____ pages/day

⑧ 210 m in 2 min

_____ m/s

⑨ 96 books in 2 years

_____ books/month

Find the speeds in km/h.

⑩  320 km in 4 h

_____

⑪ 0.6 km in 0.15 h

_____

⑫  87.5 km in 3.5 h

_____

⑬  46 km in 0.5 h

_____

Find the unit rates. Check the better buy.

⑭

Ⓐ $34.56 for 12 cans _____

Ⓑ $17.82 for 9 cans _____

⑮

Ⓐ $59.50 for 7 jugs _____

Ⓑ $50.70 for 6 jugs _____

⑯

Ⓐ $14.50 for 10 balls _____

Ⓑ $11.04 for 8 balls _____

⑰

Ⓐ $32.80 for 2 kg

_____

Ⓑ $51.60 for 3 kg

_____

Solve for the unknown in each proportion.

⑱ $\frac{9}{12} = \frac{x}{6}$

$x =$ _____

⑲ $\frac{16}{30} = \frac{96}{y}$

$y =$ _____

⑳ $\frac{3}{z} = \frac{27}{72}$

$z =$ _____

㉑ $\frac{a}{210} = \frac{6}{5}$

$a =$ _____

㉒ $\frac{2}{3} = \frac{8}{b}$

$b =$ _____

㉓ $\frac{20}{35} = \frac{4}{c}$

$c =$ _____

㉔ $\frac{5}{7} = \frac{b}{70}$

$b =$ _____

㉕ $\frac{6}{11} = \frac{e}{77}$

$e =$ _____

㉖ $\frac{12}{p} = \frac{8}{144}$

$p =$ _____

Set up a proportion for each problem. Then find the cost of each quantity.

㉗  5 tickets for $11

a. 8 tickets

b. 12 tickets

c. 3 tickets

㉘  6 rings for $4

a. 4 rings

b. 8 rings

c. 10 rings

Solve the problems.

㉙ 850 g of flour is mixed with 700 g of sugar.

    a. What is the ratio of flour to sugar?   _____

    b. How much sugar should be mixed with 5100 g of flour?   _____

㉚ Mary walks 1.5 km in 30 minutes every day. At the same rate,

    a. how far can she walk in 45 minutes?   _____

    b. how long does it take her to walk 2 km?   _____

㉛ Sunny earns $15 per hour, Frank earns $144 per 8 hours, and Paul earns $480 per 40 hours.

    a. How much does Paul earn if he works 32 hours?   _____

    b. How much does Frank earn if he works 20 hours?   _____

    c. What is the ratio of the hourly rates among Sunny, Frank, and Paul?   _____

    d. Sunny, Frank and Paul all worked the same length of shift. How much did Frank and Paul earn if Sunny earned $120?   _____

㉜ Jason spends 3 hours reading every day. What percent of a day does Jason spend reading?   _____

㉝ The price of a volleyball at a 40% discount was $18. What was its original price?   _____

㉞ Elaine drank 65% of a bottle of water. 735 mL was left over. How much water was there to start?   _____

4 Areas of Circles

- finding the areas of circles

Read This

The area of a circle is found using the formula

$$A = \pi r^2$$

where A is the area and r is the radius.

Example Find the area. Consider π as 3.14.

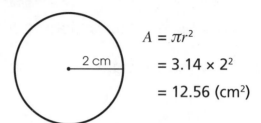

2 cm

$$A = \pi r^2$$
$$= 3.14 \times 2^2$$
$$= 12.56 \ (cm^2)$$

Try It

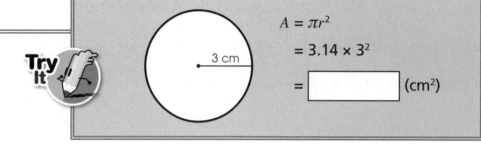

3 cm

$$A = \pi r^2$$
$$= 3.14 \times 3^2$$
$$= \boxed{} \ (cm^2)$$

Find the areas of the circles. Consider π as 3.14.

①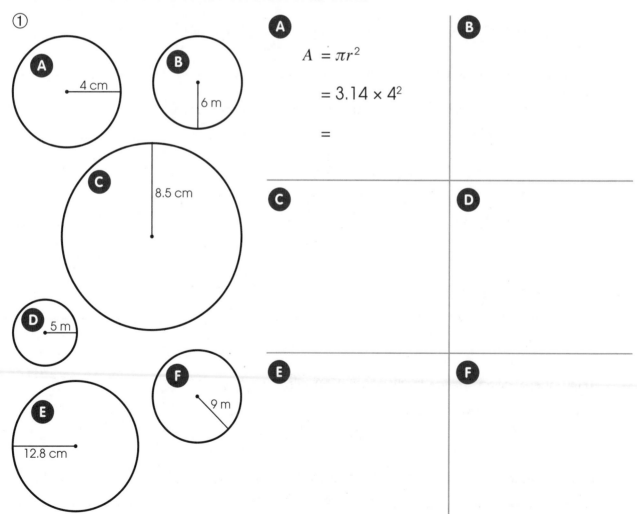

A   4 cm

B   6 m

C   8.5 cm

D   5 m

E   12.8 cm

F   9 m

A

$$A = \pi r^2$$
$$= 3.14 \times 4^2$$
$$=$$

B

C

D

E

F

Find the area of each circle with the given diameter.

② diameter = 8 cm   ③ diameter = 10 m

④ diameter = 16 cm   ⑤ diameter = 22 cm   ⑥ diameter = 25 m

Use a ruler to measure the radius of each circle. Then find the areas. Record the measurements in the table.

⑦

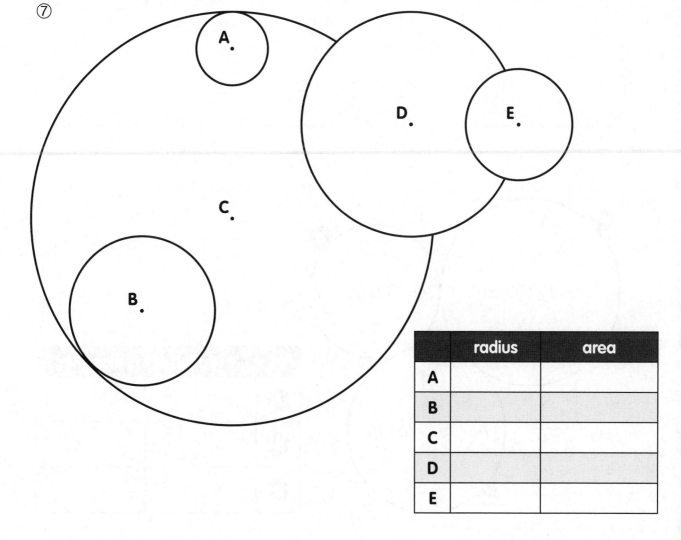

	radius	area
A		
B		
C		
D		
E		

LEVEL 2 – FURTHER YOUR UNDERSTANDING

Use the given area of each circle to find its radius and diameter.

⑧ area = 78.5 cm²   ⑨ area = 200.96 m²   ⑩ area = 3.14 cm²

radius: _____
diameter: _____

radius: _____
diameter: _____

radius: _____
diameter: _____

⑪ area = 706.5 cm²   ⑫ area = 379.94 m²   ⑬ area = 254.34 mm²

radius: _____
diameter: _____

radius: _____
diameter: _____

radius: _____
diameter: _____

⑭

Ⓐ A = 19.625 cm²

Ⓑ A = 10.1736 cm²

Ⓒ A = 15.1976 cm²

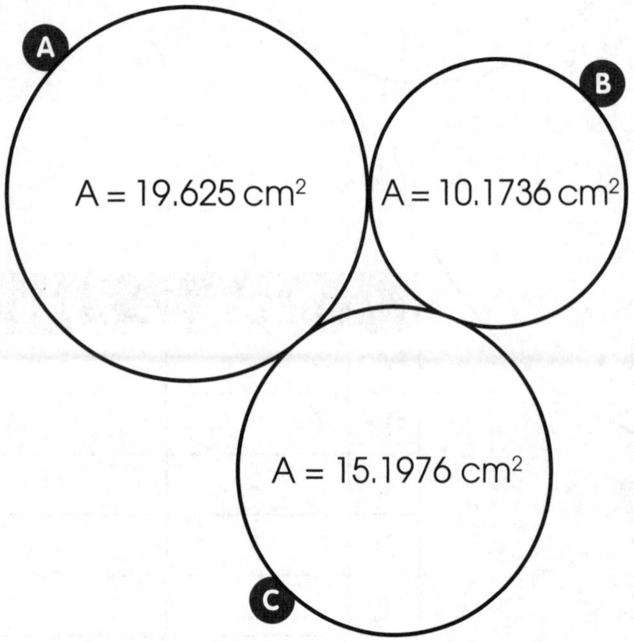

	radius	diameter
Ⓐ		
Ⓑ		
Ⓒ		

Find the areas of the shaded regions to the nearest hundredth.

⑮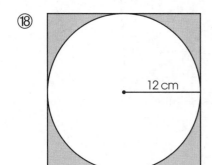

Area = _____ cm²

⑯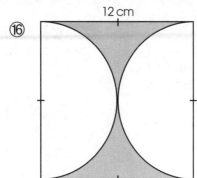

Area = _____ cm²

⑰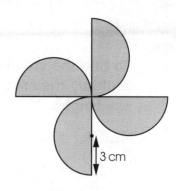

Area = _____ cm²

⑱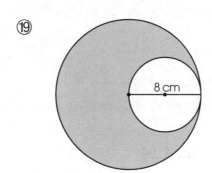

Area = _____ cm²

⑲

Area = _____ cm²

⑳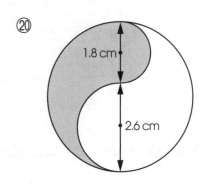

Area = _____ cm²

Find the area and circumference of each pizza. Record them in order from smallest to largest.

㉑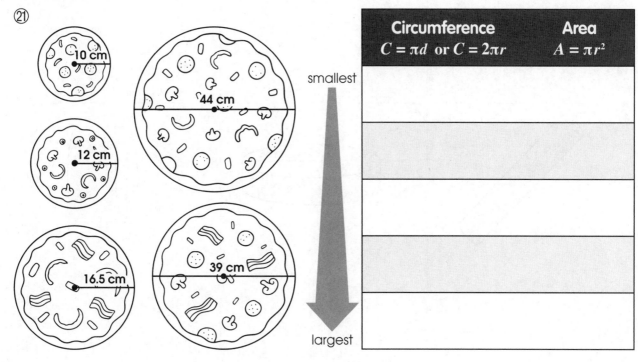

	Circumference $C = \pi d$ or $C = 2\pi r$	Area $A = \pi r^2$
smallest		
largest		

5 Cylinders

- finding the volumes and surface areas of cylinders

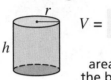 **Read This**

To find the volume of a cylinder, multiply the area of the base by the height.

$$V = \underset{\substack{\uparrow \\ \text{area of} \\ \text{the base}}}{\pi r^2} \quad \underset{\substack{\uparrow \\ \text{height}}}{h}$$

Example Find the volume. Consider π as 3.14.

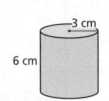

3 cm
6 cm

$V = \pi r^2 h$

$= 3.14 \times 3^2 \times 6$

$= 169.56 \ (cm^3)$

Try It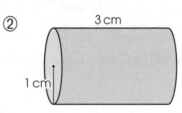

2 cm
3 cm

$V = \pi r^2 h$

$= 3.14 \times \boxed{}^2 \times \boxed{}$

$= \boxed{} \ (cm^3)$

Find the volumes. Consider π as 3.14.

①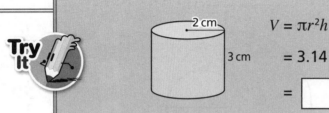

4 cm
1 cm

②
3 cm
1 cm

③
2 cm
5 cm

④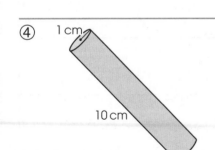

1 cm
10 cm

⑤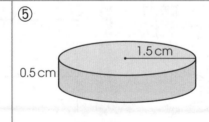

1.5 cm
0.5 cm

⑥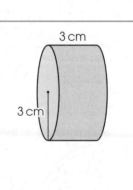

3 cm
3 cm

⑦

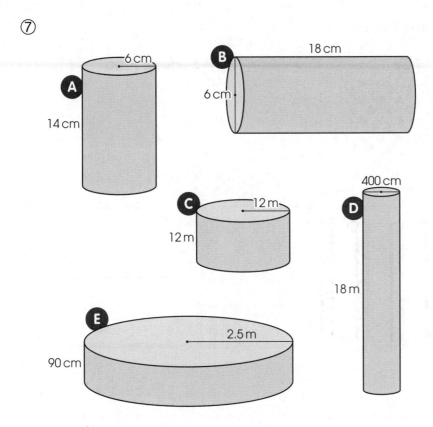

Volume

A _____

B _____

C _____

D _____

E _____

Find the surface area (S.A.) of each cylinder. Show your work.

⑧

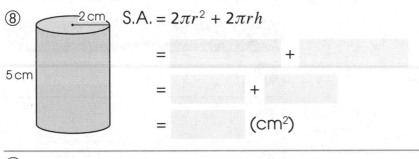

S.A. $= 2\pi r^2 + 2\pi rh$

$\quad = \underline{\hspace{3cm}} + \underline{\hspace{2cm}}$

$\quad = \underline{\hspace{2cm}} + \underline{\hspace{2cm}}$

$\quad = \underline{\hspace{2cm}}$ (cm²)

⑨

⑩

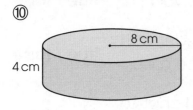

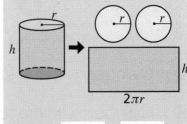

Hints

To find the surface area (S.A.) of a cylinder, add the areas of the circles and the rectangle that it comprises.

S.A. $=$ $2\pi r^2$ $+$ $2\pi rh$

area of circles · area of rectangle

Find the surface areas of the gift boxes.

⑪

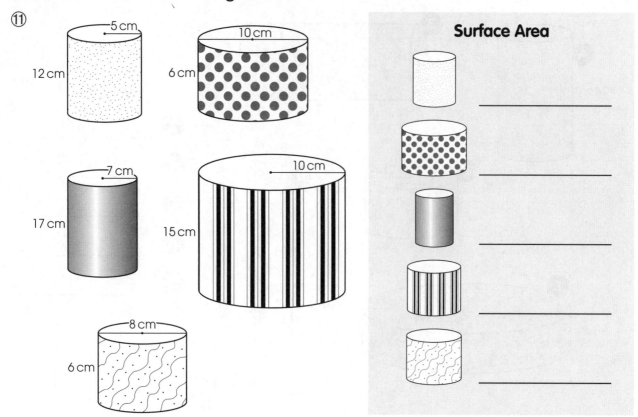

Surface Area

_____

_____

_____

_____

_____

Find the volume and surface area of each cylinder. Then circle the correct answers.

⑫

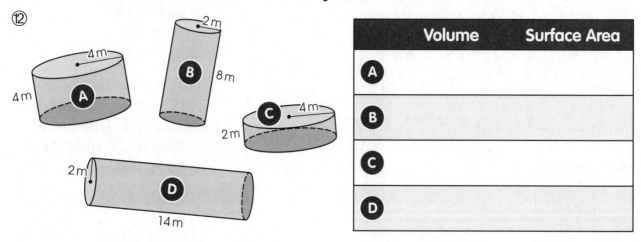

	Volume	Surface Area
Ⓐ		
Ⓑ		
Ⓒ		
Ⓓ		

⑬   Cylinders with the same volume have the same surface area.   **true / false**

⑭   Cylinders with the same surface area have the same volume.   **true / false**

⑮   For 2 cylinders that have the same base, the cylinder with the greater height has a greater volume and surface area.   **true / false**

⑯   The surface area of a cylinder is directly proportional to the area of its base.   **true / false**

Find the surface area and volume of each cylinder. Show your work.

Volume　　　　　　　　　　　　Surface Area

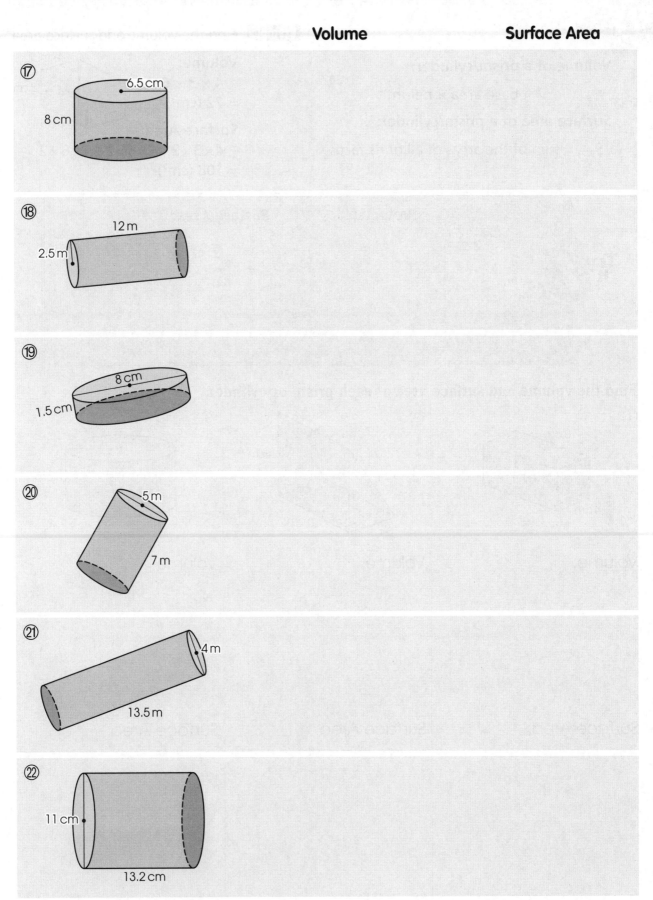

⑰ 6.5 cm   8 cm

⑱ 12 m   2.5 m

⑲ 8 cm   1.5 cm

⑳ 5 m   7 m

㉑ 4 m   13.5 m

㉒ 11 cm   13.2 cm

LEVEL 2 – FURTHER YOUR UNDERSTANDING

6 Volume and Surface Area

- finding the volumes and surface areas of prisms and cylinders

Read This

Volume of a prism/cylinder:

$$V = \text{base area} \times \text{height}$$

Surface area of a prism/cylinder:

S.A. = sum of the areas of all of its faces

Example Find the volume and surface area.

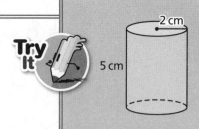

Volume:

$4 \times 3 \times 6$
$= 72 \ (\text{cm}^3)$

Surface Area:

$4 \times 3 \times 2 + 4 \times 6 \times 2 + 3 \times 6 \times 2$
$= 108 \ (\text{cm}^2)$

Try It

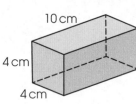

Volume: Surface Area:

Find the volume and surface area of each prism or cylinder.

①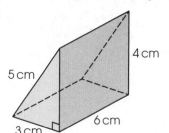

Volume:

Surface Area:

②

Volume:

Surface Area:

③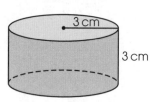

Volume:

Surface Area:

④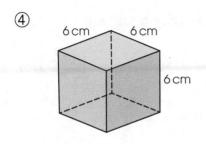

6 cm   6 cm

6 cm

Volume:

Surface Area:

⑤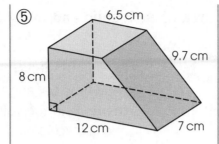

6.5 cm

9.7 cm

8 cm

12 cm   7 cm

Volume:

Surface Area:

⑥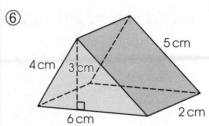

5 cm

4 cm   3 cm

6 cm   2 cm

Volume:

Surface Area:

⑦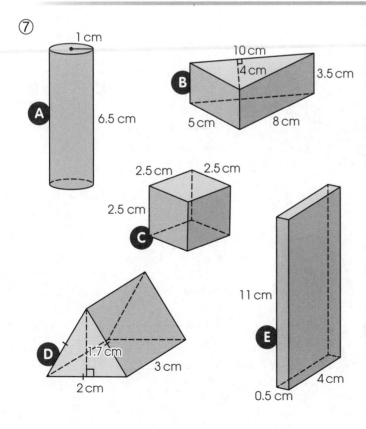

A   1 cm

6.5 cm

B   10 cm   4 cm   3.5 cm

5 cm   8 cm

C   2.5 cm   2.5 cm

2.5 cm

D   1.7 cm

2 cm   3 cm

E   11 cm

0.5 cm   4 cm

	Volume	Surface Area
A		
B		
C		
D		
E		

Find the volume and surface area of each solid and the solids they compose.

⑧

A

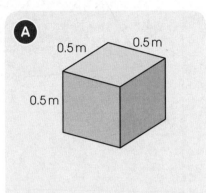

0.5 m   0.5 m

0.5 m

V = _____

S.A. = _____

I'll glue the solids as shown below and paint them. Find the volumes and surface areas.

a.

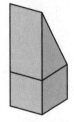

V = _____

S.A. = _____

B

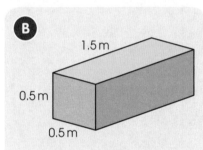

1.5 m

0.5 m

0.5 m

V = _____

S.A. = _____

b.

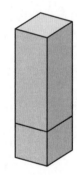

V = _____

S.A. = _____

c.

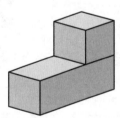

V = _____

S.A. = _____

C

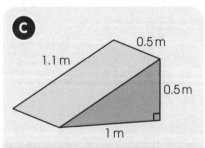

0.5 m

1.1 m

0.5 m

1 m

V = _____

S.A. = _____

d.

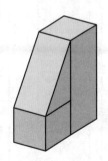

V = _____

S.A. = _____

Find the volumes and surface areas.

⑨

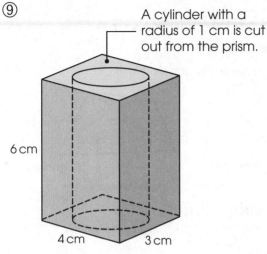

A cylinder with a radius of 1 cm is cut out from the prism.

6 cm

4 cm   3 cm

V = _____   S.A. = _____

⑩

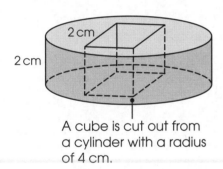

2 cm

2 cm

A cube is cut out from a cylinder with a radius of 4 cm.

V = _____   S.A. = _____

⑪

A prism is inserted into a cylinder with a diameter of 12 cm.

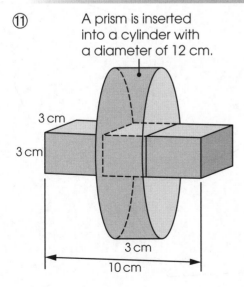

3 cm

3 cm

3 cm

10 cm

V = _____   S.A. = _____

7 2-D and 3-D Geometry

• understanding the geometric properties of polygons and polyhedrons

Diagonals are lines that join non-adjacent vertices in a polygon. They can be used to classify polygons. For example, triangles are polygons that do not have diagonals.

Example Draw the diagonals of each polygon.

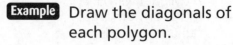
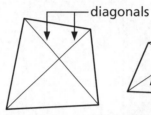
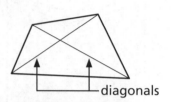

Trace the diagonals of each polygon.

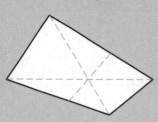

Draw the diagonals of each polygon where possible.

①

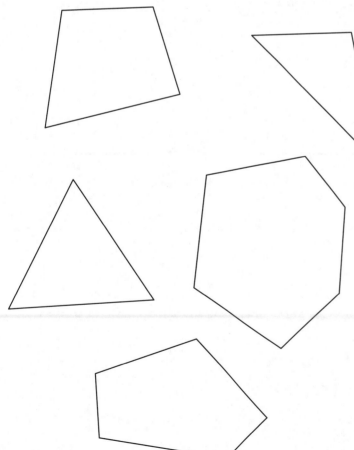
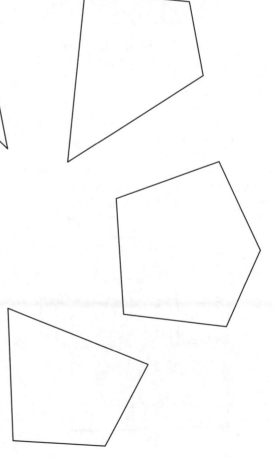

Write "T" for the true statements and "F" for the false ones. For each false statement, draw an example to show why it is false.

② **A** A triangle has no diagonals. _____

| Use the space below for drawing. Label each drawing with the corresponding letter.

B One of the diagonals of a polygon must be a line of symmetry. _____

C All the diagonals of a polygon must intersect at one point. _____

D The diagonals of a quadrilateral must intersect at one point. _____

E A line of symmetry must be a diagonal of a polygon. _____

F Polygons that have diagonals must have at least 2 diagonals. _____

LEVEL 2 – FURTHER YOUR UNDERSTANDING

Add markings to each quadrilateral and draw the diagonals. Then check its properties and answer the questions.

③ **Square**

A 4 right angles

B 2 diagonals

C 2 lines of symmetry

D 4 equal sides

 *Tips*

equal sides

parallel sides

right angles

equal angles

If there is more than one set of equal sides/ angles or parallel sides in a shape, use two or more marks to differentiate them.

e.g.

④ **Kite**

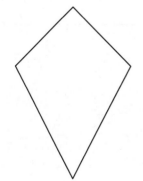

A 2 diagonals

B 2 lines of symmetry

C 1 pair of parallel sides

D must have an acute angle

⑤ **Parallellogram**

(A) no lines of symmetry   (B) 2 pairs of equal sides

(C) no diagonals   (D) same number of acute and obtuse angles

⑥ **Rhombus**

(A) 4 equal sides   (B) more than 2 diagonals

(C) 2 pairs of parallel sides   (D) same number of acute and obtuse angles

⑦ **Rectangle**

(A) 2 pairs of equal sides   (B) 2 pairs of parallel sides

(C) 4 right angles   (D) rotational symmetry of order 2

⑧ **Trapezoid**

(A) 1 pair of parallel sides   (B) cannot have lines of symmetry

(C) cannot have equal sides   (D) can have 0 or 2 right angles

⑨ Which quadrilaterals have diagonals that

a. are equal in length?   _____

b. bisect each other?   _____

c. are perpendicular?   _____

d. are perpendicular bisectors?   _____

⑩ Are the diagonals of trapezoids always equal in length? Draw an example to support your answer.

_____

Name each polyhedron. Then complete the table and answer the questions.

⑪

A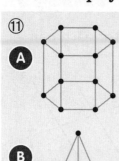

B

C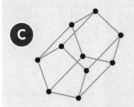

D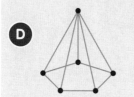

E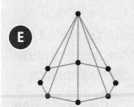

F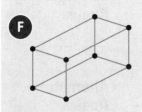

G

H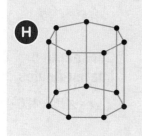

	Name	Number of			No. of faces + No. of vertices	No. of edges + 2
		faces	vertices	edges		
A						
B						
C						
D						
E						
F						
G						
H						

a. Compare the last two columns in the table. What is the relationship between the number of edges of a polyhedron and the sum of the number of faces and vertices it has? Check the equation that expresses it.

   Ⓐ No. of Faces + No. of Edges = No. of Vertices + 2

   Ⓑ No. of Faces + 2 = No. of Vertices + No. of Edges

   Ⓒ No. of Faces + No. of Vertices = No. of Edges + 2

b. A prism has 12 faces and 20 vertices. How many edges does it have? _____

c. A pyramid has 10 vertices and 18 edges. How many faces does it have? _____

8 Lines, Angles, and Triangles

- understanding angle relationships of intersecting lines, parallel lines, and triangles

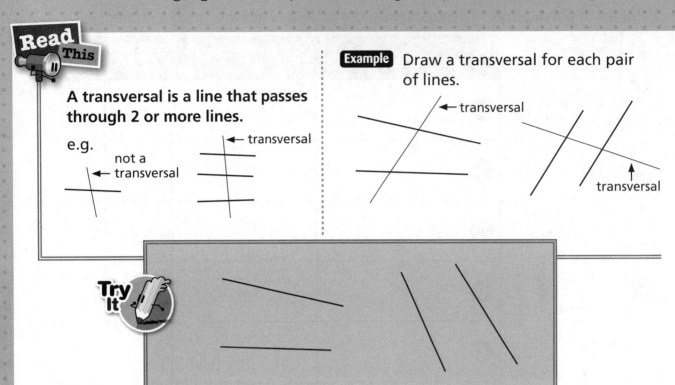

Read This

A transversal is a line that passes through 2 or more lines.

e.g.

← not a transversal

← transversal

Example Draw a transversal for each pair of lines.

← transversal

↑ transversal

Try It

Identify the angle relationship of each pair of angles.

①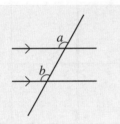

②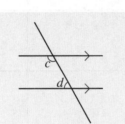

_____

③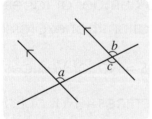

∠a and ∠b:

_____

∠a and ∠c:

_____

④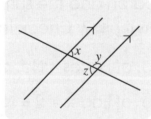

∠x and ∠y:

_____

∠x and ∠z:

_____

Hints

When parallel lines are cut by a transversal, the angles created have special relationships.

Corresponding Angles

∠a = ∠b

Alternate Angles

- interior:

  ∠a = ∠b

- exterior:

  ∠c = ∠d

Consecutive Interior Angles

∠a + ∠b = 180°

Find the unknown angles.

⑤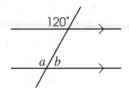

a = _____

b = _____

⑥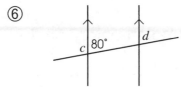

c = _____

d = _____

⑦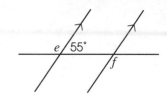

e = _____

f = _____

⑧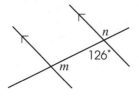

m = _____

n = _____

⑨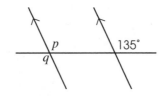

p = _____

q = _____

⑩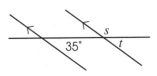

s = _____

t = _____

Identify the opposite angles. Then find the unknown angles.

⑪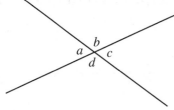

Opposite Angles

• ∠a and _____

• ∠b and _____

⑫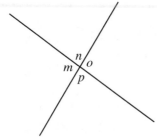

Opposite Angles

• _____ and _____

• _____ and _____

Hints

Opposite angles are congruent angles formed by two intersecting lines.

e.g.

Opposite angles: ∠a = ∠b

⑬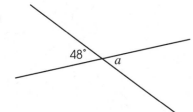

a = _____

⑭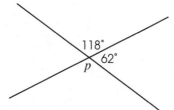

p = _____

⑮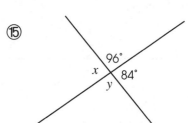

x = _____

y = _____

List the complementary and supplementary angles.

⑯

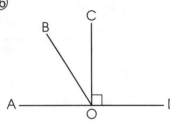

Complementary Angles:

∠AOB and _____

Supplementary Angles:

∠AOB and _____

Hints

Complementary Angles

∠a + ∠b = 90°

Supplementary Angles

∠a + ∠b = 180°

⑰

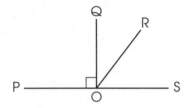

Complementary Angles:

_____

Supplementary Angles:

_____

_____

⑱

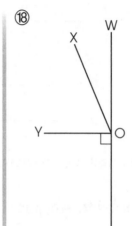

Complementary Angles:

_____

Supplementary Angles:

_____

_____

Find the unknown angles.

⑲

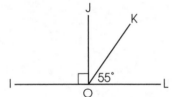

∠JOK = _____

⑳

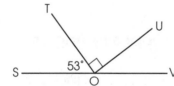

∠UOV = _____

㉑

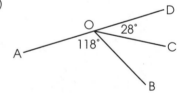

∠BOC = _____

㉒

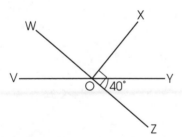

∠XOY = _____

∠VOW = _____

∠WOX = _____

㉓

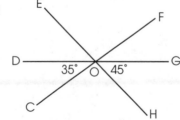

∠COH = _____

∠EOF = _____

∠FOG = _____

㉔

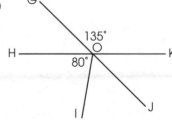

∠JOK = _____

∠IOJ = _____

∠GOH = _____

Find the third angle of each triangle. Then identify whether the triangle is scalene, isosceles, or equilateral.

Hints

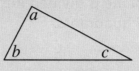

The sum of the angles in a triangle is 180°.

$\angle a + \angle b + \angle c = 180°$

㉕ 40° 100° _____ _____ triangle

㉖ 45° 60° _____ _____ triangle

㉗ 60° 60° _____ _____ triangle

LEVEL 2 – FURTHER YOUR UNDERSTANDING

Find the unknown angles.

㉘
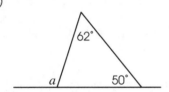

$a =$ _____

㉙
62° ... 50°

$m =$ _____

㉚
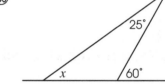

$x =$ _____

㉛
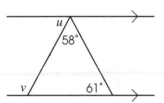

$u =$ _____

$v =$ _____

㉜
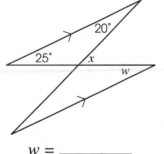

$w =$ _____

$x =$ _____

㉝
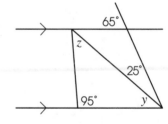

$y =$ _____

$z =$ _____

㉞
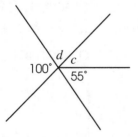

$c =$ _____

$d =$ _____

㉟
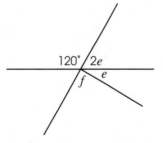

$e =$ _____

$f =$ _____

㊱
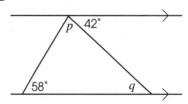

$p =$ _____

$q =$ _____

9 Cartesian Coordinate Plane

• using the Cartesian coordinate plane

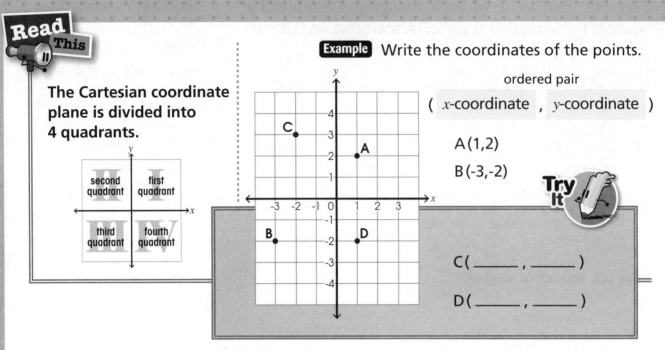

Read This

The Cartesian coordinate plane is divided into 4 quadrants.

II second quadrant	**I** first quadrant
III third quadrant	**IV** fourth quadrant

Example Write the coordinates of the points.

ordered pair

(*x*-coordinate , *y*-coordinate)

A (1,2)

B (-3,-2)

Try It

C (_____ , _____)

D (_____ , _____)

Find the coordinates and fill in the blanks.

①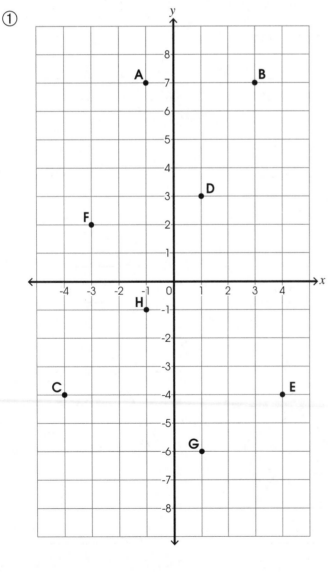

a. List the points and the coordinates under the quadrants they are in.
   • first quadrant:

   _____

   • second quadrant:

   _____

   • third quadrant:

   _____

   • fourth quadrant:

   _____

b. Investigate the signs of the *x*- and *y*-coordinates of the points. Write "+" or "–" in the boxes for each quadrant.

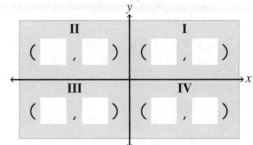

Check the correct location for each ordered pair.

② **(-5,6)**
- Ⓐ second quadrant
- Ⓑ third quadrant
- Ⓒ origin

③ **(0,-2)**
- Ⓐ x-axis
- Ⓑ y-axis
- Ⓒ third quadrant

④ **(0,0)**
- Ⓐ first quadrant
- Ⓑ third quadrant
- Ⓒ origin

⑤ **(-6,0)**
- Ⓐ x-axis
- Ⓑ y-axis
- Ⓒ second quadrant

⑥ **(3,-1)**
- Ⓐ second quadrant
- Ⓑ third quadrant
- Ⓒ fourth quadrant

⑦ **(5,3)**
- Ⓐ first quadrant
- Ⓑ second quadrant
- Ⓒ fourth quadrant

Plot the vertices and draw the shapes. Then find the perimeter and area of each.

⑧

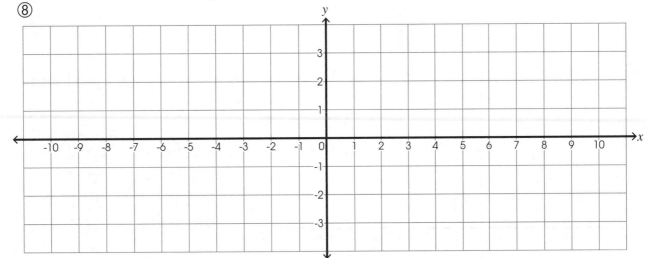

A(-4,2) B(2,2) C(2,-1) D(-4,-1)	P(-9,3) Q(-6,3) R(-9,-3)	M(7,3) N(4,0) O(7,-3) P(10,0)
Perimeter:	Perimeter:	Perimeter:
Area:	Area:	Area:

Draw the shapes with vertices at the specified coordinates. Then describe the transformations.

⑨

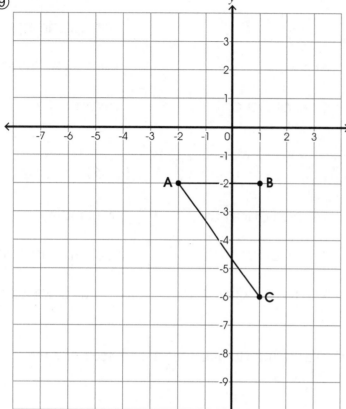

a. Plot the vertices and draw the shapes.

△DEF	△IJK
D(-7,3)	I(0,2)
E(-4,3)	J(3,2)
F(-4,-1)	K(3,-2)

b. Describe the transformations.

• △ABC to △DEF:

_____

_____

• △ABC to △IJK:

_____

_____

⑩

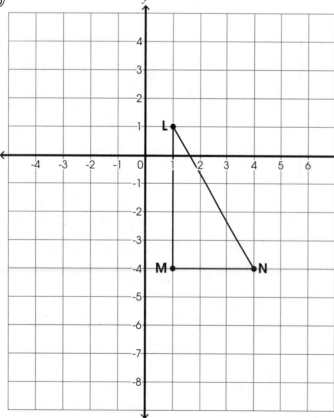

a. Plot the vertices and draw the shapes.

△PQR	△XYZ
P(1,1)	X(-1,1)
Q(6,1)	Y(-1,-4)
R(6,4)	Z(-4,-4)

b. Describe the transformations.

• △LMN to △PQR:

_____

_____

• △LMN to △XYZ:

_____

_____

Do the transformations and write the coordinates. Then answer the questions.

⑪

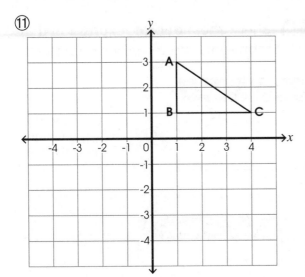

a. Draw and label the images.

- △A₁B₁C₁:
  reflection of △ABC
  in the *x*-axis

- △A₂B₂C₂:
  reflection of △ABC
  in the *y*-axis

b. List the coordinates.

△ABC	△A₁B₁C₁	△A₂B₂C₂
A(1,3)	A₁(,)	A₂(,)
B(1,1)	B₁(,)	B₂(,)
C(4,1)	C₁(,)	C₂(,)

⑫

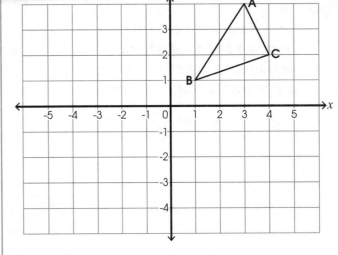

a. Draw and label the images.

- △A₁B₁C₁: rotate △ABC 90°
  clockwise about (0,0)

- △A₂B₂C₂: rotate △ABC 180°
  about (0,0)

- △A₃B₃C₃: rotate △ABC 270°
  clockwise about (0,0)

b. List the coordinates.

△ABC	△A₁B₁C₁	△A₂B₂C₂	△A₃B₃C₃
A(3,4)	A₁(,)	A₂(,)	A₃(,)
B(1,1)	B₁(,)	B₂(,)	B₃(,)
C(4,2)	C₁(,)	C₂(,)	C₃(,)

⑬ Look at each transformation above. Fill in the blanks to show the change in the coordinates.

Transformations

- reflection in the *x*-axis: (a,b) ⟶ _____

- reflection in the *y*-axis: (a,b) ⟶ _____

- 90° clockwise rotation about (0,0): (a,b) ⟶ _____

- 180° rotation about (0,0): (a,b) ⟶ _____

- 270° clockwise rotation about (0,0): (a,b) ⟶ _____

(-a,-b)

(-a,b)

(a,-b)

(-b,a)

(b,-a)

10 Linear Patterns

• understanding linear patterns

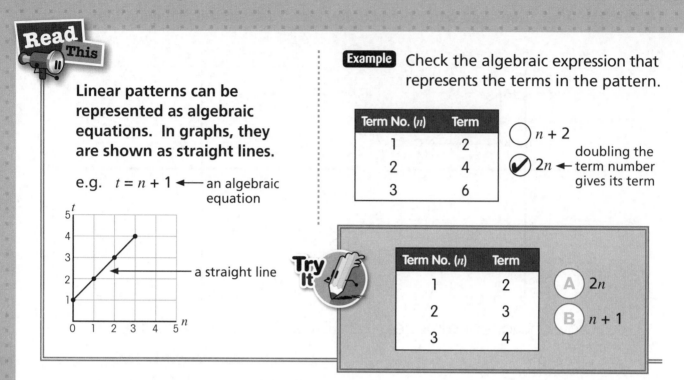

Read This

Linear patterns can be represented as algebraic equations. In graphs, they are shown as straight lines.

e.g. $t = n + 1$ ← an algebraic equation

a straight line

Example Check the algebraic expression that represents the terms in the pattern.

Term No. (n)	Term
1	2
2	4
3	6

○ $n + 2$

✓ $2n$ ← doubling the term number gives its term

Try It

Term No. (n)	Term
1	2
2	3
3	4

Ⓐ $2n$

Ⓑ $n + 1$

Count the number of sticks used to create each pattern. Complete the table for each. Then check the algebraic expression that represents the terms for term number n.

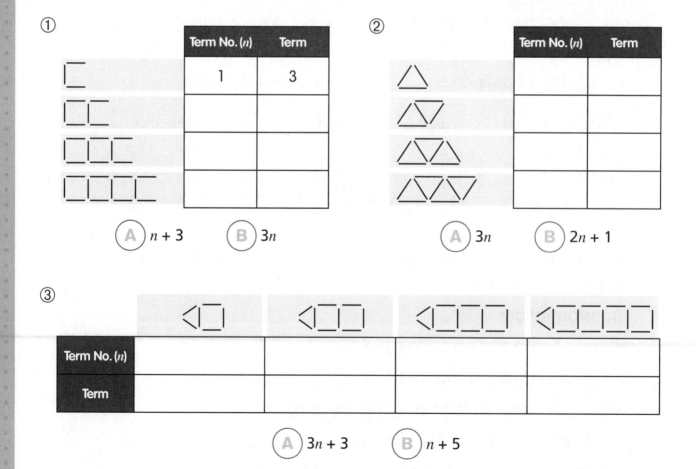

①

Term No. (n)	Term
1	3

Ⓐ $n + 3$ Ⓑ $3n$

②

Term No. (n)	Term

Ⓐ $3n$ Ⓑ $2n + 1$

③

Term No. (n)				
Term				

Ⓐ $3n + 3$ Ⓑ $n + 5$

Complete the tables and write the algebraic expressions. Then answer the questions.

④

Pattern A

Term No.	Term
1	7
2	8
3	9
4	
5	

nth term: $n +$ _____

Pattern B

Term No.	Term
1	1
2	3
3	5
4	
5	

nth term: _____

Pattern C

Term No.	Term
1	1
2	4
3	7
4	
5	

nth term: _____

⑤ Find the term of the given term number for each pattern.

a. 8th term

- Pattern A: _____
- Pattern B: _____
- Pattern C: _____

b. 10th term

- Pattern A: _____
- Pattern B: _____
- Pattern C: _____

⑥

Use the term to determine the term number for each pattern. If the term doesn't exist in the pattern, put a cross.

Term		7	9	19	22	25
Term Number in Pattern	A					
	B					
	C					

Find the terms for each pattern, where n is the term number and t is the term. Then answer the questions and match the patterns.

⑦ **Ann's Pattern:** $t = n + 2$

Term No. (n)	1	2	3	4	5
Term (t)					

Ben's Pattern: $t = n - 1$

Term No. (n)	1	2	3	4	5
Term (t)					

Carl's Pattern: $t = 3n + 1$

Term No. (n)	1	2	3	4	5
Term (t)					

Dan's Pattern: $t = 2n - 2$

Term No. (n)	1	2	3	4	5
Term (t)					

⑧ What is the 10th term in

   a. Ann's pattern? _____

   b. Ben's pattern? _____

⑨ What is the term number of 16 in

   a. Carl's pattern? _____

   b. Dan's pattern? _____

⑩ Whose pattern has each term below? Specify the term number.

   a. Term: 2

   _____

   _____

   b. Term: 9

   _____

   _____

⑪

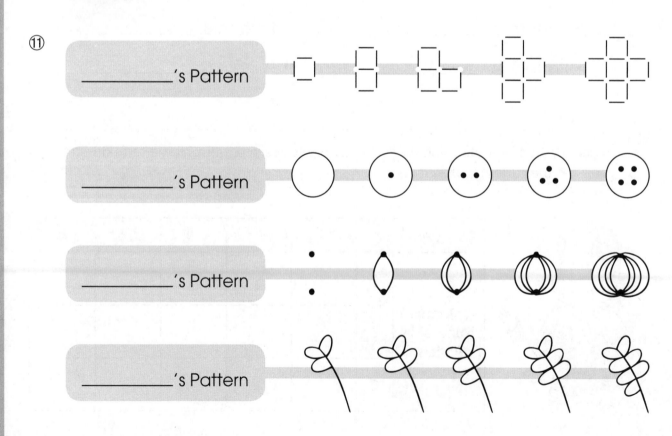

_____'s Pattern

_____'s Pattern

_____'s Pattern

_____'s Pattern

Complete the tables and graph the patterns. Then answer the questions.

⑫

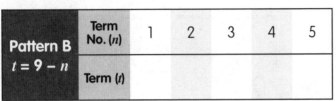

Pattern A $t = n + 1$	Term No. (n)	1	2	3	4	5
	Term (t)					

Pattern B $t = 9 - n$	Term No. (n)	1	2	3	4	5
	Term (t)					

Pattern C $t = 2n$	Term No. (n)	1	2	3	4	5
	Term (t)					

Term Numbers and Terms

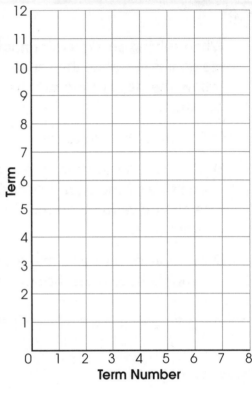

⑬ Find the common term number and term for each pair of patterns.

a. Patterns A and B

common	
term no.	term

b. Patterns A and C

common	
term no.	term

c. Patterns B and C

common	
term no.	term

⑭ Extend the lines of the patterns to find the answers.

a. Is 9 the 8th term of Pattern A? _____

b. Is 12 the 7th term of Pattern C? _____

c. Which pattern has 3 as its 6th term? _____

⑮ Does Pattern A have 0 as a term? _____

⑯ Does Pattern B have a term that is greater than 10? _____

⑰ Does Pattern C have 9 as a term? _____

⑱ Which pattern has a greater value in its 25th term,
Pattern A or Pattern C? _____

11 Linear Equations

- solving linear equations

When solving an algebraic equation, the goal is to isolate the variable. Follow the steps below to solve an equation.

❶ Combine the like terms.

❷ Move all the constant terms to one side of the equation and leave the variable on the other side.

❸ Multiply or divide to make the variable have a coefficient of 1.

Example Solve the equation.

$$6x - 5 = 13$$
$$6x - 5 + 5 = 13 + 5 \leftarrow \text{Add 5 on both sides.}$$
$$6x = 18$$
$$6x \div 6 = 18 \div 6 \leftarrow \text{Divide both sides by 6.}$$
$$x = 3$$

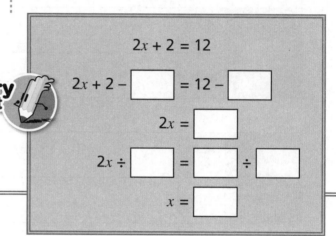

$$2x + 2 = 12$$

$$2x + 2 - \boxed{} = 12 - \boxed{}$$

$$2x = \boxed{}$$

$$2x \div \boxed{} = \boxed{} \div \boxed{}$$

$$x = \boxed{}$$

Solve the equations.

① $2x + 5 = 11$

② $\dfrac{n}{5} - 1 = 4$

③ $3y + 2 = 8$

④ $\dfrac{4}{9}k = 8$

⑤ $3 + \dfrac{m}{4} = 9$

⑥ $12 = 2 + \dfrac{a}{3}$

⑦ $6x + 7x = 52$

⑧ $6 - k = k + 2$

⑨ $3y = 32 - 5y$

Check each correct equation. Then solve it and check your answer.

⑩ The difference of 10 and the product of 5 and n is 20.

  Ⓐ $10 + 5n = 20$

  Ⓑ $5n - 10 = 20$

Check

To check your answer, substitute the answer into the equation. If the left side of the equation equals the right side, then the answer is correct.

e.g. $3a + 1 = 7$. Is $a = 2$ correct?

  $\text{left side} = 3a + 1$

  $= 3(2) + 1$

  $= 7$ ← equal to the right side

So, $a = 2$ is correct.

⑪ Multiplying m by 9 and subtracting the product by 10 gives 8.

  Ⓐ $(9 - m) \times 10 = 8$

  Ⓑ $9m - 10 = 8$

Check

⑫ x divided by 6 and then increased by 4 is 7.

  Ⓐ $x \div 6 + 4 = 7$

  Ⓑ $x \div 6 + 7 = 4$

Check

⑬ Three quarters of y minus 5 is 4.

  Ⓐ $\frac{3}{4}(y - 5) = 4$

  Ⓑ $\frac{3}{4}y - 5 = 4$

Check

⑭ Two fifths of q plus 2 is equal to 8.

  Ⓐ $\frac{2}{5}q + 2 = 8$

  Ⓑ $(q + 2) \times \frac{2}{5} = 8$

Check

Read what each child says and set up a corresponding equation. Then solve it and check your answer using substitution.

⑮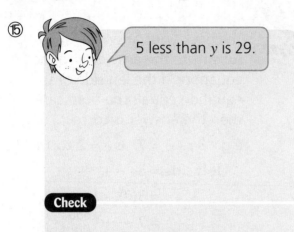

5 less than y is 29.

Check

⑯

9 subtracted from z is -4.

Check

⑰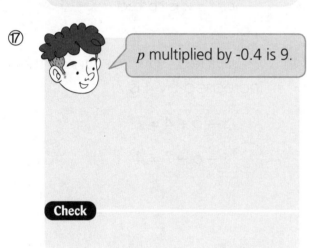

p multiplied by -0.4 is 9.

Check

⑱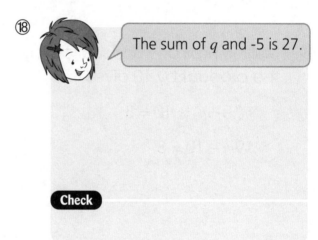

The sum of q and -5 is 27.

Check

Simplify the equations and solve them. Then check your answers using substitution.

⑲ $9y + 5 = y + 37$

⑳ $4p + 5 + 8p = 11p$

㉑ $i + 6 + 4i = 18 + 8$

Check

Check

Check

Solve the equations and write the letters to find out what Jason says.

㉒ $7c + 8 = 35 - 2c$ $c = \boxed{}$

㉓ $4y + 8 = 29 - 5y$ $y = \boxed{}$

㉔ $0.6e + 0.7 = 0.4e$ $e = \boxed{}$

㉕ $\dfrac{1}{4}t + \dfrac{1}{5}t - 4 = 5$ $t = \boxed{}$

㉖ $3 - s = 6s + 24$ $s = \boxed{}$

㉗ $5 - 2a - 0.5a = -4$ $a = \boxed{}$

㉘ $0.3b - 0.8 = 0.2b - 1.9$ $b = \boxed{}$

㉙ $\dfrac{2}{3}m - \dfrac{1}{2}m + 4 = 7$ $m = \boxed{}$

㉚ $1.4h + 0.8 = 8 - 0.2h$ $h = \boxed{}$

㉛ $i - 67 + 3.2i = -4$ $i = \boxed{}$

㉜

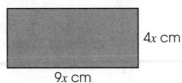

I like $\boxed{18}$ $\boxed{3\frac{3}{5}}$ $\boxed{20}$ $\boxed{4\frac{1}{2}}$ $\boxed{-3\frac{1}{2}}$ $\boxed{18}$ $\boxed{3\frac{3}{5}}$ $\boxed{20}$ $\boxed{15}$ $\boxed{3}$ $\boxed{-3}$.

Solve the problems using equations.

㉝

$4x$ cm

$9x$ cm

What is the value of x if the perimeter of the rectangle is

a. 234 cm?

b. 65 cm?

㉞

$4y$ cm

What is the value of y if the area of the square is

a. 64 cm²?

b. 256 cm²?

12 Graphs

- reading and analyzing graphs

A scatter plot is used to find the relationship between two sets of data. A line of best fit is a straight line that best represents the trend of the data on a scatter plot.

A Scatter Plot

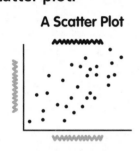

Example What trend does the scatter plot show?

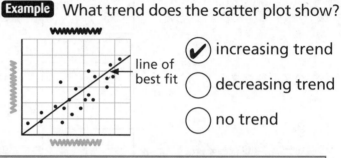

line of best fit

✓ increasing trend

◯ decreasing trend

◯ no trend

Try It

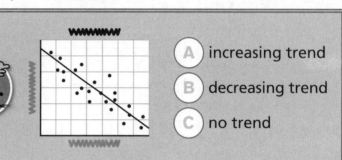

A increasing trend

B decreasing trend

C no trend

For each scatter plot, draw a line of best fit. Then identify the trend and fill in the blanks with "increased" or "decreased".

① Paul recorded the number of swimmers at the pool and the temperature outside.

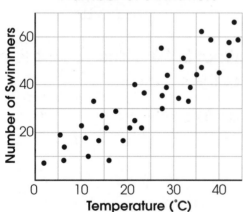

Temperature vs. Number of Swimmers

_____ trend

As the temperature increased, the number of swimmers at the pool _____ .

② Tony tracked how long it took him to bike to the park each weekend.

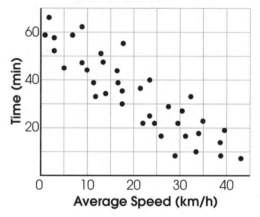

Average Speed vs. Time Spent Biking

_____ trend

As Tony's speed increased, the amount of time it took to reach the park _____ .

For each scatter plot, draw a line of best fit. Then answer the questions.

③ Thomas recorded the number of traffic lights he passed by during his car rides around the city.

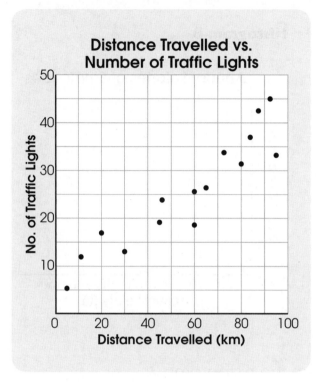

a. Describe the trend.

_____

_____

b. Would Thomas expect to pass by more traffic lights travelling 50 km or travelling 70 km? Explain.

_____

_____

c. About how many traffic lights would Thomas pass by if he travelled 40 km?

_____

_____

④ Mr. Drakam recorded the number of classes his students missed and their Math grades.

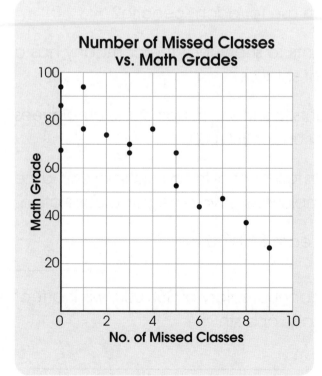

a. Describe the trend.

_____

_____

b. Janice missed 3 classes. Predict her Math grade.

_____

_____

c. What conclusion can you draw from the scatter plot?

_____

_____

_____

Read the histograms and answer the questions.

⑤ Ms. Smith owns ABC Company. She keeps a record of her employees' salaries. She created two histograms to represent the same set of data.

Histogram A

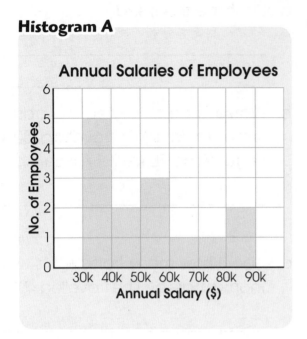

Histogram B

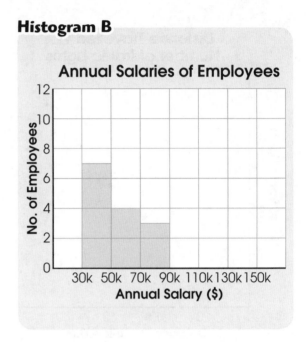

a. Describe two differences between the histograms.

• _____

• _____

b. Which histogram should Ms. Smith use for each scenario?

Scenario A

Ms. Smith wants to show that the company has a wide range of salaries.

Scenario B

Ms. Smith wants to show that half of the employees have a salary under $50 000.

Scenario C

Ms. Smith wants to show that the annual salaries and the number of employees have a negative correlation.

c. What percent of the employees earn $40 000 to $50 000 a year? _____

d. If a new employee is hired at an annual salary of $65 000, will it affect the median salary, the mode salary, or both?

_____

Read the graphs and answer the questions.

⑥ Ali recorded the ice cream orders from children and adults below.

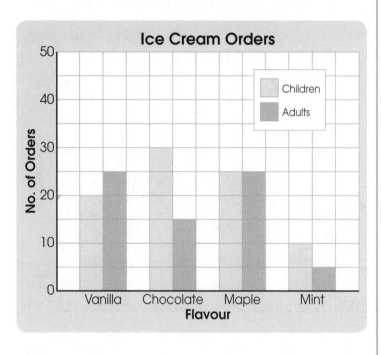

Ice Cream Orders

a. Which flavours were twice as popular among children as adults?

_____

b. Find the mean, median, and mode adult ice cream orders.

- mean: _____ orders
- median: _____ orders
- mode: _____ orders

c. Do you think a histogram is suitable for representing the data? Explain.

_____

_____

⑦ The tickets sold for a concert at different times are shown in the graphs below.

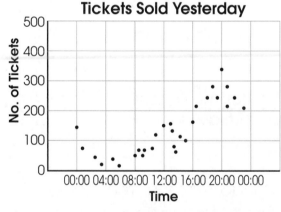

Tickets Sold Yesterday

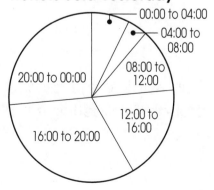

Tickets Sold Yesterday

00:00 to 04:00
04:00 to 08:00
08:00 to 12:00
12:00 to 16:00
16:00 to 20:00
20:00 to 00:00

a. Describe the trend of ticket sales shown in the scatter plot.

_____

_____

b. What percent of the tickets were sold

- from 00:00 to 12:00? _____
- from 12:00 to 00:00? _____

c. What reason(s) would you give for the results you found in question b. Explain.

_____

_____

_____

_____

* understanding theoretical and experimental probabilities

Read This

Theoretical probability is the chance that an event occurs in theory.

e.g. flipping a coin

$$P(H) = \frac{1}{2} \qquad P(T) = \frac{1}{2}$$

Experimental probability is the chance that an event occurs based on experimental results.

e.g. flipping a coin 5 times: 2 heads and 3 tails

$$P(H) = \frac{2}{5} \qquad P(T) = \frac{3}{5}$$

Example Billy spins the spinner. Find the probabilities.

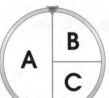

Probability of spinning
* A: <u>50%</u> ⎤
* B: <u>25%</u> ⎬ theoretical probabilities
* C: <u>25%</u> ⎦

Try It

Billy spins the spinner 20 times. He got 9 As, 5 Bs, and 6 Cs.

Probability of spinning

A: _____   B: _____   C: _____

Read each description. Determine whether it is about theoretical probability (TP) or experimental probability (EP).

①

$$\text{Probability} = \frac{\text{no. of favourable outcomes}}{\text{total no. of possible outcomes}}$$ _____

②

$$\text{Probability} = \frac{\text{no. of times an outcome occurs}}{\text{total no. of trials}}$$ _____

③ Klay recorded the results of the trials to find the probabilities of the events.

_____

④ Ronda made a tree diagram to find all the possible outcomes.

_____

⑤ To find the probabilities, Liza counted the number of trials.

_____

⑥ Danny rolled the dice to find the probability of getting each number.

_____

Find the probabilities.

⑦ **Flip the coin!**

Andrea flipped the coin 10 times and got 4 heads and 6 tails.

Theoretical Probability | Experimental Probability

• heads: _____ • tails: _____ | • heads: _____ • tails: _____

⑧ **Roll the dice!**

Tommy rolled the dice 15 times. He got five 1s, two 2s, two 3s, two 4s, zero 5s, and four 6s.

Theoretical Probability | Experimental Probability

• 1: _____ • 2: _____ | • 1: _____ • 2: _____

• 3: _____ • 4: _____ | • 3: _____ • 4: _____

• 5: _____ • 6: _____ | • 5: _____ • 6: _____

⑨ **Spin it!**

Janice spun the wheel 20 times and got 12 As, 5 Bs, and 3 Cs.

Theoretical Probability | Experimental Probability

• A: _____ • B: _____ • C: _____ | • A: _____ • B: _____ • C: _____

⑩ **Pick a ball!**

Nelson picked a ball 30 times. He got 10 , 14 , and 6 .

Theoretical Probability | Experimental Probability

• : _____ • : _____ | • : _____ • : _____

• : _____ | • : _____

Find a coin and a dice for this activity. Then draw a tree diagram and complete the table to find the probabilities.

⑪

> For this activity, a coin is flipped and a dice is rolled. Complete the tree diagram to show the theoretical probabilities. Then flip a coin, roll a dice, and record your results to find the experimental probabilities.

a.

Coin   Dice   Result

        1 ——— H1
       2 ——— H2
    H < 3 ——— H3

Theoretical Probability

What is the probability of getting

- heads and a 3?　　　_____

- tails and a 1?　　　_____

- heads?　　　_____

- tails and an even number?　　　_____

- heads and a prime number?　　　_____

b.

Repeat the activity 24 times and record your results.

1 □　2 □　3 □　4 □

5 □　6 □　7 □　8 □

9 □　10 □　11 □　12 □

13 □　14 □　15 □　16 □

17 □　18 □　19 □　20 □

21 □　22 □　23 □　24 □

Experimental Probability

What is the probability of getting

- tails and a 2?　　　_____

- heads and a 5?　　　_____

- tails?　　　_____

- 6?　　　_____

- heads and an odd number?　　　_____

- tails and a prime number?　　　_____

Read what Maggy says. Find the probabilities and check the correct answers.

⑫

> A coin is flipped. Find the theoretical probability of getting heads and getting tails. Then flip a coin yourself. Use tally marks to record your results and find the experimental probabilities.

Theoretical Probability

P(H): _____

P(T): _____

Experimental Probability

	4 trials	20 trials	50 trials
H			
T			

4 trials
P(H): _____
P(T): _____

20 trials
P(H): _____
P(T): _____

50 trials
P(H): _____
P(T): _____

a. Which number of trials yielded experimental probabilities that are closest to the theoretical probabilities?

(A) 4 trials   (B) 20 trials   (C) 50 trials

b. Which statement is correct?

(A) Increasing the number of trials changes the theoretical probability.

(B) As the number of trials increases, the experimental probability gets closer to the theoretical probability.

Check the complementary event for each.

⑬ **Complementary Event**

a.
flipping heads on a coin
(A) flipping heads twice
(B) flipping tails

b.
spinning red on a spinner
(A) not spinning red
(B) spinning yellow

c.
rolling a 1 on a dice
(A) rolling a 6
(B) rolling a number that is not 1

d.
not picking a blue ball
(A) picking a blue ball
(B) picking a blue or green ball

Hints

Complementary events are two or more non-overlapping outcomes that account for all possible outcomes.

e.g.   Roll a dice.

roll an even number   roll an odd number

complementary events

LEVEL 3
APPLICATIONS

1 Powers and Roots

- solving word problems involving powers and roots

Try It

Fred made a big square with 81 square tiles. He then took one row of tiles and rearranged them into a small square. How many tiles are there in one row of the small square?

No. of tiles in one row of big square: $\sqrt{81}$ = ☐

No. of tiles in one row of small square: $\sqrt{☐}$ = ☐

There are ☐ tiles in one row of the small square.

Read This

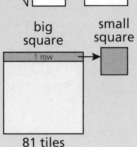

A = Area   s = side length

$$A = s^2 \quad | \quad s = \sqrt{A}$$

big square   small square

1 row

81 tiles

Answer the questions.

① Conrad made a big square with 256 blocks. He then rearranged one row of blocks into a medium square. After that, he rearranged one row of the medium square into a small square. How many blocks are there in one row of the small square?

_____

② Look at the solutions Alex and Doris have.

a. Who has a better answer to Question 1? Explain.

_____

_____

Question 1

Alex	Doris
$\sqrt{8} \times \sqrt{50}$	$\sqrt{8} \times \sqrt{50}$
$= \sqrt{8 \times 50}$	$= 2.83 \times 7.07$
$= \sqrt{400}$	$= 20.01$
$= 20$	

b. Whose way of finding the answer to Question 2 is more efficient? Explain.

_____

_____

Question 2

Alex	Doris
$\sqrt{64} \times \sqrt{81}$	$\sqrt{64} \times \sqrt{81}$
$= \sqrt{5184}$	$= 8 \times 9$
$= 72$	$= 72$

③ Find the exact answers without a calculator.

a. Find the square of the square root of 3.

_____

b. Find the square root of the square of 0.2137.

_____

④ a. Write each number as a product of prime factors.

| 36 | 81 | 144 | 210 | 500 | 900 |

- 36 = _____   • 81 = _____

- 144 = _____   • 210 = _____

- 500 = _____   • 900 = _____

b. Which numbers are perfect squares? Look at how perfect squares differ from non-perfect squares when written as products of prime numbers. What do you find?

_____

_____

⑤ Determine the smallest possible integer that, when multiplied by 20, will result in a perfect square. Explain how you found the answer.

_____

_____

_____

⑥ Find all the factors of 2160 that are perfect squares.

Tips

Find the number as a product of prime factors first.

_____

Solve the problems. Show your work.

⑦ A rectangular mosaic wall is made up of 25 rows of 80 tiles. If it is rebuilt into the biggest possible square, how many tiles will be left over?

_____

⑧ An astronaut has spent 439 days in space. How long is this in minutes? Write your answer in scientific notation.

_____

⑨ Canada has a population of about 37 million. If, on average, every Canadian buys 1.26 books per year, how many books are sold each year to Canadians in all? Write your answer in scientific notation.

_____

⑩ In 2018, the national debt of Canada was about 755 billion dollars and the population was about 37 million. If every person in Canada paid the same amount to pay off this debt, how much would each person have to pay? (Round to the nearest cent.)

_____

⑪ The distance from Earth to the sun is about 1.5×10^8 km. The next closest star is Alpha Centauri, which is 270 000 times as far from Earth as the sun.

a. Determine in scientific notation the distance from Earth to Alpha Centauri.

_____

b. A light year is the distance light travels in one year in kilometres. Alpha Centauri is 4.28 light years away from Earth. Determine the distance of 1 light year. Write your answer in scientific notation.

_____

⑫ Pluto has a mass of 1.32×10^{22} kg and Jupiter has a mass of 1.9×10^{27} kg. How many times as heavy is Jupiter as Pluto?

_____

⑬ As of 2017, Vatican City's population is about 1000 while India's is about 1.3 billion. How many times as many people live in India as in Vatican City? Write your answer in expanded form and in scientific notation.

_____

⑭ An amusement park in Canada had about 3.7 million visitors in 2016. If this attendance is projected to double every 5 years, how many visitors are expected in 2026? Write the answer in scientific notation.

_____

⑮ On a house plant, there are 600 microscopic spider mites. If the number doubles every 30 minutes, how many mites will there be in 2 hours?

_____

⑯ Steve designed his backyard. On his blueprint, the flower bed has an area of 4.84 cm².

a. If the actual area of the flower bed is 1.21 m², how many times as small is the area of the planned flower bed as the actual one?

_____

b. If the actual area of his backyard is 9 m², what is its area on the blueprint?

_____

2 Fractions

• solving word problems involving fractions

Try It

George and Harry raced each other down a waterslide. George lost by $\frac{1}{4}$ seconds. If it took Harry $7\frac{4}{5}$ seconds, how long did it take George?

When answering questions involving fractions, always write the answer in simplest form.

$7\frac{4}{5} + \frac{1}{4}$

$= 7\frac{\boxed{}}{20} + \frac{\boxed{}}{20}$

$= \boxed{}$ It took George $\boxed{}$ seconds.

Solve the problems. Show your work. Write the answers in simplest form.

① Sammy purchased $2\frac{1}{2}$ m of fabric at $\$5\frac{3}{5}$ for each metre. How much did Sammy spend?

_____

② Joseph has a batting average of $\frac{8}{25}$ and Conner has a batting average of $\frac{7}{20}$. Who has a better batting average and by how much?

_____

③ Kelly biked $2\frac{3}{5}$ km to the library. If Kelly biked for $\frac{1}{4}$ h, what was her speed?

_____

④ $\frac{3}{7}$ of a $3\frac{1}{2}$-L bowl of fruit punch is orange juice. How much orange juice is there?

_____

⑤ Ivan can plant a flower in $\frac{3}{10}$ min.

  a. How long does it take him to plant 250 flowers?

  _____

  b. How many flowers can he plant in 20 min?

  _____

  c. If he plants a flower in $\frac{1}{4}$ min, how much time will he save when planting 250 flowers?

  _____

⑥ ABC Hamburger House sells half-pound hamburgers for $3 each. They recently began selling three-eighth-pound hamburgers for $2 each. Which is a better deal?

  _____

⑦ Pizza Uno offers $\frac{2}{3}$ of a pizza for $3. Pizza Duo offers $\frac{3}{4}$ of a pizza for $4. How much does each restaurant charge for a whole pizza?

  _____

⑧ Every litre of gasoline used produces about $2\frac{1}{2}$ g of carbon dioxide. An average family car uses about 8 litres of gasoline every 100 km travelled. How much carbon dioxide does a car produce on a 75-km trip?

  _____

⑨ David earns $12/h selling flowers. He earns $1\frac{1}{2}$ times his regular wage on weekends. How much does David earn if he works $8\frac{1}{2}$ h on Thursday and 3 h on Sunday?

  _____

⑩ A local charity raised $3300 this year.

a. $\frac{2}{15}$ of the donations came from Mr. Smith and $\frac{1}{12}$ from Ms. Brown. How much did they donate altogether?

_____

b. $\frac{1}{20}$ of the donations are used to cover administrative costs. Of the remaining money, $\frac{10}{19}$ will be given to a home for seniors. How much money will the seniors' home receive?

_____

⑪ Corel stock was worth $\$1\frac{13}{20}$ per share in September 2018 and $\$40\frac{19}{20}$ in November 2019.

a. How did the value of each share change between September 2018 and November 2019?

_____

b. Clive bought 100 Corel shares in September 2018 and sold them in November 2019. How much profit did he make?

_____

c. Write decimal representations of the value of 1 Corel share in September 2018 and in November 2019.

_____

⑫ When a jug is $\frac{1}{2}$ full, it contains enough juice to fill 3 glasses.

a. How full is the jug if it has enough juice to fill 5 glasses?

_____

b. If a full jug holds 1200 mL of juice, how much juice can one glass hold?

_____

⑬ A hiking trail around a park is divided into 4 sections.

a. What is the total length of the trail?

_____

b. What fraction of the trail does Section D take up?

_____

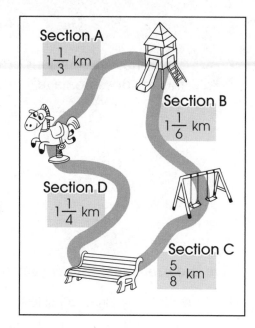

Section A
$1\frac{1}{3}$ km

Section B
$1\frac{1}{6}$ km

Section D
$1\frac{1}{4}$ km

Section C
$\frac{5}{8}$ km

c. A shortcut halves the total length of Sections C and D. How much distance is saved by using the shortcut?

_____

⑭ A recipe for crepes is shown below.

Classic Crepes

makes 4 crepes

Ingredients

• 2 eggs

• $\frac{1}{2}$ cup of flour

• $\frac{1}{3}$ cup of milk

• $1\frac{1}{2}$ tbsp* of butter

• $\frac{3}{4}$ tbsp* of sugar

*tbsp = tablespoon

How much of each ingredient is needed to make

a. 1 crepe?

_____

b. 6 crepes?

_____

3 Decimals

- solving word problems involving decimals

Jason has 2469 nickels. How much money does he have?

When giving answers as money amounts, always round the amount to the nearest cent (hundredth).

He has $ ☐ .

Solve the problems. Show your work.

① Eric drew 2 zig-zag lines. Their measurements are shown below.

> **Line A: 2 m + 5 cm + 17 mm**
> **Line B: 3 m + 20 cm + 20 mm**

What is their difference in length in metres?

_____

② A bacterium has a length of 0.00002 cm. Determine its length when viewed through a microscope with 500x magnification.

_____

③ For a pizza party, a Grade 8 class ordered 5 pizzas at $7.99 each, 8 juice boxes at $0.75 each, 24 chicken wings at $0.55 each, and 12 cans of pop at $0.49 each.

a. What is the total cost of the food items?

_____

b. If 25 students split the cost, how much would each student pay?

_____

④ In space, the Andromeda Galaxy is the farthest object we can see with the naked eye. It is 2.4×10^{19} km away. If 1 light year is 9.46×10^{12} km, what is the distance from Earth to the Andromeda Galaxy in light years?

_____

⑤ 10 friends are at a lunch buffet. The cost of the buffet is $14.95 (tax included) for each person.

a. What is the total cost?

_____

b. If 3 of the friends use a half-price coupon, what is the total cost?

_____

⑥ Erica has 2 part-time jobs. She earns $14.25/h at a toy store and $16.50/h at a gas station. One weekend she worked 3.5 h at the toy store and 4.5 h at the gas station. How much did she earn?

_____

⑦ 45 Grade 8 students at Riverview School went on a trip to the theatre. The bus cost $60.50 in total and the theatre tickets cost $15.25 for each student.

a. What was the total cost?

_____

b. How much did each student have to pay?

_____

⑧ 4 friends rented a car for $30/day plus 10¢/km. How much would each person pay if they rented the car for 3 days and drove 1000 km?

_____

⑨ Each month, the Kerr family makes 75 minutes of long distance phone calls within North America. Their long distance plan rate has just dropped from $0.15 per minute to $0.12 per minute.

  a. How much money will they save per month?

_____

  b. How much money will they save annually?

_____

⑩ Norris has 5 quarters, 7 dimes, and 8 nickels.

  a. How many candy bars can he buy if they cost $0.55 each?

_____

  b. How many lollipops can he buy if they cost $0.85 each?

_____

⑪ Neil spent a total of $125.50 on holiday gifts. He spent $35 on a sweater for his dad, $32.95 on a blouse for his mom, and $19.95 and $18.50 on 2 CDs for his sisters. He spent the rest on a gift for his friend, James. How much did he spend on that gift?

_____

⑫ A snail travelled 0.141 km on Day 1, 0.098 km on Day 2, and 0.118 km on Day 3. What was the mean distance travelled each day?

_____

⑬ Conrad earns $17.50/h and Jacky earns $19.35/h. If they both work on the same shift from 1:00 p.m. to 4:30 p.m.,

a. how much will their employer pay the two of them in total?

_____

b. how much more will Jacky earn than Conrad?

_____

⑭ Brian is filling party bags with candy. Each bag has 0.2 kg of red candy and 0.35 kg of green candy.

a. If he needs to fill 15 party bags, how many kilograms of candy does he need in all?

_____

b. If there is 1.6 kg of red candy and 3.15 kg of green candy, will there be enough candy to fill 8 party bags?

_____

c. If there is 3 kg of candy in each colour, how many party bags can he fill? How much candy in each colour will be left over?

_____

4 Percents

- solving word problems involving percents

Ms. Jones, a salesperson, earns a 7% commission on the sale price. If she sells a $129.99 dress, how much is her commission?

$129.99 × 7%

= $ ⬚

Her commission is $ ⬚ .

Read This

Commission is an amount of money earned for selling a product or providing a service.

Solve the problems. Round the answers to the nearest hundredth.

① Uncle Matthew received an 8% commission on the sale of a car for $26 500. How much did he receive?

_____

② A table costs $180 before a 9% tax. What is the total cost?

_____

③ Ken's monthly salary is $3600. What will his salary be after a 20% increase?

_____

④ A truck priced at $106 000 was sold at a 7% discount. If the sales tax was 7%, how much did the buyer pay?

_____

⑤ A basketball costs $12.50. Coach Jackson buys 20 basketballs and gets a 12% discount.

a. How much do the basketballs cost in total? _____

b. Bob the salesperson gets a 4% commission on the final price of the sale. What is his commission from Coach Jackson's purchase? _____

Solve the problems. Show your work.

⑥ A manufacturer found that 300 of 50 000 units produced are defective. What percent of the units are defective?

_____

⑦ 27% of the books in a school library are hardcover. If there are 7200 books in the library, how many books are hardcover?

_____

⑧ Mary spends 35% of her salary on utilities every month. If Mary earns $700 a month, how much does she spend on utilities?

_____

⑨ Joe had $550 in his bank account. If he withdrew $110 yesterday, what percent of his money did he withdraw?

_____

⑩ Eric deposits $2000 in an account at an interest rate of 2.4% per year and $1500 at 2.8% per year. What is the total simple interest he will receive after 3 years?

_____

⑪ 60% of the students in Mr. Wick's class have pets at home. If 21 students in his class have pets at home, how many students are there in Mr. Wick's class?

_____

⑫ An appliance store has a "Pay No Tax" day. Mr. and Mrs. Lee decide to buy a washer and dryer in this special sale. The washer costs $699.99 and the dryer costs $599.99. How much money will Mr. and Mrs. Lee save if the tax rate is 15%?

_____

⑬ A toy that previously sold for $1 now sells for 75¢. Calculate the percent decrease in the cost of the toy.

_____

⑭ The cost of dry cleaning at Carrie's Cleaners has just gone up. Cleaning a jacket used to cost $7.50 but now costs $10.

a. What is the percent increase in the cost of dry cleaning a jacket?

_____

b. The cost of cleaning pants also went up by the same percent. How much would John pay to have a jacket and a pair of pants cleaned if cleaning pants used to cost $5.70?

_____

⑮ Between 2000 and 2010, the number of vehicles in a country went from 10 256 000 to 12 811 000.

a. What was the percent increase in the number of vehicles?

_____

b. How many vehicles were there in 2020 if the rate of increase remained the same?

_____

c. 75% of vehicles 20 years old or older were dismantled in 2019. How many old vehicles would still be in service after 2019?

_____

⑯ Bill earns a 5% commission on every car he sells. One month he earned $5750 in commission. What was the total value of the cars he sold?

_____

⑰ The price of a local newspaper went up from 50¢ to 65¢. If the price of milk increased by the same percent, what would be the price of a bag of milk which previously cost $3.29?

_____

⑱ Mr. Singh invested $2520 at $7\frac{1}{2}$ % for $2\frac{1}{2}$ years. Mrs. Brown invested $2720 at 7% for the same time period. Who earned more interest?

_____

⑲ Sam received a 20% pay raise, increasing his weekly pay by $70. What was his weekly pay before the raise?

_____

⑳ The table below shows the changes in a city's rail transportation.

Year	Number of Locomotives	Number of Freight Cars	Number of Passenger Cars
1987	4821	197 907	5942
2017	3855	121 679	926

a. Determine the percent decrease in the number of passenger cars between 1987 and 2017.

_____

b. Determine the percent decrease in the number of freight cars between 1987 and 2017.

_____

• solving word problems involving ratios, rates, and proportions

Read This

Ratios and proportions are closely related. A proportion is an expression of two equivalent ratios.

Try It

In Valleyview Public School, there is a total of 35 students in Grade 8. If there are 20 girls in Grade 8, what is the ratio of boys to girls?

No. of boys: 35 – 20 = [   ]

Ratio of boys to girls: [:20] = [:   ]

The ratio of boys to girls is [   ].

Solve the problems. Show your work.

① 150 mL of lemonade is mixed with 950 mL of water.

  a. What is the ratio of lemonade to water?

  _____

  b. Using the same ratio, how much lemonade will be mixed with 2.85 L of water?

  _____

② $1500 is divided between Barry and Helen at a ratio of 2:3 respectively. How much money does Helen get?

  _____

③ The ratio of pizza combos to burger combos sold was 3:5. How many combos were sold in total if 45 burger combos were sold?

  _____

④ A discount of 16% results in saving $12.80. What is the sale price of the item?

_____

⑤ 45% of the flowers in a garden are red. What is the ratio of red flowers to non-red flowers in the garden?

_____

⑥ A mail courier can deliver 20 letters in 30 minutes. How many letters can be delivered in 4 and a half hours?

_____

⑦ A beekeeper collected 6 L of honey from 32 beehives. How much honey can be collected from 48 beehives?

_____

⑧ Tom drove at 62 km/h on local roads and then 50% faster on a highway. What is the ratio of his local road speed to his highway speed?

_____

⑨ ABC Mart sells bananas for $1.30/kg. Bestmart sells them for $4.41/3 kg. Which store offers a better buy?

_____

⑩ If 1.2 m² of carpet costs $7.50, what area of carpet can be purchased for $100?

_____

⑪ A video game sells 20 gems for $5.99 and 50 gems for $12.99. Which is a better buy?

_____

⑫ May cycles 25 km in 2 hours.

   a. How far can she cycle in 3 hours?

   _____

   b. How long does it take her to cycle 40 km?

   _____

⑬ Simon checked his pulse. He counted 27 beats in 15 seconds. How many beats would he count in 1 minute?

   _____

⑭ Barbara made 12 phone calls in 9 days. Lydia made 7 phone calls in 5 days. Who made more calls per day?

   _____

⑮ Team Tiger has a win-loss ratio of 7:5 and Team Wolf has a loss-win ratio of 3:5. Which team has a higher win percentage?

   _____

⑯ Sound travels in water at a speed of 1460 m/s.

   a. How far does sound travel in water in 3.5 seconds?

   _____

   b. How long does it take for sound to travel through a lake that is 292 km long?

   _____

⑰ The table below shows the speeds of 3 animals. Complete the table and rank the animals from the fastest (1) to the slowest (3).

Animal	Speed	Speed (m/s)	Rank
cat	200 m per 15 s		
elephant	370 m per 30 s		
zebra	390 m per 20 s		

⑱ Mike earns $37.50 for 3 hours' work. How much will he earn for 5 hours' work?

_____

⑲ Jo runs 100 m in 13 seconds, Ken runs 500 m in 60 seconds, and Leo runs 200 m in 25 seconds. Who is the fastest?

_____

⑳ Jill is making a science-fiction movie. A 12-m-tall monster is represented by a 16-cm-tall lizard. The film set is 50 cm tall. The lizard moves at a speed of 12.5 cm/s.

a. How long does it take for the lizard to cover a distance of 30 cm?

_____

b. How tall does the set appear to be in the movie?

_____

c. Using the same scale, how tall is the model of a 15-m-tall building?

_____

㉑ Amy reads 2 books a week. Beth reads 7 books a month. Connie reads 90 books a year. Debbie reads $\frac{1}{4}$ of a book per day. Rank the girls from the one who reads the fewest books in a year to the one who reads the most.

_____

_____

㉒ Jill is drawing a map of her neighbourhood. The 20-m-long basketball court is 5 cm long on her map. How long should a 56-m-long lake be on the map?

_____

㉓ Pineville has 2 fire hydrants for every 3 city blocks.

a. If there are 36 city blocks in Pineville, how many fire hydrants are there?

_____

b. How many city blocks do you have to walk in order to pass 12 fire hydrants?

_____

6 Integers

• solving word problems involving integers

On January 5, Toronto's temperature dropped from -2°C in the daytime to -10°C at night. What was the temperature change from day to night?

Positive numbers can be written without the positive sign (+) but negative numbers must include the negative sign (-).

Temperature change: -10 – (-2) = ☐

The temperature change from day to night was ☐ .

Solve the problems. Show your work.

① Temperatures during the day and at night in Townsville and Pleasantville are shown in the table.

Town	Temperature	
	Day	Night
Townsville	12°C	-5°C
Pleasantville	15°C	-3°C

a. What was the temperature change from day to night in

• Townsville? • Pleasantville?

_____ _____

b. What was the two towns' average

• day temperature? • night temperature?

_____ _____

c. What was the temperature change going from

• Townsville to Pleasantville at night? • Townsville during the day to Pleasantville at night?

_____ _____

② The temperature of a water bottle dropped by 15°C when placed in the freezer. If the freezer is set to -5°C, what was the original temperature of the water bottle?

_____

③ On a typical winter day, the temperature is -15°C in Inuvik and 7°C in Vancouver.

    a. What is the difference in temperature between Vancouver and Inuvik?

    _____

    b. What is the average temperature of Inuvik and Vancouver?

    _____

④ In one week in March, the following temperatures were recorded in Oakville: -2°C, 3°C, 5°C, -1°C, 7°C, -5°C, and 4°C. Determine the average daily temperature for the week. (Correct to the nearest 0.1°C.)

_____

⑤ During a week in December, the temperature in Thunder Bay was -3°C for 5 days and -7°C for 2 days. Determine the average temperature over the 7 days. (Correct to the nearest 0.1°C.)

_____

⑥ On January 13, the temperature in Edmonton was -5°C. Over the next 7 days, the temperature dropped by 2°C per day. What was the temperature on January 20?

_____

⑦ Last month, Janet withdrew $30.90 from her chequing account. Then she deposited $27.50 in the account and later withdrew $122.25. Calculate the overall change in her account balance last month.

_____

⑧ International Time Zones are defined relative to the Prime Meridian, which goes through Greenwich, England. +2 means 2 hours ahead of the time in Greenwich and -3 means 3 hours behind.

a. Toronto is at -5 and Hong Kong is at +8. If it is 6 a.m. in Toronto, what time is it in Hong Kong?

_____

b. Honolulu, Hawaii is at -10 and Sydney, Australia is at +10. If it is noon on Monday in Sydney, what time is it in Honolulu?

_____

⑨ Read the table below. Then solve the problems.

Stock Market Indices

Market Index	Tuesday		Wednesday	
	Close	Change	Close	Change
TSE 300	7625.31	-21.35	7631.43	+6.12
Consumer	8132.43	+32.43	8130.00	-2.43
Oil & Gas	4831.17	+7.12	4812.08	-19.09
Biotech	1023.41	-12.31	1010.91	-12.50

a. Which index showed the greatest increase on Tuesday?

_____

b. Which index showed the greatest decrease on Wednesday?

_____

c. What was the value of the TSE 300 Index on Monday?

_____

d. What was the value of the Consumer Index on Monday?

_____

⑩ Read the chart and solve the problems.

> An air temperature of -12°C and a wind speed of 8 km/h will produce a wind chill index of -14°C.

Wind Chill Index

Wind Speed (km/h)	Temperature (°C)						no wind
	4	2	-1	-4	-7	-9	-12
8	3	1	-3	-6	-9	-11	-14
16	-2	-6	-9	-13	-17	-19	-23
24	-6	-9	-12	-17	-21	-24	-28
32	-8	-11	-16	-20	-23	-27	-31
40	-9	-14	-18	-22	-26	-30	-34
48	-11	-15	-19	-24	-28	-32	-36

a. What is the wind chill index when the air temperature is -4°C and the wind speed is 40 km/h?

_____

b. List both sets of conditions that produce a wind chill index of -17°C.

_____

c. If the wind speed is 24 km/h and the wind chill index is -24°C, what is the air temperature?

_____

d. A wind chill index of -30°C or lower is considered extremely cold. What is the minimum wind speed needed to create extremely cold weather if the air temperature is -9°C?

_____

⑪ The average of two integers is 4. If one of the integers is -10, what is the other integer?

_____

7 Circles

- solving word problems involving circles

A circular flower bed has a diameter of 2 m. What is the area of the flower bed?

Radius: 2 ÷ 2 = 1

Area: $\pi \times (1)^2 = 3.14 \times 1 =$ ☐

The area of the flower bed is ☐ m².

 Read This

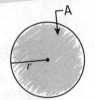

Area of a Circle

$$A = \pi r^2$$

Circumference of a Circle

$$C = \pi d$$
$$= 2\pi r$$

Solve the problems. Show your work. Use $\pi = 3.14$.

① Paul uses a 63-cm rope to form a circle. Determine the area of this circle. (Correct to 2 decimal places.)

_____

② A regular hexagon is enclosed in a circle. If the radius of the circle is 10 cm, what is

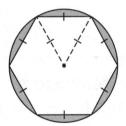

  a. the perimeter of the hexagon?

_____

  b. the circumference of the circle?

_____

③ The diagram shows an archery target.

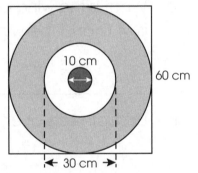

Determine the area of

  a. the smallest circle.

_____

  b. the unshaded ring.

_____

  c. the shaded ring.

_____

  d. the outermost part not covered by the circles.

_____

④ The radius of a circular mat is 10 cm.

a. Determine the area of the mat.

_____

b. Determine the length of fringe required to border the mat.

_____

⑤ Determine the area of the circular pathway shown.

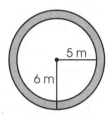

_____

⑥ A circular pool with a radius of 3 m is in the centre of a square lot. Calculate the area of the square lot around the pool.

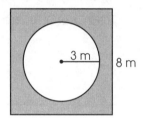

_____

⑦ Look at the circular design.

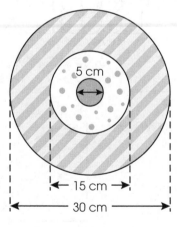

How many times

a. the area of the smallest circle is the area of the dotted ring?

_____

b. the area of the dotted ring is the area of the striped ring?

_____

⑧ Milly is making a circular tablecloth with an area of 2 m². Determine the length of trimming she needs to sew around the outer edge of the tablecloth.

_____

⑨ The two inside circles have a radius of 2 cm each. Determine the unshaded area of the larger circle.

_____

⑩ The diagram shows the design of a 6 cm by 6 cm square quilt. Determine the total area of the shaded portions.

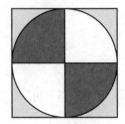

_____

⑪ The Norman window shown is a rectangular pane of glass with a semi-circular pane above it. Determine the area of the glass in the window.

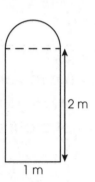

2 m

1 m

_____

⑫ Circles are cut from two 40 cm-by-40 cm pieces of cardboard. Is the amount of waste the same in both cases? If not, what is the difference?

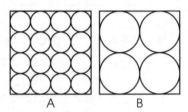

A   B

_____

⑬ A quarter-circle-shaped lot is divided as shown. Determine the shaded area of the lot.

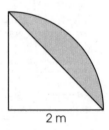

2 m

_____

⑭ A rectangular backyard pool is 6 m by 10 m in size. A circular pool has the same area. Determine the diameter of the circular pool.

_____

Write answers in terms of π.

⑮ The area of the square OABC is 36 cm². Determine the area of the shaded quarter-circle.

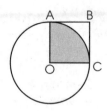

_____

⑯ James drew a circle with a circumference of 6π units. Determine the radius of the circle.

_____

⑰ A 100-cm rope is used to make a circle with the greatest area possible. Determine the radius of the circle.

_____

⑱ In the diagram, the diameter of the largest circle is the sum of the diameters of Circle A and Circle B. Determine the ratio of the area of the largest circle to the sum of the areas of Circle A and Circle B.

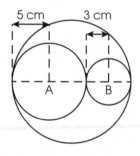

_____

⑲ The difference between the radii of 2 circles is 10 cm. Determine the difference between their circumferences.

_____

⑳ A line segment is 8 cm long. It is divided into 8 equal parts and semi-circles are drawn as shown. Determine the ratio of the length of the upper path A → C → E to the length of the lower path A → D → E.

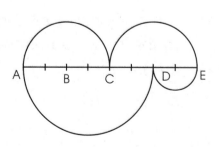

_____

Volume and Surface Area

- solving word problems involving volume and surface area

An aquarium is in the shape of a rectangular prism and has a capacity of 4 L. If the area of its base is 200 cm², what is its height?

Read This

Capacity: 4 L = 4000 mL
Volume: 4000 cm³

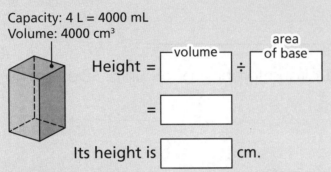

Height = ⌐volume⌐ ÷ ⌐area of base⌐

[____] ÷ [____]

= [____]

Its height is [____] cm.

Capacity is the greatest amount that a container can hold. It is closely related to volume.

$$1 \text{ mL} = 1 \text{ cm}^3$$

↑ capacity   ↑ volume

Solve the problems. Show your work.

① A rectangular container has a base that measures 20 cm by 16 cm.

a. If 10 L of water is poured into the container, what is the height of the water?

_____

b. Dropping a rock into the container raises the water level by 1.5 cm. What is the volume of the rock?

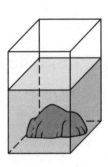

_____

② The cylindrical tank shown has a diameter of 2 m. 6 m³ of water is added to the tank. Determine the depth of the water. (Round to the nearest cm.)

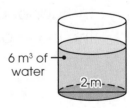

6 m³ of water

2 m

_____

③ Katie is making the tent shown. How much canvas is needed to make the tent?

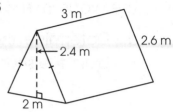

_____

④ Bill is going to form a triangular prism with the net shown. The base of the prism is an equilateral triangle.

    a. Determine the surface area of the prism.

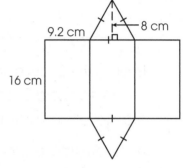

_____

    b. Determine the volume of the prism.

_____

⑤ ACD Chocolate Bars are available in the 2 sizes shown.

    a. How much cardboard is needed to package each bar?

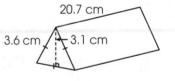

_____

    b. What is the volume of each chocolate bar package? (Round to the nearest whole number.)

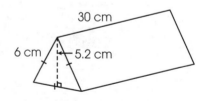

_____

    c. If the small one costs $1.99 and the large one costs $5.99, which is a better buy?

_____

⑥ The diagram shows the dimensions of a shed.

a. Determine the amount of wood needed to build the shed.

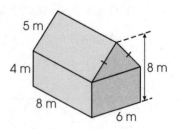

_____

b. Determine the space occupied by the shed.

_____

⑦ There are 2 cylindrical soup cans in Tim's kitchen. One soup can has a diameter of 6.8 cm and a height of 9.7 cm. The other soup can has a diameter of 10 cm and a height of 11.8 cm.

a. Determine the surface area of each soup can. (Correct to 1 decimal place.)

_____

b. Determine the volume of each soup can. (Correct to 1 decimal place.)

_____

⑧ Popcorn is available in the 3 containers shown.

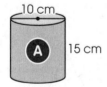 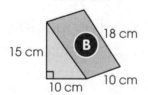 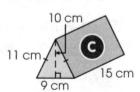

a. Which container has the largest surface area, assuming the containers are closed?

_____

b. Which container has the largest volume?

_____

⑨ The bases of three 10-cm-tall containers are shown below. What are their volumes?

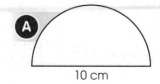 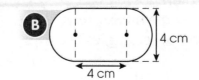 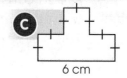

A   10 cm

B   4 cm   4 cm

C   6 cm

_____

⑩ A cylindrical pool with a diameter of 2.4 m is filled with water to a depth of 1 m. Determine the volume of the water in the pool in litres.

_____

⑪ A wooden napkin ring has the dimensions shown. Determine its volume.

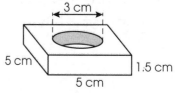

3 cm   5 cm   1.5 cm   5 cm

_____

⑫ A solid has the dimensions shown. Determine its volume and surface area.

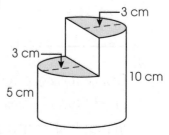

3 cm   3 cm   10 cm   5 cm

_____

⑬ A cylindrical tank has a radius of 12 cm and a uniform thickness of 1 cm. What is the capacity of the tank?

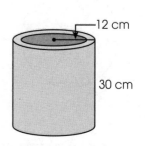

12 cm   30 cm

_____

9 Angles

• solving word problems involving angles

Try It

Alison constructed an isosceles triangle with one angle measuring 100°. What are the other angles?

The other angles are [ ] and [ ] .

Read This

Draw diagrams whenever necessary to help visualize word problems.

Equilateral Triangles
• 3 sides equal
• 3 angles equal (60° each)

Isosceles Triangles
• 2 sides equal
• 2 angles equal

Bob drew the shapes below. Help him solve the problems.

① Bob drew the side view of a house below. Determine the size of ∠EBC.

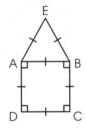

_____

② Bob drew a triangle as shown. He then drew Line ST through Point P. Determine the sum of ∠QPS and ∠TPR.

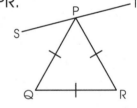

_____

③ Bob drew a circle with Centre O and two radii, OA and OB. What is the measure of ∠OAB?

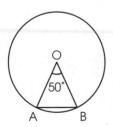

_____

④ Bob built the shape below with 6 sticks of equal lengths. What is the sum of Angles A, B, C, D, E, and F?

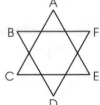

_____

Solve the problems. Show your work.

⑤ The diagram represents a sail for Carol's boat. Determine the values of *a*, *b*, and *c*.

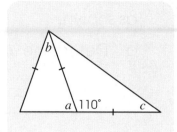

_____

⑥ Kyle divided the pentagonal tile shown into 3 non-overlapping triangles to find the sum of the angles of the tile. What is the sum?

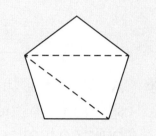

_____

⑦ Marc drew the octagon shown. Divide it into non-overlapping triangles. Then find the sum of the angles of the octagon.

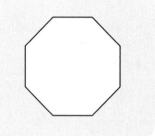

_____

⑧ Leonard is standing 5.8 m away from a tree. His eye level is 1.5 m above the ground and makes a 45° angle to the top of the tree.

   a. Check the diagram that correctly illustrates the scenario.

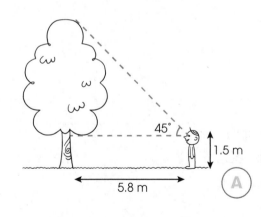

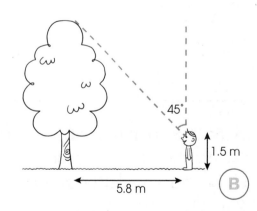

   b. What is the height of the tree?

_____

⑨ Charlie wears an asymmetrical bow tie as shown.

  a. Determine a, b, and c.

  _____

  b. Determine d.

  _____

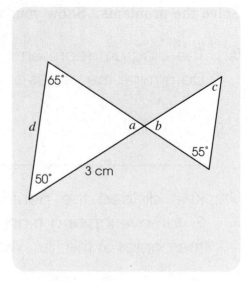

⑩ A 10-m-tall tree casts an 8-m-long shadow on the ground. How tall is a building that casts a 32-m-long shadow?

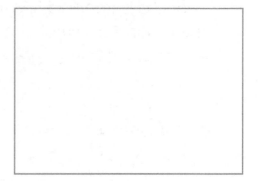

_____

Draw a diagram to illustrate each problem. Then solve it.

⑪ In △PQR, ∠Q is 36° greater than ∠P and ∠R is 6 times as large as ∠P. What is the measure of ∠R?

  _____

⑫ A field is in the shape of a rhombus. Given that the measure of ∠A is 60°, show that the field can be divided into 2 equilateral triangles.

  _____

Answer the questions. You may draw diagrams to help you.

⑬ The sum of the angles in a quadrilateral is 360°. Explain why this is true for all quadrilaterals using the properties of triangles.

⑭ Allie draws 2 diagonals to divide the rectangle below into 4 triangles.

If at least one of the centre angles is 35°, is it possible to find the sizes of the angles of all the triangles? Explain.

⑮ △ABC is a scalene triangle. The measure of ∠B is double that of ∠A, and ∠A is $\frac{1}{3}$ of ∠C.

a. Determine the measure of each angle.

b. Sketch the triangle. Which side is the longest?

c. What is the relationship between the measures of the angles and the lengths of the sides?

⑯
This straw is 31 cm long. I want to bend it into a triangle so that two of its sides are 9 cm and 16 cm.

Is it possible? Explain.

_____

_____

10 Angles in Parallel Lines

• solving word problems involving parallel lines

Try It

Are the lines in bold parallel? Explain.

$70° + 105° = $ [ ]

_____

_____

_____

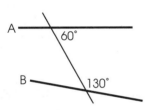

Read This

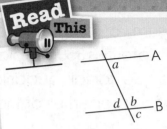

Two lines (Lines A and B) are parallel if

• the corresponding angles are equal ($\angle a = \angle c$), and/or

• the alternate angles are equal ($\angle a = \angle d$), and/or

• the interior angles have a sum of 180° ($\angle a + \angle b = 180°$).

Kawhi drew some lines. Check whether Lines A and B are parallel in each case. Explain why or why not.

①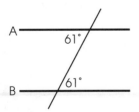

◯ parallel   ◯ not parallel

_____

_____

②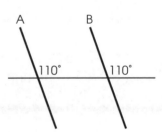

◯ parallel   ◯ not parallel

_____

_____

③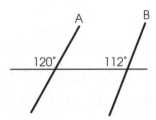

◯ parallel   ◯ not parallel

_____

_____

④

◯ parallel   ◯ not parallel

_____

_____

Answer the questions.

⑤ Determine the sum of x and y.

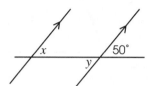

⑥ Why are the lines in bold below not parallel?

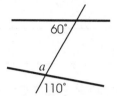

_____

⑦ Find the values of a, f, and g.

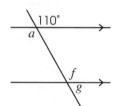

⑧ Which angles are the supplementary angles of Angle e?

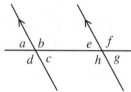

_____

⑨ In the given diagram, Line DE passes through Point A and is parallel to Line BC. Use the diagram to show that the sum of the angles of the triangle is 180°.

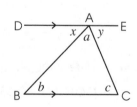

_____

⑩ Look at the diagram.

a. Find the value of a.

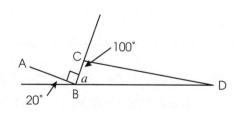

_____

b. Are Lines AB and CD parallel? Explain.

_____

⑪ Find the answers about the quadrilateral on the right. Explain your findings.

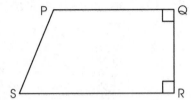

a. Name a pair of parallel lines.

_____

_____

b. Name 2 pairs of supplementary angles.

_____

c. Find the sum of the 4 angles.

_____

⑫ ABCD is a parallelogram. BD is a diagonal.

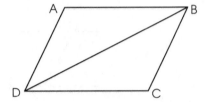

a. Identify 2 pairs of alternate angles.

_____

b. What is the relationship between ∠ABC and ∠BCD?

_____

c. Are △ABD and △CDB congruent? Explain.

_____

⑬ The figure is formed by 3 pairs of equal and parallel lines. Show that ∠FED is equal to ∠ABC.

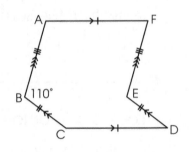

_____

⑭ △ABC is an equilateral triangle. The two vertical lines are parallel. Find the value of x.

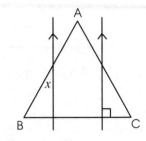

_____

Solve the problems.

⑮ 2 railway tracks cross each other at an angle of 70°. Determine the value of b.

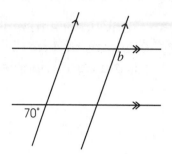

_____

⑯ Andy used wire to create the design as shown.

a. Determine the values of the unknown angles.

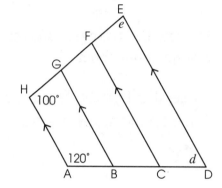

_____

b. If Lines DA and EH are extended to meet at a point called Point X, what is the value of ∠EXD?

_____

_____

⑰ The diagram shows the side view of a magazine holder. Divide the diagram into 2 rectangles and a right triangle. Then find the measure of ∠ABC.

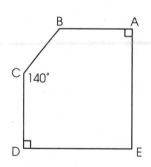

_____

⑱ Danny put some sticks together as shown.

a. Determine the values of a and b.

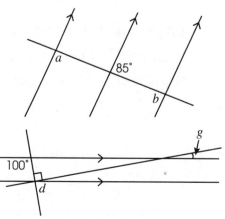

_____

b. Determine the values of d and g.

_____

11 Pythagorean Relationship

• solving word problems using the Pythagorean relationship

Try It

Tony drew a triangle that has lengths of 4 cm, 5 cm, and 6 cm. Is it a right triangle?

Read This

The Pythagorean relationship: In any right triangle, the square of the hypotenuse is the sum of the squares of the other two sides.

$$a^2 + b^2 = c^2$$

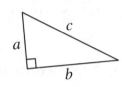

↑ This formula only applies to right triangles.

Marc drew the triangles shown. Answer the questions about them.

① Use the Pythagorean relationship to determine which triangles are right triangles.

A

B

C

D

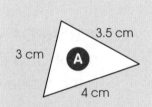

② What are the areas and perimeters of the right triangles? Round your answers to the nearest hundredth if necessary.

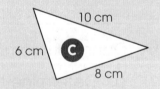

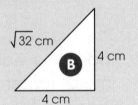

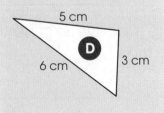

Solve the problems. Show your work.

③ A rectangular field measures 24 m by 7 m. What is the length of the diagonal?

_____

④ An isosceles right triangle has 2 sides of 3 cm each. Determine the perimeter of the triangle.

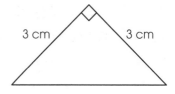

_____

⑤ A rectangular field has a side of 32 m and a diagonal of 40 m. Determine the area of the field.

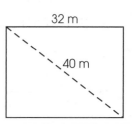

_____

⑥ The area of a square is 36 cm². What is the length of the diagonal?

_____

⑦ Determine the area and the perimeter of a square playground which has a diagonal of 16 m.

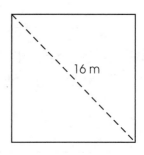

_____

⑧ Look at the diagram of Jim's backyard. A new fence will be built from A to B. How long will this fence be?

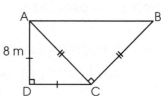

_____

⑨ Jim also wants a rectangular in-ground pool with a circular concrete pad around it. What will the area of the concrete pad be?

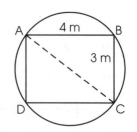

_____

⑩ Jim is going to buy flowers for his triangular garden. What is the area of his garden?

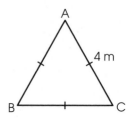

_____

⑪ Jim parked at A and the flower store is at C. How much distance can Jim save by cutting across the parking lot instead of walking all the way around?

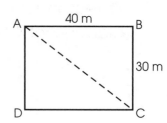

_____

⑫ Jim has a triangular office as shown. He has a desk at △ABE and a window from B to C.

a. Determine the length of the window.

_____

b. Carpet (Shape BCDE) is installed beside Jim's desk. What is the area of the carpet?

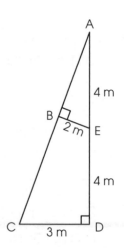

_____

⑬ Two sides of a right triangle have lengths of 9 cm and 7 cm. Determine 2 possible values for the perimeter.

_____

⑭ A 10-m ladder is leaning against a wall. The ladder reaches 8 m up the wall. What is the distance from the base of the wall to the bottom of the ladder?

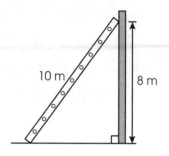

_____

⑮ Debbie has put 4 thumbtacks at A, B, C, and D and wrapped an elastic band around them as shown. Determine the length of AD.

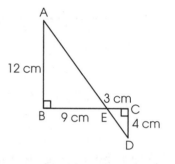

_____

⑯ A 5-m ladder is leaning against a 10-m-tall wall. The foot of the ladder is 3 m from the base of the wall. Determine the distance from the top of the ladder to the top of the wall.

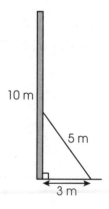

_____

⑰ PR is the diameter of a semicircle. Determine the area of the shaded parts.

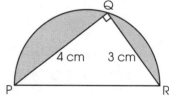

_____

⑱ Two vertical poles stand 12 m apart. One is 8 m tall and the other is 3 m tall. Determine the distance between the tops of the poles.

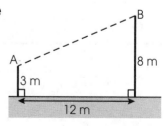

_____

- solving word problems involving coordinates and transformations

Try It

Draw a shape with vertices at (4,2), (-2,-2), and (4,-2). Then find its perimeter.

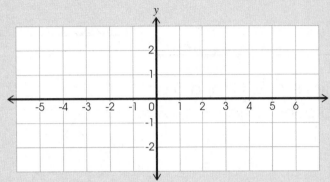

Read This

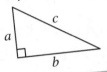

When finding the length of a line on a coordinate plane, consider using the Pythagorean relationship.

$$a^2 + b^2 = c^2$$

The perimeter is ⬚ units.

Draw the shapes on the coordinate planes. Then solve the problems. Show your work.

① The location of the old field is shown. The new field is a reflection of the old field in the y-axis.

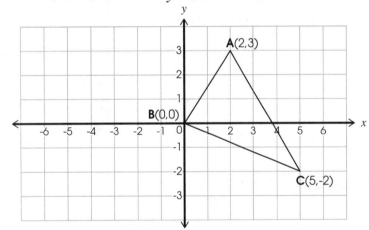

a. Draw the new field. What are the coordinates of its vertices?

_____

b. What is the total area of the fields?

_____

② A rug is positioned with its corners at D, E, F, and G. It is rotated 180° about the origin.

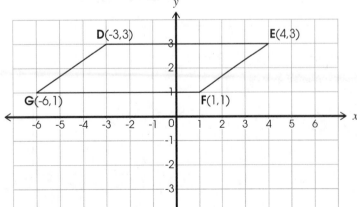

a. What are the rug's new coordinates?

_____

b. What is the area of the rug?

_____

Solve the problems. Show your work.

③ Sharon designed a shape as shown below. Translate the shape 4 units to the right and 1 unit up. What are the coordinates of the image?

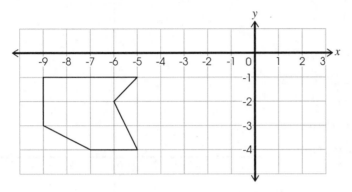

_____

_____

④ Jaclyn drew Shape A and transformed it into Shapes B, C, and D. Describe a transformation from Shape A to

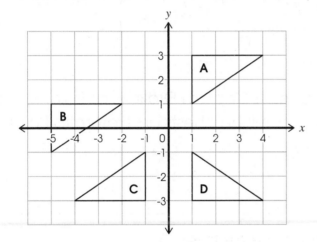

a. Shape B.

_____

b. Shape C.

_____

c. Shape D.

_____

⑤ The map below shows the positions of 4 landmarks.

a. The school and the bridge have the same y-coordinates. The school is the same distance from the bridge and the tower. Label the school on the map. What are its coordinates?

_____

b. If the mall is 7 km from City Hall, how far is the school from City Hall?

_____

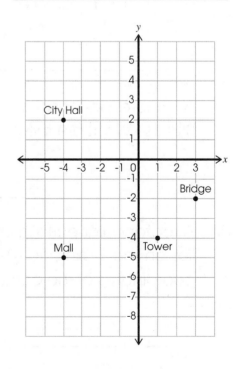

⑥ Captain Drake has a map which shows the locations of three hidden treasure chests: A(-2,4), B(3,4), and C(3,-6).

a. Plot Points A, B, and C on the grid and connect them.

b. Captain Drake does not want anybody to know the locations of the chests. Help him rotate △ABC 90° counterclockwise about the point (-2,0) and draw the image △A'B'C'.

c. What are the coordinates of A, B, and C if △ABC is translated 2 units to the left and 3 units up?

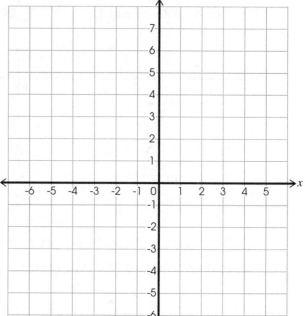

_____

d. The distance from A to B is 20 m. If Captain Drake is at Point A, how far does he have to travel to find all the chests and return to Point A? (Correct to 2 decimal places.)

_____

e. What is the area of △ABC in square metres?

_____

⑦ A square park has one corner at (2,2). The park has a perimeter of 8 units. What are the possible coordinates of the other corners?

_____

⑧ A rectangular parking lot has an area of 10 square units. One of its sides lies on the x-axis and (0,-2) is one of its corners. What are other possible coordinates of the corners?

_____

⑨ The diagram shows two triangles. Describe two ways the unshaded triangle can be transformed into the shaded one.

Way 1

_____

_____

Way 2

_____

_____

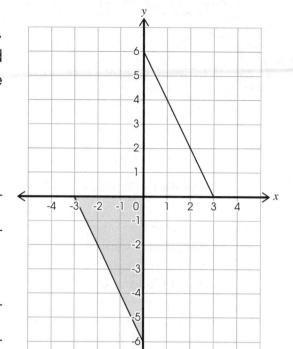

Read what the children say. Then answer the questions.

⑩ a.

Plot these points and connect them.

(-2,-1)   (-1,0)   (0,1)
(1,2)   (2,3)   (3,4)

What is the relationship between the *x*-coordinate and *y*-coordinate of each point?

_____

_____

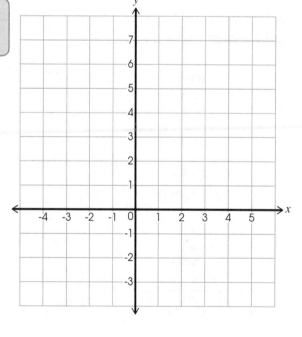

b.

Plot the vertices of Shape ABCD.

A(0,6)   B(3,6)   C(-1,2)   D(-4,2)

• What is the area of the shape?

_____

• Reflect the shape in the line you drew for Question a.

• solving word problems involving patterning

Consider the pattern below.

Diagram 1   Diagram 2   Diagram 3   Diagram 4

How many squares will there be in Diagram 10?

Diagram No. (d)	1	2	3	4
No. of Squares (s)	1	4		

$$s = \boxed{} \, d - \boxed{}$$

There will be $\boxed{}$ squares in Diagram 10.

Read This

It is easier to identify the pattern rule with more terms in the pattern.

e.g.

Term No. (n)	Term (t)
1	3
2	6

Term No. (n)	Term (t)
1	3
2	6
3	8

Is it $t = 3n$ or $t = 2n + 2$?

$t = 2n + 2$

Danny drew triangles and coloured them by following a pattern. Extend the pattern and answer the questions.

①

Frame 1

Frame 2

Frame 3

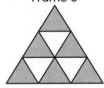

Frame 4

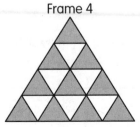

a. Unshaded triangles:

0 _____ _____ _____ _____ _____

b. Shaded triangles:

1 _____ _____ _____ _____ _____

c. Which frame will have

• 21 unshaded triangles? _____

• 28 shaded triangles? _____

d. Complete the table and check the correct equation.

Frame No. (f)	1	2	3	4
Total No. of Triangles (t)	1	4		

Ⓐ $t = 2f$

Ⓑ $t = f^2$

The given squares create a pattern. Complete the table and answer the questions.

②

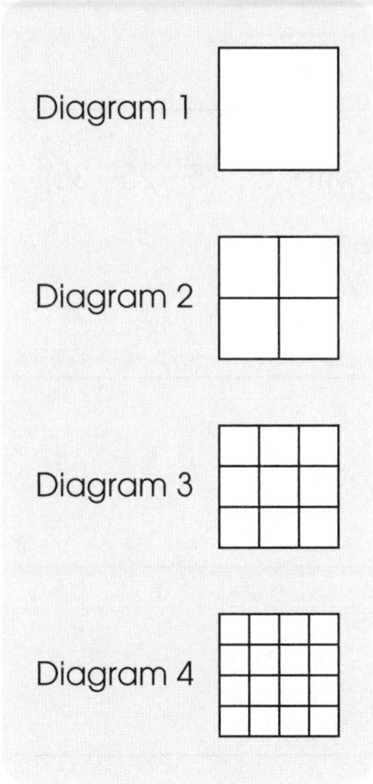

Diagram 1

Diagram 2

Diagram 3

Diagram 4

a.

Diagram No. (d)	1	2	3	4
No. of Squares (s)	1	4		

b. Write an equation to represent the pattern. _____

c. How many squares will there be in
- Diagram 5? _____
- Diagram 7? _____

d. Which diagram will have
- 36 squares? _____
- 64 squares? _____

Answer the questions.

③ Study the numbers in the triangular pattern shown.

a. Complete the table and check the correct equations.

Row No. (r)	No. of Numbers (n)
1	
2	
3	
4	

Ⓐ $n = 2r - 1$

Ⓑ $n = r + 1$

Row No. (r)	Middle Term (m)
1	
2	
3	
4	

Ⓐ $m = r + 1$

Ⓑ $m = r(r - 1) + 1$

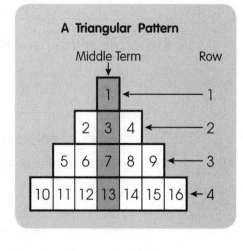

A Triangular Pattern

b. How many numbers will there be in Row 9? _____

c. What will the middle term be in Row 15? _____

④ Janet starts counting backward by 7's from 763. Will she say the number 203?

_____

⑤ You are given a series of numbers that begins with: 5^2, 15^2, 25^2, 35^2...

   a. Write the square numbers as whole numbers.

_____

   b. Determine the next 4 numbers.

_____

   c. Find the pattern rule of the whole numbers.

_____

⑥ There is a famous series of numbers called the Fibonacci Sequence.

Fibonacci Sequence

1, 1, 2, 3, 5, 8, 13...

   a. Describe the pattern rule of the Fibonacci Sequence in words.

_____

   b. Determine the next 8 terms of the Fibonacci Sequence.

_____

   c. Two of the consecutive terms are 4181 and 6765. What is the term that comes before 4181?

_____

   d. List the first 15 terms and circle the odd numbers. What relationship do you notice between the circled and uncircled numbers?

_____

⑦ Jill is folding a large piece of paper and counting the number of layers after each fold.

a. Complete the table.

No. of Folds	No. of Layers
1	
2	
3	
4	
5	

b. How many layers are there after n folds?

_____

c. How many layers will she get after 10 folds?

_____

d. After how many folds will she get 128 layers?

_____

⑧ Complete the table.

Shape	Quadrilateral	Pentagon	Hexagon	Heptagon	Polygon with n Sides
No. of Sides	4	5	6	7	n
No. of Diagonals from One Vertex	1				
No. of Triangles Created by Diagonals	2				

⑨ Will the number 103 appear in the patterns below? If so, identify the term numbers.

Pattern A: 3, 5, 7, 9...　　　　**Pattern B:** 4, 7, 10, 13...

_____

⑩ Each number in a pattern is obtained by adding the 2 previous numbers. Three consecutive terms are 42, 68, and 110. What is the 2nd term in the pattern if the 1st term is 0?

_____

⑪ The number 2^5 has 6 (or 5 + 1) factors. $2^5 = 32$; the factors of 32 are 1, 2, 4, 8, 16, and 32. Use this pattern to determine the number of factors of 3^7.

_____

14 Linear Equations

- solving word problems involving linear equations

Try
It

Bob subtracts 5 from a number and then adds 7 to the difference to get the final answer of -20. What is the number?

Let n represent the number.

$$n - \boxed{} + \boxed{} = -20$$

The number is $\boxed{}$.

Follow the steps to solve problems with equations.

❶ Use a variable to represent the unknown value in a problem.

❷ Set up an equation with the variable to represent the problem.

❸ Solve the equation.

Write equations and solve the problems. Show your work.

① The perimeter of a triangle is 13 cm.

   a. If two of its sides are 3 cm and 6 cm, how long is its third side?

_____

   b. If only one side is 7 cm and it is an isosceles triangle, how long are the other two sides?

_____

② The triangle on the right has a perimeter of 24 cm and an area of 24 cm².

   a. What are the lengths of the sides?

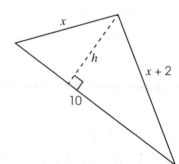

_____

   b. What is the height (h) of the triangle?

_____

③ Dan sleeps 8 hours each night, which is one hour less than twice the amount an elephant sleeps. How long does an elephant sleep?

_____

④ Bob has $30 in his wallet, which is $5 more than half the amount Kate has in her purse. How much does Kate have?

_____

⑤ Adam and Nadine participated in a gift exchange. Adam contributed a gift which cost $12. His gift was $3.50 more than half the cost of Nadine's gift. How much did Nadine's gift cost?

_____

⑥ Jamal's age is 10, which is 4 less than double Jane's age. How old is Jane?

_____

⑦

My dog had 9 pups in her third litter, which is one more than double the number of pups in her second litter. Her second litter had one fewer pup than her first litter.

a. How many pups were there in her dog's first litter?

_____

b. How many pups did her dog have altogether?

_____

⑧ Brian's car costs him $4000 per year, plus $0.20 per km in gas.

a. Determine the total yearly cost of the car if he travels 40 000 km per year.

_____

b. How far did he travel in a year if the total cost was $8200?

_____

⑨ A box contains 144 tea bags, which is 16 more than 8 times the number of tea bags in a smaller box.

a. How many tea bags are there in the smaller box?

_____

b. If the smaller box costs $0.75 and the larger one costs $5.99, which is a better buy?

_____

⑩ Each week, Bonnie earns $25 more than double Betty's earnings.

a. If Betty earns $225 weekly, how much does Bonnie earn?

_____

b. If Bonnie earns $225 weekly, how much does Betty earn?

_____

c. Betty earns n dollars weekly. Write an expression for Bonnie's weekly earnings.

_____

⑪ Adam and Ron both hosted holiday parties. Adam boasted that the number of guests at his party was 10 more than double the number of guests at Ron's party. If 48 people attended Adam's party, how many attended Ron's party?

_____

⑫ A number was decreased by 10 and then divided by 2 to get -11. What was the original number?

_____

⑬ In the year 2015, the population was about 7.33 billion. This is 1.33 billion more than 20 times what it was in the year 1 CE. What was the population in 1 CE in billions?

_____

⑭ The length of a rectangle is 5 cm greater than the width. The perimeter is 70 cm. What is the area of the rectangle?

_____

⑮

Renting a canoe has a fixed cost of $25 plus an extra cost of $5.25/h.

Jake

a. How long is a canoe rental that costs $40.75?

_____

b. How long can Jake rent a canoe with $50?

_____

15 Graphs

• identifying and analyzing sources and data

Read
This

David is studying the world population from 2000 to 2015. Below are some of the data he found.

Year	2000	2001	2002	2003
Population (in billions)	6.122	6.204	6.283	6.4

Identify the data set's source and type, and the most appropriate graph to represent it.

Identifying the source and type of a data set can help you choose an appropriate graph to represent it.

Sources and types of data:
• primary/secondary data
• sample/census
• discrete/continuous data

_____

_____

Make a scatter plot to represent the data. Then answer the questions.

① Davis did a study on how running affects body weight. The 25 participants started at the same weight and ran different distances each week. Their weekly running distances and final weights are recorded in the table.

Distance (km)	Weight (kg)
0.5	85
0.5	90
1	88
1.5	86
1.5	85
2	83
2	82
2	85
2.5	80
2.5	76
3	79
3	78
3.5	80
4	75
4	71
4	73
4.5	75
5.5	70
5.5	71
6	72
6.5	70
7	67
7.5	76
7.5	63
8	65

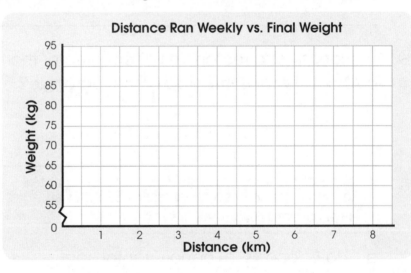

Distance Ran Weekly vs. Final Weight

a. Make a scatter plot and draw a line of best fit.

b. Describe the correlation between the distance ran each week and the final weight.

_____

c. Estimate the final weight of a person who ran 6 km each week.

_____

Decide the most appropriate graph for the given scenario and the set of data. Then make the graph and answer the questions.

② Sarah, Jane, Alvis, and Jim ran for Student Council President. The table found on the school's website shows the number of boys and girls that voted for each candidate.

Votes for Each Candidate

Candidate	Voter	
	Boy	Girl
Sarah	21	40
Jane	16	9
Alvis	38	35
Jim	24	32

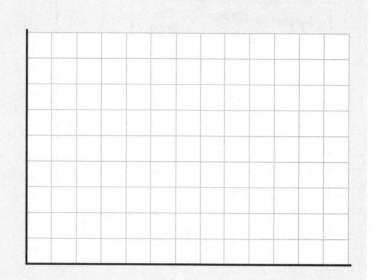

a. Identify the data set's source and type. Explain why you chose the graph you used to represent the data.

_____

_____

b. Which candidate received almost twice as many votes from boys than girls?

_____

c. Which candidate received the most

  • votes from girls?

_____

  • votes from boys?

_____

d. Which candidate won? With how many votes?

_____

Read about the set of data. Then use the most appropriate graph to represent the data and answer the questions.

③ Anna went online and found the total rainfall each week in the spring and fall in her city. She recorded the data in the table.

Rainfall Each Week in Spring and Fall

Week	Spring (mm)	Fall (mm)
1	8.4	20.4
2	10.8	21.2
3	12.3	19.1
4	14.1	17.9
5	15.3	17
6	16.5	16.1
7	18.9	16.9
8	20.7	17.5
9	21	18.4
10	20.1	19
11	18.9	12.3
12	17.8	10.7
13	16.3	9.6

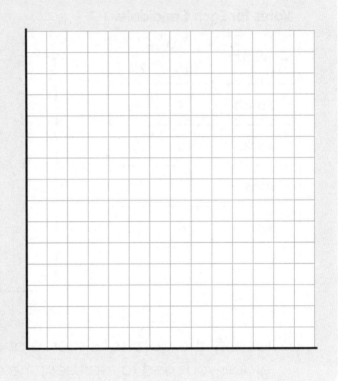

a. Explain why you chose to use the graph above.

_____

_____

b. In which week of the seasons was there almost the same amount of rainfall?

_____

c. Anna's friend loves rainy days. Which weeks in the spring and fall would she have enjoyed most?

_____

d. Make predictions on how much rainfall there was in the first week of summer and the first week of winter.

_____

Make a frequency table and a histogram to represent the set of data. Then answer the questions.

④ Mr. Moo measured the weights of 30 of the sheep on his farm. Their weights are shown below.

Weights of 30 Sheep (kg)

86.3	55.5	36.3	76	42	54.2	61.2	73	82	90.5
102.1	47.9	55	40.2	52.8	38.4	110.8	89.8	50.2	106
63.1	39.7	60.1	115	74.5	119	49.3	35.9	97.1	37

Weight (kg)	Frequency
30 – 39.9	

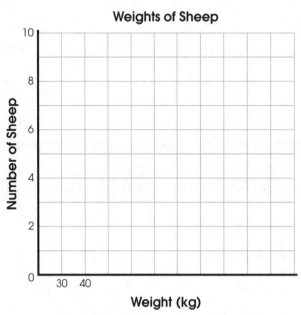

Weights of Sheep

a. Identify the data set's source and type.

_____

b. Do you think a histogram is an appropriate graph for this set of data? Explain.

_____

c. Mr. Moo has 800 sheep on his farm. Extrapolate from the sample above to answer the questions.

• If he considers all sheep under 40 kg to be lambs (young sheep), about how many lambs are there?

_____

• Sheep that are over 100 kg are usually mature male sheep. About how many mature male sheep are there on the farm?

_____

16 Probability

Try It

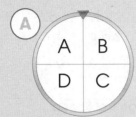

Jordan spun a spinner 80 times and got 20 As, 19 Bs, 18 Cs, and 23 Ds. Check the spinner he probably spun and find the theoretical probabilities.

Read This

Sometimes, knowing the experimental probabilities of an experiment can help us find the theoretical probabilities, especially when the number of trials is large.

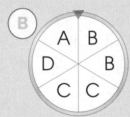

The theoretical probabilities of getting A, B, C, and D are ____ , ____ , ____ , and ____ respectively.

Match each table with the correct spinner. Then find the theoretical probabilities.

①

A	100 spins		B	120 spins		C	80 spins
• 37 As			• 31 As			• 11 As
• 22 Bs			• 29 Bs			• 9 Bs
• 20 Cs			• 32 Cs			• 32 Cs
• 21 Ds			• 28 Ds			• 28 Ds

Tips

P(A) represents the probability of Event A.

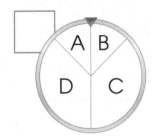

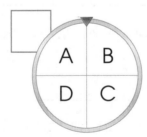

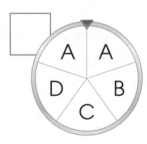

P(A) = ____   P(A) = ____   P(A) = ____

P(B) = ____   P(B) = ____   P(B) = ____

P(C) = ____   P(C) = ____   P(C) = ____

P(D) = ____   P(D) = ____   P(D) = ____

For each event in the table, determine whether its possible outcomes are equally likely.

②

Event	Possible Outcomes	Equally Likely? ✔ or ✗
flipping a coin	heads, tails	
giving birth to a baby	boy, girl	
the weight of an egg	over 1 kg, under 1 kg	
the weather in Winnipeg in August	snowy, rainy, sunny	
how a tossed pop can lands	right side up, on its side, upside down	
choosing a number from 1 to 10	greater than 4, smaller than 4	

Solve the problems. Show your work.

③ Brian flips a coin and rolls a dice.

a. What is the probability that he will

- flip heads?

  _____

- flip heads and roll a 6?

  _____

- roll a 6?

  _____

- flip tails and roll a 4 or 5?

  _____

Make a tree diagram here.

b. Write two sets of complementary events: one set for the coin and one set for the dice.

- Coin: _____

- Dice: _____

④ Davis rolls two dice simultaneously. He adds to find the sum of the numbers rolled.

a. Help Davis complete the table.

+	1	2	3	4	5	6
1						
2						
3						
4						
5						
6						

b. What is the probability of rolling

• a sum of 6?

_____

• a sum that is a multiple of 6?

_____

• a 6 on either dice?

_____

⑤ Mary flipped a coin 3 times and got tails every time. What is the probability that she will get tails on the 4th flip?

Tips Do the previous results affect her 4th flip?

_____

⑥ Joanna is designing a spinner with 5 colours: red, green, blue, yellow, and white. Draw to complete the spinners according to the descriptions.

a. The chance of landing on each colour is the same.

b. The chance of landing on red is double that of any other colour.

c. Joanna spins each spinner 120 times. How many times more should she expect Spinner B to stop on red than Spinner A?

_____

Handy Reference

Order of Operations

BEDMAS

B rackets
E xponents
D ivision
M ultiplication
A ddition
S ubtraction

Squares and Square Roots

$$\sqrt{a \times b} = \sqrt{a} \times \sqrt{b}$$

$$\sqrt{a \div b} = \sqrt{a} \div \sqrt{b}$$

$$\sqrt{a^2} = a$$

$$\sqrt{a^{\,2}} = a$$

Operations with Integers

Addition	Subtraction	Multiplication	Division
+ + ➡ +	– + ➡ –	(+) × (+) ➡ +	(+) ÷ (+) ➡ +
+ – ➡ +	– – ➡ +	(+) × (–) ➡ –	(+) ÷ (–) ➡ –
		(–) × (+) ➡ –	(–) ÷ (+) ➡ –
		(–) × (–) ➡ +	(–) ÷ (–) ➡ +
e.g. 3 + (-2)	e.g. 3 – (-2)	e.g. (-2) × (+3)	e.g. (-8) ÷ (-4)
= 3 – 2	= 3 + 2	= -6	= +2
= 1	= 5		

Perimeter and Area of Polygons

Perimeter

P = 4s

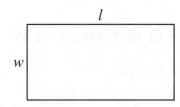

P = 2(l + w)

Area

A = s^2

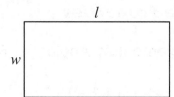

A = lw

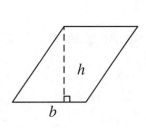

A = bh

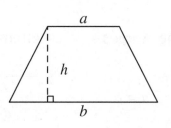

A = (a + b)h ÷ 2

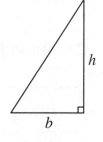

A = bh ÷ 2

Circumference and Area

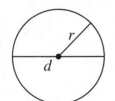

$C = \pi d = 2\pi r$

$A = \pi r^2$

Volume and Surface Area

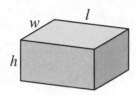

$V = l \times w \times h$

$S.A. = 2lw + 2lh + 2wh$

$V = (bh \div 2) \times t$

$S.A. = 2(bh \div 2) + at + bt + ct$

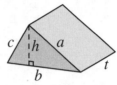

$V = \pi r^2 h$

$S.A. = 2\pi r^2 + 2\pi rh$

Pythagorean Relationship

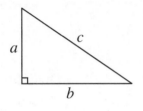

$a^2 + b^2 = c^2$

Unit Conversions

Length	Mass	Capacity and Volume
1 km = 1000 m	1 kg = 1000 g	1 L = 1000 mL
1 m = 100 cm	1 g = 1000 mg	1 L = 1000 cm³
1 cm = 10 mm		1 mL = 1 cm³

Angle Properties

Complementary Angles

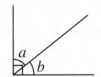

$a + b = 90°$

Supplementary Angles

$c + d = 90°$

Opposite Angles

$e = f$

Corresponding Angles

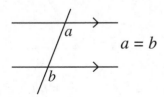

$a = b$

Alternate Angles

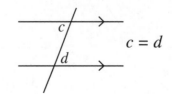

$c = d$

Consecutive Interior Angles

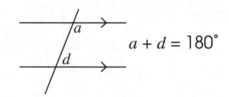

$a + d = 180°$

Grade 8
QR Code

QR Code – a quick way to access our fun-filled videos

Our QR code provides you with a quick and easy link to our fun-filled videos, which can help enrich your learning experience while you are working on the workbook. Below is a summary of the topics that the QR code brings you to. You may scan the QR code in each unit to learn about the topic or the QR code on the right to review all the topics you have learned in this book.

Scan this QR code or visit our Download Centre at **www.popularbook.ca**.

The topics introduced with the QR code:

1 **What is a perfect square?** (p. 19)
Discover what makes a number a perfect square.

2 **How to Divide Fractions** (p. 23)
Learn how to divide fractions.

3 **How to Multiply Decimal Numbers** (p. 27)
Learn how to multiply decimal numbers.

4 **How to Divide Decimal Numbers** (p. 29)
Learn how to divide decimal numbers.

5 **What is π?** (p. 43)
Learn what π is and how it relates to circles.

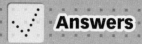

Level 1

1 Exponents

Try It

4^3 ; 4 ; 3

1. 2 ; 3   2. 7 ; 4   3. 5 ; 2
4. 3 ; 4   5. 10 ; 6
6. A: 4^6 B: 3^6 C: 6^4
   D: 5^4 E: 2^7 F: 8^5
   D ; C ; F ; B ; A ; E
7. 2^3 ; 3^2 8. $4^2 \times 5^4$
9. $3^4 \times 4^3$ 10. $2^5 \times 7^2$
11. $3^3 \times 4^2 \times 5^2$ 12. $2^3 \times 5^4 \times 7^2$
13. $3 \times 3 \times 3 \times 4 \times 4 \times 4 \times 4$
14. $5 \times 5 \times 7 \times 7 \times 7$
15. $2 \times 2 \times 2 \times 2 \times 3 \times 3 \times 5 \times 5 \times 5$
16. $3 \times 3 \times 4 \times 4 \times 4 \times 4 \times 4 \times 8 \times 8$
17. 4   18. 27   19. 36   20. 16   21. 64
22. 81   23. 7   24. 5   25. 1   26. 1
27. 72   28. 400   29. 100
30. 243   31. 405   32. 576
33. 40 960   34. 21 600
35. 4   36. 8   37. 0   38. 12   39. 2
40. 1   41. 2   42. 2   43. 2   44. 2
45. 3   46. 1 ; 2 ; 1
47a. =   b. >   c. >   d. <   e. >
   f. <   g. >   h. <   i. <   j. <
   k. <   l. >   m. =   n. =
48a. 0^3 ; 6^0 ; 7^1 ; 2^3 b. $1^{10} < 2^2 < 10^1 < 5^2$
   c. $4^3 < 3^4 < 3^5 < 4^5$ d. $5^1 < 3^3 < 5^3 < 3^5$
   e. $7^0 < 9^1 < 2^4 < 5^2$ f. $5^2 < 2^5 < 4^3 < 3^4$
49. 10 ; ten
   100 ; one hundred
   1000 ; one thousand
   10 000 ; ten thousand
   100 000 ; one hundred thousand
   1 000 000 ; one million
50. 20 ; 4   51. 100 ; 70 ; 2
   2×10 ; 4×1 1×100 ; 7×10 ; 2×1
   2×10^1 ; 4×10^0 1×10^2 ; 7×10^1 ; 2×10^0
52. $8 \times 10^2 + 1 \times 10^1 + 3 \times 10^0$
53. $7 \times 10^2 + 9 \times 10^0$
54. $1 \times 10^3 + 2 \times 10^2 + 4 \times 10^1$
55. $3 \times 10^4 + 2 \times 10^3 + 1 \times 10^0$
56. $1 \times 10^4 + 5 \times 10^2$
57. 546   58. 902   59. 7034
60. 2503   61. 50 320

2 Scientific Notation

Try It
B
1. B   2. A   3. C
4. C   5. A   6. C
7.   8.
9a. 3.8 ; 10^7 b. 1.05×10^5
   c. 4.2×10^6 d. 1.98×10^5
   e. 2.35×10^6 f. 4.09×10^6
   g. 3.3×10^6 h. 8.1×10^4
   i. 2.71×10^8
10a. 4600   b. 850 000
   c. 64 000   d. 97 000
   e. 1060   f. 4 080 000
   g. 6 300 000   h. 207 000 000
   i. 39 000 000   j. 42 900 000
11. A   12. B   13. A
14. B   15. A   16. B
17. A   18. C   19. A
20. 5.2×10^{-3} 21. 1.3×10^{-4}
22. 9×10^{-4} 23. 1.02×10^{-6}
24. 8.8×10^{-4} 25. 3.07×10^{-3}
26. 4.13×10^{-6} 27. 5.2×10^{-7}
28. 0.0071   29. 0.00012
30. 0.000085   31. 0.00133
32. 0.000972   33. 0.00000806
34. 0.00000408   35. 0.000000027
36a. 1.3×10^4 ; 3.5×10^3
   b. 3.84×10^5 ; 1.496×10^8
37a. 7.2×10^{-4} ; 5×10^{-5} ; 1.1×10^{-5}
   b. 1.44×10^{-3}
38a. 1×10^{-3} ; 1×10^5 b. 3.8×10^{-7} ; 7×10^{-7}
   c. 3×10^{-9} ; 3×10^{-7}

3 Prime Factorization

Try It
2 ; 3 ; 2 ; 3
1. 2 ; 2 ; 2×2 2. 3 ; 3 ; 3×3
3. 2 ; 5 ; 2×5 4. 2 ; 7 ; 2×7
5. 3 ; 5 ; 3×5 6. 3 ; 7 ; 3×7
7. 5 ; 5 ; 5×5 8. 5 ; 7 ; 5×7
9.   10.   11.

$2 \times 2 \times 3$ $2 \times 2 \times 5$ $2 \times 2 \times 2 \times 3$
12. 2×5 ; 3×5 ; 5

13. 2 x 2 x 2 x 2 ; 2 x 2 x 7 ; 4
14. 2 x 3 x 3 ; 2 x 2 x 2 x 2 x 2 ; 2
15. 2 x 3 x 5 ; 2 x 2 x 2 x 5 ; 10
16. 2 x 2 x 3 x 3 ; 3 x 3 x 5 ; 2 x 2 x 3 x 5 ; 3
17. 3 x 5 ; 2 x 2 x 2 x 5 ; 2 x 5 x 5 ; 5
18. 2 ; 2 ; 2 ; 3   19. 2, 2, 3, 5
    2 ; 2 ; 2 ; 3 ; 24   2 x 2 x 3 x 5 = 60
20. 2, 2, 2, 3, 3
    2 x 2 x 2 x 3 x 3 = 72
21. 2, 3, 3, 5   22. 2, 2, 2, 3, 5
    2 x 3 x 3 x 5 = 90   2 x 2 x 2 x 3 x 5 = 120
23. 2, 2, 2, 2, 3, 3
    2 x 2 x 2 x 2 x 3 x 3 = 144
24. 2 x 2 x 5 ; 2 x 3 x 5 ; 60
25. 2 x 2 x 2 x 2 ; 2 x 2 x 3 x 3 ; 144
26. 2 x 7 ; 2 x 2 x 7 ; 28
27. 5 x 5 ; 3 x 3 x 5 ; 225
28. 3 x 7 ; 5 x 7 ; 105
29. 2 x 2 x 2 x 2 x 3 ; 2 x 2 x 3 x 5 ; 240
30. 100 = 2 x 2 x 5 x 5
    120 = 2 x 2 x 2 x 3 x 5
    150 = 2 x 3 x 5 x 5
    180 = 2 x 2 x 3 x 3 x 5
    210 = 2 x 3 x 5 x 7
    GCF: 50 ; 20 ; 30
    LCM: 360 ; 900 ; 1260
31. (Individual answer)

4 Squares and Square Roots

Try It

A ; B

1. 1 ; 4 ; 9 ; 16 ; 25 ; 36 ; 49 ; 64 ; 81 ; 100 ;
    121 ; 144 ; 169 ; 196 ; 225 ; 256 ; 289 ; 324 ; 361 ; 400
2. 1 ; 2 ; 3 ; 4 ; 5 ; 6 ; 7 ; 8 ; 9 ; 10 ;
    11 ; 12 ; 13 ; 14 ; 15 ; 16 ; 17 ; 18 ; 19 ; 20
3. 9   4. 9   5. 5   6. 4
7. 0   8. 1   9. 1   10. 6
11. 6   12. 4   13. 9   14. 9
15. A   16. B   17. A   18. B
19-24. (Individual estimates)
19. 7.7   20. 8.8   21. 10.9
22. 9.4   23. 13.2   24. 15.5
25. $6 < \sqrt{49} < 8 < \sqrt{81}$
26. $\sqrt{110} < \sqrt{120} < 11 < 12$
27. $\sqrt{169} < \sqrt{260} < 130 < 16^2$
28. $\sqrt{120} < 12 < \sqrt{150} < 4^2$
29. 7   30. 7   31. 11   32. 10
33. 8   34. 21   35. 38   36. 19

37. 45   38. 51   39. 64   40. 75
41. 36   42. $= \sqrt{49}$
    6              $= 7$
43. $= \sqrt{100}$ 44. $= \sqrt{16}$
    $= 10$ $= 4$
45. 5 ; 20   46. $= \sqrt{2 \times 18}$
    100          $= \sqrt{36}$
    10           $= 6$
47. $= \sqrt{108 \div 3}$ 48. $= \sqrt{100 \div 4}$
    $= \sqrt{36}$ $= \sqrt{25}$
    $= 6$ $= 5$
49. $= \sqrt{147 \div 3}$ 50. $= \sqrt{5 \times 45}$
    $= \sqrt{49}$ $= \sqrt{225}$
    $= 7$ $= 15$
51. $= (\sqrt{2 \times 8})^2$ 52. $= \sqrt{100} - 10$
    $= (\sqrt{16})^2$ $= 10 - 10$
    $= 16$ $= 0$
53. $= 9 + 9$ 54. $= 5^2 - 3$
    $= 18$ $= 25 - 3$
                  $= 22$
55. $= \sqrt{16} + 7$ 56. $= 6^2 - \sqrt{4}$
    $= 4 + 7$ $= 36 - 2$
    $= 11$ $= 34$
57. $= 3 \times 5 - 18 \div 2$ 58. $= 41 - 16$
    $= 15 - 9$ $= 25$
    $= 6$
59. $= \sqrt{169 - 144} + 2$ 60. $= (\sqrt{64 \div 16})^2$
    $= \sqrt{25} + 2$ $= (\sqrt{4})^2$
    $= 5 + 2$ $= 4$
    $= 7$

5 Fractions

Try It

$\dfrac{1 \times 1}{2 \times 3} ; \dfrac{1}{6}$

1. $= \dfrac{1 \times 2}{3 \times 3}$ 2. $= \dfrac{3 \times 2}{4 \times 5}$
   $= \dfrac{2}{9}$ $= \dfrac{6}{20}$
                 $= \dfrac{3}{10}$

3. $= \dfrac{5 \times 2}{6 \times 5}$ 4. $= \dfrac{2 \times 3}{7 \times 4}$
   $= \dfrac{10}{30}$ $= \dfrac{6}{28}$
   $= \dfrac{1}{3}$ $= \dfrac{3}{14}$

5. $= \dfrac{6 \times 7}{12}$ 6. $= \dfrac{4 \times 3}{5 \times 4}$
   $= \dfrac{42}{12}$ $= \dfrac{12}{20}$
   $= 3\dfrac{1}{2}$ $= \dfrac{3}{5}$

7. $= \dfrac{9}{4} \times \dfrac{1}{3}$

$= \dfrac{9 \times 1}{4 \times 3}$

$= \dfrac{9}{12}$

$= \dfrac{3}{4}$

8. $= \dfrac{3}{5} \times \dfrac{7}{6}$

$= \dfrac{3 \times 7}{5 \times 6}$

$= \dfrac{21}{30}$

$= \dfrac{7}{10}$

9. $= \dfrac{11}{4} \times \dfrac{4}{3}$

$= \dfrac{11 \times 4}{4 \times 3}$

$= \dfrac{44}{12}$

$= 3\dfrac{2}{3}$

10. $= \dfrac{6}{5} \times \dfrac{11}{4}$

$= \dfrac{6 \times 11}{5 \times 4}$

$= \dfrac{66}{20}$

$= 3\dfrac{3}{10}$

11. $= \dfrac{\overset{1}{\cancel{4}}}{\underset{3}{\cancel{9}}} \times \dfrac{\overset{1}{\cancel{3}}}{\underset{2}{\cancel{8}}}$

$= \dfrac{1 \times 1}{2 \times 3}$

$= \dfrac{1}{6}$

12. $= \dfrac{\overset{3}{\cancel{9}}}{\underset{2}{\cancel{10}}} \times \dfrac{\overset{1}{\cancel{3}}}{\underset{2}{\cancel{6}}}$

$= \dfrac{3 \times 1}{2 \times 2}$

$= \dfrac{3}{4}$

13. $= \dfrac{\overset{3}{\cancel{9}}}{\underset{4}{\cancel{8}}} \times \dfrac{\overset{1}{\cancel{2}}}{\underset{5}{\cancel{15}}}$

$= \dfrac{3 \times 1}{4 \times 5}$

$= \dfrac{3}{20}$

14. $= \dfrac{\overset{2}{\cancel{14}}}{\underset{1}{\cancel{5}}} \times \dfrac{\overset{2}{\cancel{10}}}{\underset{1}{\cancel{7}}}$

$= \dfrac{2 \times 2}{1 \times 1}$

$= 4$

15. $\dfrac{3}{20}$ 16. $\dfrac{2}{7}$ 17. $1\dfrac{3}{4}$ 18. $15\dfrac{5}{6}$

19. $1\dfrac{1}{15}$ 20. $9\dfrac{3}{5}$ 21. $3\dfrac{3}{4}$ 22. $\dfrac{2}{15}$

23. $\dfrac{7}{24}$ 24. $6\dfrac{6}{7}$ 25. $7\dfrac{1}{3}$ 26. $\dfrac{1}{10}$

27. $2\dfrac{1}{4}$ 28. The film is $2\dfrac{1}{2}$ hours long!

29. $\dfrac{5}{2}$ 30. $\dfrac{4}{3}$ 31. $\dfrac{6}{1}$ 32. $\dfrac{1}{4}$

33. $\dfrac{5}{8}$ 34. $\dfrac{2}{7}$ 35. $\dfrac{4}{5}$ 36. $\dfrac{5}{11}$

37. $= \dfrac{3}{5} \times \dfrac{2}{1}$

$= \dfrac{3 \times 2}{5 \times 1}$

$= \dfrac{6}{5}$

$= 1\dfrac{1}{5}$

38. $= \dfrac{\overset{2}{\cancel{4}}}{\underset{1}{\cancel{3}}} \times \dfrac{\overset{1}{\cancel{3}}}{\underset{1}{\cancel{2}}}$

$= \dfrac{2 \times 1}{1 \times 1}$

$= 2$

39. $= \dfrac{5}{6} \times \dfrac{1}{2}$

$= \dfrac{5 \times 1}{6 \times 2}$

$= \dfrac{5}{12}$

40. $= 4 \times \dfrac{4}{3}$

$= \dfrac{4 \times 4}{1 \times 3}$

$= \dfrac{16}{3}$

$= 5\dfrac{1}{3}$

41. $= \dfrac{11}{\underset{3}{\cancel{6}}} \times \dfrac{\overset{1}{\cancel{2}}}{1}$

$= \dfrac{11 \times 1}{3 \times 1}$

$= 3\dfrac{2}{3}$

42. $= \dfrac{7}{3} \times \dfrac{4}{5}$

$= \dfrac{7 \times 4}{3 \times 5}$

$= \dfrac{28}{15}$

$= 1\dfrac{13}{15}$

43. $= 5 \times \dfrac{5}{11}$

$= \dfrac{5 \times 5}{1 \times 11}$

$= \dfrac{25}{11}$

$= 2\dfrac{3}{11}$

44. $= \dfrac{\overset{5}{\cancel{10}}}{3} \times \dfrac{1}{\underset{2}{\cancel{4}}}$

$= \dfrac{5 \times 1}{3 \times 2}$

$= \dfrac{5}{6}$

45. $= \dfrac{17}{\underset{2}{\cancel{8}}} \times \dfrac{\overset{1}{\cancel{4}}}{1}$

$= \dfrac{17 \times 1}{2 \times 1}$

$= 8\dfrac{1}{2}$

46. $2\dfrac{4}{5}$ 47. $\dfrac{1}{2}$ 48. $\dfrac{21}{25}$ 49. $5\dfrac{1}{3}$

50. 2 51. $\dfrac{5}{8}$ 52. $\dfrac{3}{4}$ 53. $1\dfrac{1}{3}$

54. $2\dfrac{1}{14}$ 55. $1\dfrac{13}{20}$

56. $= \left(\dfrac{3}{10} + \dfrac{3}{2}\right) \times \dfrac{7}{2}$

$= \dfrac{9}{5} \times \dfrac{7}{2}$

$= \dfrac{63}{10}$

$= 6\dfrac{3}{10}$

57. $= \dfrac{7}{3} \div 1\dfrac{3}{4}$

$= \dfrac{7}{3} \times \dfrac{4}{7}$

$= \dfrac{4}{3}$

$= 1\dfrac{1}{3}$

58. $= \dfrac{5}{2} \times \dfrac{\overset{1}{\cancel{3}}}{\underset{3}{\cancel{9}}} \times \dfrac{\overset{1}{\cancel{3}}}{\underset{2}{\cancel{10}}}$

$= \dfrac{5 \times 1 \times 1}{2 \times 3 \times 2}$

$= \dfrac{5}{12}$

59. $= \dfrac{8}{\underset{1}{\cancel{3}}} \times \dfrac{\overset{1}{\cancel{3}}}{7} \times \dfrac{\overset{4}{\cancel{12}}}{\underset{1}{\cancel{3}}}$

$= \dfrac{8 \times 1 \times 4}{1 \times 7 \times 1}$

$= \dfrac{32}{7}$

$= 4\dfrac{4}{7}$

60. $= 2\dfrac{3}{4} + \dfrac{\overset{8}{\cancel{16}}}{\underset{1}{\cancel{5}}} \times \dfrac{\overset{1}{\cancel{5}}}{\underset{3}{\cancel{6}}}$

$= 2\dfrac{3}{4} + 2\dfrac{2}{3}$

$= 5\dfrac{5}{12}$

61. $= \dfrac{29}{\underset{2}{\cancel{6}}} \times \dfrac{\overset{1}{\cancel{3}}}{8} - \dfrac{3}{4}$

$= \dfrac{29}{16} - \dfrac{3}{4}$

$= 1\dfrac{1}{16}$

62. $= \dfrac{63}{10} \div \dfrac{7}{5}$

$= \dfrac{\overset{9}{\cancel{63}}}{\underset{2}{\cancel{10}}} \times \dfrac{\overset{1}{\cancel{5}}}{\underset{1}{\cancel{7}}}$

$= 4\dfrac{1}{2}$

63. $= \dfrac{\overset{17}{\cancel{35}}}{\underset{12}{\cancel{6}}} \times \dfrac{\overset{1}{\cancel{3}}}{\underset{1}{\cancel{7}}} \times \dfrac{\overset{2}{\cancel{4}}}{\underset{1}{\cancel{5}}} + 3\dfrac{1}{2}$

$= 2 + 3\dfrac{1}{2}$

$= 5\dfrac{1}{2}$

6   Decimals

Try It

4.404

1. 14.401

$\begin{array}{r} 10.250 \\ +\quad 4.151 \\ \hline 14.401 \end{array}$

2. 5.211

$\begin{array}{r} 8.252 \\ -\quad 3.041 \\ \hline 5.211 \end{array}$

3. 33.317

$\begin{array}{r} 25.114 \\ +\quad 8.203 \\ \hline 33.317 \end{array}$

4. 5.878

$\begin{array}{r} 15.320 \\ -\quad 9.442 \\ \hline 5.878 \end{array}$

5. 38.579
```
        20.349
   +   18.230
   ─────────
       38.579
```

6. 34.487
```
        61.680
   -   27.193
   ─────────
       34.487
```

7. 16.131
```
         4.890
   +   11.241
   ─────────
       16.131
```

8. 3.826
```
         5.940
   -    2.114
   ─────────
        3.826
```

9. 6.385
```
        18.390
   -   12.005
   ─────────
        6.385
```

10. 6.009
```
         3.410
   +    2.599
   ─────────
        6.009
```

11. 13.386   12. 9.806   13. 39.57
14. 23.827   15. 120.55   16. 40.205
17. 49.138   18. 10.295   19. 25.425
20. 212.19   21. 288.182   22. 50.63
23. 303.77   24. 187.24   25. 5.49

26.
```
      21.2
   x   4.8
   ─────────
      1696
      8480
   ─────────
    101.76
```
27.
```
      3.02
   x    25
   ─────────
      1510
      6040
   ─────────
     75.50
```
28.
```
      30.4
   x    1.7
   ─────────
      2128
      3040
   ─────────
     51.68
```

29.
```
      2.38
   x    2.5
   ─────────
      1190
      4760
   ─────────
     5.950
```
30.
```
     15.35
   x    4.1
   ─────────
      1535
     61400
   ─────────
    62.935
```

31. 83.4   32. 5.125   33. 11.64
34. 5.452   35. 6.929   36. 37.764

37. A: 4.95
```
          4.95
   4)   19.80
        16
      ─────
         38
         36
      ─────
         20
         20
```
B: 20.7
```
          20.7
   5)  103.5
        10
      ─────
         35
         35
```

C: 203
```
          203
   8)  1624
        16
      ─────
         24
         24
```
D: 2.49
```
          2.49
   7)   17.43
        14
      ─────
         34
         28
      ─────
         63
         63
```

E: 3.47
```
           3.47
   19)   65.93
         57
       ─────
          89
          76
       ─────
         133
         133
```
F: 5.6
```
           5.6
   102)  571.2
         510
       ─────
         612
         612
```

G: 5.4
```
           5.4
   34)  183.6
        170
      ─────
        136
        136
```
H: 6.05
```
           6.05
   28)  169.40
        168
      ─────
         140
         140
```

38. A: = 4.75 + 2.825   B: = 310 - 0.94
     = 7.575   = 309.06
    C: = 3.3 x 1.27   D: = 10.5 x 0.8
     = 4.191   = 8.4
    4.191 ; 309.06 ; 7.575 ; 8.4
    36.591

39. A: = 12.39 - 1.48   B: = 5.4 ÷ 0.6
     = 10.91   = 9
    C: = 5.95 ÷ 1.7   D: = 4.5 x 7.19
     = 3.5   = 32.355
    32.355 ; 10.91 ; 3.5 ; 9
    66.0575

7   Percents

Try It
0.6 ; 3

1. 7 x 50%
    = 7 x 0.5
    = 3.5

2. 25 x 8%
    = 25 x 0.08
    = 2

3. 50 x 12%
    = 50 x 0.12
    = 6

4. 24 x 37.5%
    = 24 x 0.375
    = 9

5. 200 x 0.5%
    = 200 x 0.005
    = 1

6. 250 x 0.4%
    = 250 x 0.004
    = 1

7.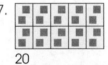
20

8.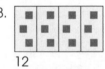
12

9.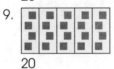
20

10.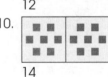
14

11a. 5   b. 6

12. increase ; 1500   13. decrease ; 30
    1500 ; 60 $\frac{30}{120}$; 25

14. increase ; 8   15. increase ; 8
    $\frac{8}{16}$; 50 $\frac{8}{64}$; 12.5

16. $2000 x 5% x 6 = $600
17. $150 x 10% x 3 = $45
18. $5000 x 2.5% x 5 = $625
19. $3500 x 4.8% x 2 = $336

20-21.

		Principal	Rate	Years	Interest
Ann	A	$5000	2%	4	$5000 × 2% × 4 = $400
	B	$2000	5%	2	$2000 × 5% × 2 = $200
	Ⓒ	$3000	3%	5	$3000 × 3% × 5 = $450
Sam	A	$3000	5%	2	$3000 × 5% × 2 = $300
	Ⓑ	$5000	4%	3	$5000 × 4% × 3 = $600
	C	$1000	13.5%	1	$1000 × 13.5% × 1 = $135

22. Plan A: $400

Plans B and C: $200 + $450 = $650

Difference: $650 – $400 = $250

She will earn $250 more in interest by splitting her principal into Plans B and C.

23. Amount saved: $80 x 20% = $16

Sale price: $80 – $16 = $64

24. Tax amount: $50 x 13% = $6.50

Total price: $50 + $6.50 = $56.50

25. Amount saved: $300 x 15% = $45

Sale price: $300 – $45 = $255

26. Tax amount: $110 x 7% = $7.70

Total price: $110 + $7.70 = $117.70

27.

Amount Saved	Sale Price	Tax Amount	Total Price
$18.50 × 10% = $1.85	$18.50 – $1.85 = $16.65	$16.65 × 13% = $2.16	$16.65 + $2.16 = $18.81
$28 × 10% = $2.80	$28 – $2.80 = $25.20	$25.20 × 13% = $3.28	$25.20 + $3.28 = $28.48
$32.50 × 10% = $3.25	$32.50 – $3.25 = $29.25	$29.25 × 13% = $3.80	$29.25 + $3.80 = $33.05
$37.75 × 10% = $3.78	$37.75 – $3.78 = $33.97	$33.97 × 13% = $4.42	$33.97 + $4.42 = $38.39

8 Proportions

Try It

2

1. $a \times 4 = 3 \times 8$
$4a = 24$
$a = 6$

2. $n \times 1 = 4 \times 2$
$n = 8$

3. $v \times 9 = 12 \times 3$
$9v = 36$
$v = 4$

4. $h \times 13 = 78 \times 2$
$13h = 156$
$h = 12$

5. $n \times 4 = 5 \times 2$
$4n = 10$
$n = 2.5$

6. $m \times 5 = 2 \times 6$
$5m = 12$
$m = 2.4$

7. $y \times 8 = 12 \times 11$
$8y = 132$
$y = 16.5$

8. $g \times 15 = 16 \times 3$
$15g = 48$
$g = 3.2$

9. $x \times 8 = 6 \times 5$
$8x = 30$
$x = 3.75$

10. $k \times 5 = 25 \times 4$
$5k = 100$
$k = 20$

11. $x \times 4 = 16 \times 3$
$4x = 48$
$x = 12$

12. $h \times 5 = 3 \times 15$
$5h = 45$
$h = 9$

13. 14 ; 14

14. 8
$\frac{16}{100} = \frac{x}{50}$
$100x = 800$
$x = 8$

15. 54
$\frac{30}{100} = \frac{x}{180}$
$100x = 5400$
$x = 54$

16. 18
$\frac{20}{100} = \frac{x}{90}$
$100x = 1800$
$x = 18$

17. 30
$\frac{15}{100} = \frac{x}{200}$
$100x = 3000$
$x = 30$

18. 104
$\frac{65}{100} = \frac{x}{160}$
$100x = 10\,400$
$x = 104$

19. Check A, C, D, E, and H.

20. $\frac{5}{10} = \frac{x}{8}$
$10x = 40$
$x = 4$
4

21. $\frac{4.5}{3} = \frac{x}{2}$
$3x = 9$
$x = 3$
$3

22. $\frac{7.5}{6} = \frac{x}{8}$
$6x = 60$
$x = 10$
$10

23. $\frac{6.8}{8} = \frac{x}{12}$
$8x = 81.6$
$x = 10.2$
$10.20

24a. $\frac{2.1}{3} = \frac{x}{2}$
$3x = 4.2$
$x = 1.4$
$1.40

$\frac{0.95}{2} = \frac{x}{3}$
$2x = 2.85$
$x = 1.425$
$1.43

b. $\frac{1}{1.69} = \frac{x}{8.45}$
$1.69x = 8.45$
$x = 5$
5 cartons

$\frac{3}{2.1} = \frac{x}{2.8}$
$2.1x = 8.4$
$x = 4$
4 boxes

25a. $\frac{2}{4} = \frac{x}{8}$
$4x = 16$
$x = 4$
4 cups

$\frac{2}{4} = \frac{x}{6}$
$4x = 12$
$x = 3$
3 cups

b. $\frac{\frac{1}{4}}{4} = \frac{x}{12}$
$4x = 3$
$x = \frac{3}{4}$
$\frac{3}{4}$ teaspoon

$\frac{\frac{1}{4}}{4} = \frac{x}{10}$
$4x = 2\frac{1}{2}$
$x = \frac{5}{8}$
$\frac{5}{8}$ teaspoon

c. $\dfrac{4}{2} = \dfrac{x}{9}$ 　　　　$\dfrac{4}{1\frac{1}{3}} = \dfrac{x}{4}$

　　$2x = 36$ 　　　　$1\frac{1}{3}x = 16$

　　$x = 18$ 　　　　$x = 12$

　　18 servings 　　12 servings

d. $\dfrac{1}{1\frac{1}{2}} = \dfrac{x}{3}$ 　　　　$\dfrac{1}{\frac{1}{4}} = \dfrac{x}{2}$

　　$1\frac{1}{2}x = 3$ 　　　　$\frac{1}{4}x = 2$

　　$x = 2$ 　　　　$x = 8$

　　2 cups 　　　　8 cups

9　Integers

Try It

D

1. $2 - 5$ 　　　2. $= -9 - 6$ 　　3. $= -2 + 3$
   -3 　　　　　$= -15$ 　　　　$= 1$
4. $= 5 + 9$ 　　5. $= 7 - 5$ 　　6. $= -8 - 3$
   $= 14$ 　　　　$= 2$ 　　　　$= -11$
7. $= -6 - 8$ 　8. $= 1 + 9$ 　　9. $= -4 + 5$
   $= -14$ 　　　$= 10$ 　　　　$= 1$
10. $= 7 - 6$ 　11. $= -5 - 2$ 　12. $= 4 - 7$
    $= 1$ 　　　　$= -7$ 　　　　$= -3$
13. 30 　　14. 20 　　15. -3 　　16. 10
17. -6 　　18. -12 　　19. -12 　　20. 2
21. 28 　　22. 4 　　23. -7 　　24. -36
25. 21 　　26. 3 　　27. -3 　　28. 35
29. -33 　　30. 4 　　31. 30 　　32. -5
33. $-, +$; $+, -$ 　　34. $+, +$; $-, -$
35. $+, -$; $-, +$ 　　36. $+, +$; $-, -$
37. $+, +$; $-, -$ 　　38. $+, +$; $-, -$
39. $-, +$; $+, -$ 　　40. $+, +$; $-, -$
41. -1 　　42. -20 　　43. -9 　　44. 18
45. -18 　　46. 14 　　47. -5 　　48. -8
49. 29 　　50. 3 　　51. 5 　　52. -2
53. $-$ 　　54. $+$ 　　55. $-$ 　　56. $-$
57. $-$ 　　58. $-$ 　　59. $+$ 　　60. $-$
61. $+, -$ 　　62. $+, +$ 　　63. $+, -$ 　　64. $+, +$
65. $+$ 　　66. $-$
67. +5 　　68. -3 　　69. -4 　　70. +3
71. $= 10 - (-12)$ 　72. $= 25 - (-6)$
    $= 22$ 　　　　　$= 31$
73. $= 19 - 13 \times (-2)$ 　74. $= 18 + 25 \times (-2)$
    $= 19 - (-26)$ 　　　　$= 18 + (-50)$
    $= 45$ 　　　　　　$= -32$
75. $= \dfrac{1 - 4 - 9}{-1 + 2 + 3}$ 　76. $= \dfrac{49 - 1 \times 25}{1 - 4}$

    $= \dfrac{-12}{4}$ 　　　　$= \dfrac{24}{-3}$

    $= -3$ 　　　　　$= -8$

77. $= \dfrac{12 + 13}{25 \div (-5)}$ 　78. $= \dfrac{-6 - (5 \times 4)}{(9 - 1) \div (-2)}$

    $= \dfrac{25}{-5}$ 　　　　$= \dfrac{-26}{-4}$

    $= -5$ 　　　　　$= 6\frac{1}{2}$

79. $= \dfrac{2 - 7}{4 \times (-3)}$ 　80. $= \dfrac{1 - 4 + 7}{-12 - 4}$

    $= \dfrac{-5}{-12}$ 　　　　$= \dfrac{4}{-16}$

    $= \dfrac{5}{12}$ 　　　　$= -\dfrac{1}{4}$

10　Circumferences of Circles

Try It

3 cm ; 1.5 cm

1.
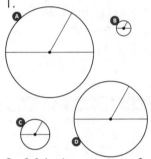

A: 6 cm ; 3 cm
B: 1 cm ; 0.5 cm
C: 2 cm ; 1 cm
D: 5 cm ; 2.5 cm
　　two

2. 3.14 ; 6 　　　3. 2 x 3.14 x 4
   18.84 　　　　　25.12 (cm)
4. 3.14 x 3 　　　5. 2 x 3.14 x 2.5
   9.42 (cm) 　　　15.7 (cm)
6. A: 3.14 x 12 ; 37.68 (cm)
   B: 3.14 x 8.6 ; 27.004 (cm)
   C: 3.14 x (15 – 8.6) ; 20.096 (cm)
   D: 2 x 3.14 x 2.5 ; 15.7 (cm)
   E: 2 x 3.14 x (2.5 x 2) ; 31.4 (cm)
7. C = 3.14 x 18 　　8. C = 2 x 3.14 x 6
   = 56.52 (cm) 　　　= 37.68 (m)
9. C = 2 x 3.14 x 13 　10. C = 3.14 x 15
   = 81.64 (m) 　　　　= 47.1 (mm)
11. C = 2 x 3.14 x 8.5 　12. C = 3.14 x 26.5
    = 53.38 (cm) 　　　　= 83.21 (m)

13.

6 cm	3 cm	7.6 cm	4.6 cm	2.2 cm
3 cm	1.5 cm	3.8 cm	2.3 cm	1.1 cm
18.84 cm	9.42 cm	23.864 cm	14.444 cm	6.908 cm

14. d = 12.56 ÷ 3.14 　15. d = 31.4 ÷ 3.14
    = 4 (cm) 　　　　　= 10 (m)
16. d = 78.5 ÷ 3.14 　17. d = 18.84 ÷ 3.14
    = 25 (cm) 　　　　= 6 (cm)
18. d = 17.584 ÷ 3.14
    = 5.6 (m)

19.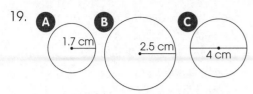

A: 3.4 cm ; 1.7 cm ; 10.676 cm
B: 5 cm ; 2.5 cm ; 15.7 cm
C: 4 cm ; 2 cm ; 12.56 cm

11 Congruence and Similarity

Try It
similar

1.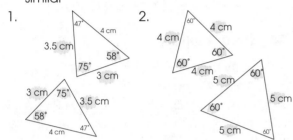
2.

congruent   similar

3. 2 ; 2 ; 2 ; is
4. $\frac{4}{5}$; 0.8 ; $\frac{5}{6.4}$ = 0.78 ; $\frac{3}{4}$ = 0.75 ; is not
5. $\frac{3}{6}$ = 0.5 ; $\frac{5}{10}$ = 0.5 ; $\frac{4}{8}$ = 0.5 ; is
6. $\frac{8}{24}$ = 0.33 ; $\frac{9}{27}$ = 0.33 ; $\frac{10}{30}$ = 0.33 ; is
7. 2:3   8. 4:3

9. 3:2   10. 2:1

11. Condition C   12. Condition B
13. Condition A   14. Condition C
15. Condition B
16-18. (Suggested drawings)
16. 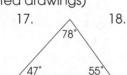   17.   18.

12 Pythagorean Relationship

Try It

1.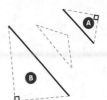
   a. A: 3 ; 4 ; 25
      B: $6^2 + 8^2 = 100$
   b. A: 5 ; 25
      B: $10^2 = 100$
c. The answers in a and b of each triangle are the same.
2. 25 ; 5
3. $5^2 + 12^2 = c^2$ 4. $6^2 + 8^2 = c^2$
      $c^2 = 169$ $c^2 = 100$
      $c = 13$ $c = 10$
5. $10^2 + 24^2 = c^2$ 6. $8^2 + 15^2 = c^2$
      $c^2 = 679$ $c^2 = 289$
      $c = 26$ $c = 17$
7. $x^2 + 5^2 = 10^2$ 8. $2^2 + 2^2 = y^2$
      $x^2 = 75$ $y^2 = 8$
      $x = 8.66$ $y = 2.83$
9. $2^2 + 8^2 = a^2$ 10. $b^2 + 3^2 = 7^2$
      $a^2 = 68$ $b^2 = 40$
      $a = 8.25$ $b = 6.32$
11. $m^2 + 10^2 = 12^2$ 12. $5^2 + 6^2 = n^2$
      $m^2 = 44$ $n^2 = 61$
      $m = 6.63$ $n = 7.81$
13. $4^2 + 5^2 = k^2$ 14. $6^2 + 9^2 = n^2$
      $k^2 = 41$ $n^2 = 117$
      $k = 6.40$ $n = 10.82$
15. $2^2 + 6.5^2 = a^2$
      $a^2 = 46.25$
      $a = 6.80$
16. It is not a right triangle.
17. It is not a right triangle.
18. $b^2 + 25^2 = 40^2$ 19. $a^2 + 10^2 = 26^2$
      $b^2 = 975$ $a^2 = 576$
      $b = 31.22$ $a = 24$
20. $15^2 + 15^2 = d^2$ 21. $e^2 + 20^2 = 24^2$
      $d^2 = 450$ $e^2 = 176$
      $d = 21.21$ $e = 13.27$
22. $f^2 + 7^2 = 22^2$
      $f^2 = 435$
      $f = 20.86$
23. 7.21 ; 17.21   24. 10.07 ; 29.97
25. 16.97 ; 40.97   26. 8.65 ; 23.05
27. 6 ; 48   28. 11.18 ; 111.8
29. 7.75 ; 15.5   30. 15.35 ; 69.08

13 Algebraic Expressions

Try It
$8y$; $4y$

1-6. (Individual examples)

1. $4a$; $-a$
2. $6j$; $0.2j$
3. $\frac{1}{5}y$; $3y$
4. $4xy$; $-xy$
5. ab ; $3ab$
6. m^2n ; $-0.3m^2n$
7. $4x$
8. y
9. $3a$
10. $4i^2$
11. $5m - 5n$
12. $2x^2 - 4x$
13. $8p^2 + 2pq - 8q^2$
14. $3a$; $3b$
    $7a - 3b$
15. $6x$; $6y$
    $-2x + 6y$
16. $= -10a + 5b - 6b$
    $= -10a - b$
17. $= 56x^3$
18. $= -6x^4$
19. $= 12x^3 - 2x^3$
    $= 10x^3$
20. $= -3xy^2$
21. $= \dfrac{a^3b^6}{3}$
22. $= -2ab^2 + ab^2$
    $= -ab^2$
23. $= \dfrac{1}{2}j - \dfrac{1}{2}j$
    $= 0$
24. $8a^2 - 8a + 3$
25. $3b^3 + 4b^2 - 6b - 5$
26. $2n^3 - 7n^2 - 2n - 9$
27. $a^2 - ab + 2$
28. $-4mn + 7n^2$
29. $-4x^2 + 7x^2y + y^2$
30. $2n - 9$
    a. $2 \times 8 - 9 = 7$
    b. $2 \times (-1) - 9 = -11$
    c. $2 \times 0.5 - 9 = -8$
31. $9a^2 - 6$
    a. $9 \times 2^2 - 6 = 30$
    b. $9 \times 0^2 - 6 = -6$
    c. $9 \times (-2)^2 - 6 = 30$
32. $2t + 6$
    a. $2 \times 5 + 6 = 16$
    b. $2 \times \dfrac{1}{2} + 6 = 7$
    c. $2 \times (-5) + 6 = -4$
33. $= 3a + 2b$
    $= 3 \times 3 + 2 \times (-4)$
    $= 1$
34. $= c + cd$
    $= (-1) + (-1) \times 5$
    $= -6$
35. $= 7e + 2f$
    $= 7 \times 0.2 + 2 \times (-4)$
    $= -6.6$
36. $= -2m + 3n$
    $= -2 \times (-\dfrac{1}{3}) + 3 \times \dfrac{2}{3}$
    $= 2\dfrac{2}{3}$
37. $= 4pq - 2p$
    $= 4 \times \dfrac{1}{4} \times \dfrac{2}{5} - 2 \times \dfrac{1}{4}$
    $= -\dfrac{1}{10}$
38. $= 2x^2 + 2xy$
    $= 2 \times (-0.1)^2 + 2 \times (-0.1) \times (-9)$
    $= 1.82$
39. $= -a^3 + 3bc$
    $= -(2)^3 + 3 \times 4 \times 6$
    $= 64$
40. $= -ij - i - k$
    $= -3 \times 1 - 3 - (-2)$
    $= -4$
41. $= 4d + 2ef$
    $= 4 \times 1.2 + 2 \times \dfrac{1}{2} \times (-0.2)$
    $= 4.6$
42. $(a + 2b) \times 7$
    $= 7a + 14b$
43. $(3a)(b - 1) \div 2$
    $= \dfrac{3ab - 3a}{2}$

44. $(2a - b)(a) - (a - 0.5a)(2a - b - a)$
    $= 2a^2 - ab - (0.5a)(a - b)$
    $= 2a^2 - ab - 0.5a^2 + 0.5ab$
    $= 1.5a^2 - 0.5ab$
45. $(3a)(b + 5) - (2a)(b + 1) \div 2$
    $= 3ab + 15a - (ab + a)$
    $= 3ab + 15a - ab - a$
    $= 2ab + 14a$
46. $7 \times 8 + 14 \times 4 = 112$; 112
    $\dfrac{3 \times 8 \times 4 - 3 \times 8}{2} = 36$; 36
    $1.5 \times 8^2 - 0.5 \times 8 \times 4 = 80$; 80
    $2 \times 8 \times 4 + 14 \times 8 = 176$; 176

14 Data Analysis

Try It

45 ; 41 ; none

1. A: 54 ; 51.5 ; 65   B: 62 ; 60.5 ; 60, 95
   C: 53 ; 50.5 ; 16   D: 47 ; 42 ; none
2. F   3. F   4. T   5. F   6. F
7. 41 ; 32   8. 65 ; 41   9. 60 ; 61 ; 62
10. 88 ; 88 ; 84   11. 14 ; 11 ; 11
    Mean: 64   Median: 16.5
12. 45 ; 45 ; 26 ; 26
    Mode: 26, 45
13a. primary ; sample ; discrete
   b. 22.5 ; 21.5 ; 17, 19, 29
   c. No, it is not because there is more than one mode.
14a. primary ; sample ; continuous
   b. 0.63 ; 0.68 ; 0.8
   c. mode ; mean
15. increasing ; no ; decreasing
   a. They are secondary sets of data because the data were gathered second-hand.
   b. They are samples because they only cover the prices over 7 days.
   c. (Suggested answers)
      Stock A: The price will increase to reach about $12.
      Stock B: The price will stay steady. It will be about $30.
      Stock C: The price will come down to under $1.

15 Graphs

Try It

5 ; 5 ; 3 ; 2

1. 2 ; 2 ; 1 ; 7 ; 3   2. 3 ; 6 ; 2 ; 3 ; 1
3. 4 ; 3 ; 5 ; 2 ; 1

4a. A ; Each interval should have the same range.

b. A ; The end values of each interval should not overlap with other intervals.

c. B ; Combine every two intervals to get half as many intervals.

5. double bar graph ; Using double bar graphs is a convenient way to show comparisons of discrete data values.

6. double line graph ; Using double line graphs is a preferred way to show comparisons of continuous data values.

7. circle graph ; Parts of a whole are best displayed using a circle graph.

8. scatter plot ; A scatter plot can display the correlation between 2 different sets of data.

9a. circle graph ; comedy

b. double bar graph ; 5 girls

c. circle graph ; 50%

10a. scatter plot ; no correlation

b. line graph ; about 4°C

c. scatter plot ; no

Level 2

1 Rational Numbers

Try It

$\frac{1}{2}$; $\frac{0}{4}$; 2^3

1. $\frac{5}{1}$; $-\frac{4}{1}$; $\frac{9}{5}$; $\frac{7}{2}$

$\frac{0}{1}$; $\frac{2}{1}$; $\frac{9}{1}$; $\frac{5}{1}$

$\frac{5}{2}$; $\frac{1}{1}$; $-\frac{26}{5}$; $\frac{3}{10}$

2.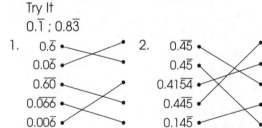

0.2 ; 0.$\overline{36}$; 0.6 ; 0.$\overline{2}$; 0.875 ; 0.8$\overline{3}$

3. -3   4. $\frac{0}{3}$ 5. $\sqrt{9}$

6. 0.$\overline{3}$ 7. 1.0881   8. $3\frac{1}{2}$

9. $\sqrt{1}$ 10. $\sqrt{64}$ 11. 2.$\overline{72}$

12. 1.62   13. $\sqrt{7}^2$ 14. 3×10^{-2}

15. 2^4 16. $-\sqrt{121}$ 17. $\sqrt{81}$

18. (Individual examples)

a. rational   b. rational   c. rational
d. rational   e. irrational   f. rational
g. irrational   h. rational   i. rational
j. rational

19. ✔ ; $\frac{4}{7}$ 20.   21. ✔ ; 3^2

22.   23. ✔ ; 2.$\overline{3}$ 24.

25. ✔ ; 8×10^2 26.   27. ✔ ; $-\sqrt{4}$

28. $\sqrt{16.9}$; $1.6\overline{9} < \sqrt{169} < 1.69 \times 10^3$

29. $\sqrt{525}$; $5.\overline{255} < 5\frac{2}{5} < 5^2$

30. $\frac{\sqrt{3}}{2}$; $-0.\overline{6} < \frac{0.25}{5} < \frac{\sqrt{9}}{4}$

31. $\sqrt{441}$; $\sqrt{441} < 44.\overline{1} < 4.14 \times 10^2$

32. $\sqrt{12 \times 4}$; $\sqrt{108 \div 3} < \sqrt{32 + 32} < \sqrt{96 - 15}$

33. F   34. T   35. F   36. F

37. F   38. T   39. T

40. $= 100 - 15$ 41. $= 1150 \div 5$
    $= 85$ $= 230$
    R   R

42. $= \sqrt{16 \times 2}$ 43. $= \sqrt{7} \times \sqrt{7} \times \sqrt{7} \times 5 \times 1$
    $= \sqrt{32}$ $= 7 \times \sqrt{7} \times 5$
    IR $= 35\sqrt{7}$
                             IR

44. $= \sqrt{\dfrac{36 + 24}{40 \div 2}}$ 45. $\dfrac{16 + 2}{49 - 25}$
    $= \sqrt{3}$ $= \dfrac{3}{4}$
    IR   R

46. $= \sqrt{450} \div \sqrt{2}$ 47. $= \dfrac{12 - 4 \times 3}{6 + 16 \times 2}$
    $= \sqrt{225}$ $= \dfrac{0}{38}$
    $= 15$ $= 0$
    R   R

48. $= 15\sqrt{6} \div 4\sqrt{6}$
    $= \dfrac{15}{4}$
    R

2 Fractions, Decimals, and Percents

Try It

0.$\overline{1}$; 0.8$\overline{3}$

1. 0.$\overline{6}$ 2. 0.$\overline{45}$
   0.0$\overline{6}$ 0.4$\overline{5}$
   0.$\overline{60}$ 0.41$\overline{54}$
   0.0$\overline{66}$ 0.4$\overline{45}$
   0.00$\overline{6}$ 0.14$\overline{5}$

3. 55.$\overline{5}$%   4. 3.$\overline{3}$%   5. 28.$\overline{28}$%

6. 14.$\overline{414}$%   7. 144.$\overline{4}$%   8. 508.$\overline{8}$%

9. 7.$\overline{1}$%   10. 0.$\overline{50}$%   11. 52.$\overline{43}$%

12. 32.$\overline{49832}$%   13. $\frac{7}{9}$; $\frac{7}{9}$

14. $\frac{2}{11}$ 15. $\frac{23}{99}$ 16. $\frac{5}{11}$

$99x = 18$ $99x = 23$ $99x = 45$

$x = \dfrac{18}{99}$ $x = \dfrac{23}{99}$ $x = \dfrac{45}{99}$

$x = \dfrac{2}{11}$ $x = \dfrac{5}{11}$

17. 0.58   18. 0.4$\overline{5}$ 19. $\frac{49}{50}$ 20. 1.32%

21. 0.1   22. $\frac{21}{100}$ 23. $0.2\overline{0}$ 24. $2\frac{1}{9}$

25. 0.8 ; 80%   26. 40% ; $\frac{2}{5}$

27. 175% ; $1\frac{3}{4}$ 28. 2.5 ; $2\frac{1}{2}$

29. 7.6 ; 760%   30. 8% ; $\frac{2}{25}$

31. 1% ; $\frac{1}{100}$ 32. $33.\overline{3}$% ; $\frac{1}{3}$

33. $122.\overline{2}$% ; $1\frac{2}{9}$ 34. $5.1\overline{3}$; $513.\overline{3}$%

35. $0.0\overline{1}$; $1.\overline{1}$%   36. $0.0\overline{8}$; $\frac{4}{45}$

37. $= \frac{\overset{3}{\cancel{21}}}{\underset{5}{\cancel{25}}} \times \frac{\overset{2}{\cancel{10}}}{\underset{1}{\cancel{7}}} + 1\frac{4}{7}$
    $= \frac{6}{5} + 1\frac{4}{7}$
    $= 2\frac{27}{35}$

38. $= 9\frac{1}{5} + \frac{24}{5} \div \frac{1}{25}$
    $= 9\frac{1}{5} + \frac{24}{\underset{1}{\cancel{5}}} \times \frac{\overset{5}{\cancel{25}}}{1}$
    $= 9\frac{1}{5} + 120$
    $= 129\frac{1}{5}$

39. $= 2\frac{1}{5} - \frac{\overset{4}{\cancel{20}}}{\underset{1}{\cancel{5}}} \times \frac{\overset{2}{\cancel{10}}}{\underset{1}{\cancel{7}}}$
    $= 2\frac{1}{5} - 8$
    $= -5\frac{4}{5}$

40. $= \frac{1}{5} \times \frac{1}{4} + 2\frac{1}{10}$
    $= \frac{1}{20} + 2\frac{1}{10}$
    $= 2\frac{3}{20}$

41. $= \frac{3}{4} + \frac{\overset{1}{\cancel{5}}}{2} \times \frac{1}{\underset{1}{\cancel{5}}}$
    $= \frac{3}{4} + \frac{1}{2}$
    $= 1\frac{1}{4}$

42. $= \frac{4}{5} - \frac{1}{5} \times \frac{8}{5}$
    $= \frac{4}{5} - \frac{8}{25}$
    $= \frac{12}{25}$

43. $= 0.8 \div 0.8 + 1.7$
    $= 1 + 1.7$
    $= 2.7$

44. $= 0.5 + 0.8 \times 1.5$
    $= 0.5 + 1.2$
    $= 1.7$

45. $= 3.6 \div (0.3 - 0.9)$
    $= 3.6 \div (-0.6)$
    $= -6$

46. $= 4 \times 0.15 - 5 \times 0.3$
    $= 0.6 - 1.5$
    $= -0.9$

47. $= 0.5 \times 0.5 + 0.4 \times 0.4$
    $= 0.25 + 0.16$
    $= 0.41$

48. $= 6.5 - 1.5 \times 0.6$
    $= 6.5 - 0.9$
    $= 5.6$

3   Ratios, Rates, and Proportions

Try It

3:2 ; 5:6

1.

Bolts	Spikers	Movers	Royals
3:1	1:3	2:3	1:1
1:5	3:7	2:7	1:2
1:5	3:7	3:7	1:4
3:1:1	1:3:3	2:3:2	1:1:2
3:1:5	1:3:7	2:3:7	1:1:4

a. the Bolts   b. the Spikers

2. 40   3. 22.5   4. 1.20   5. 40

6. 40   7. 105   8. 1.75   9. 4

10. 80 km/h   11. 4 km/h

12. 25 km/h   13. 92 km/h

14. A: $2.88/can   B: ✔ ; $1.98/can

15. A: $8.50/jug   B: ✔ ; $8.45/jug

16. A: $1.45/ball   B: ✔ ; $1.38/ball

17. A: ✔ ; $16.40/kg   B: $17.20/kg

18. 4.5   19. 180   20. 8

21. 252   22. 12   23. 7

24. 50   25. 42   26. 216

27a. $\frac{11}{5} = \frac{x}{8}$ b. $\frac{11}{5} = \frac{x}{12}$ c. $\frac{11}{5} = \frac{x}{3}$

$x = 17.6$ $x = 26.4$ $x = 6.6$

$17.60 $26.40 $6.60

28a. $\frac{4}{6} = \frac{x}{4}$ b. $\frac{4}{6} = \frac{x}{8}$ c. $\frac{4}{6} = \frac{x}{10}$

$x = 2.67$ $x = 5.33$ $x = 6.67$

$2.67 $5.33 $6.67

29a. 17:14   b. 4200 g

30a. 2.25 km   b. 40 minutes

31a. $384   b. $360   c. 5:6:4

d. Frank earned $144 and Paul earned $96.

32. 12.5%   33. $30   34. 2100 mL

4   Areas of Circles

Try It

28.26

1. A: 50.24 (cm²)   B: 3.14×6^2
                                    $= 113.04$ (m²)

   C: 3.14×8.5^2 D: 3.14×5^2
      $= 226.865$ (cm²) $= 78.5$ (m²)

   E: 3.14×12.8^2 F: 3.14×9^2
      $= 514.4576$ (cm²) $= 254.34$ (m²)

2. $r = 8 \div 2 = 4$
   $A = 3.14 \times 4^2 = 50.24$ (cm²)

3. $r = 10 \div 2 = 5$
   $A = 3.14 \times 5^2 = 78.5$ (m²)

4. $r = 16 \div 2 = 8$
   $A = 3.14 \times 8^2 = 200.96$ (cm²)

5. $r = 22 \div 2 = 11$
   $A = 3.14 \times 11^2 = 379.94$ (cm²)

6. $r = 25 \div 2 = 12.5$
   $A = 3.14 \times 12.5^2 = 490.625$ (m²)

7. A: 1 cm ; 3.14 cm²
   B: 2 cm ; 12.56 cm²
   C: 5.5 cm ; 94.985 cm²
   D: 3 cm ; 28.26 cm²
   E: 1.5 cm ; 7.065 cm²

8. $\pi r^2 = 78.5$
$r^2 = 78.5 \div 3.14$
$r^2 = 25$
$r = 5$
5 cm ; 10 cm

9. $\pi r^2 = 200.96$
$r^2 = 200.96 \div 3.14$
$r^2 = 64$
$r = 8$
8 m ; 16 m

10. $\pi r^2 = 3.14$
$r^2 = 3.14 \div 3.14$
$r^2 = 1$
$r = 1$
1 cm ; 2 cm

11. $\pi r^2 = 706.5$
$r^2 = 706.5 \div 3.14$
$r^2 = 225$
$r = 15$
15 cm ; 30 cm

12. $\pi r^2 = 379.94$
$r^2 = 379.94 \div 3.14$
$r^2 = 121$
$r = 11$
11 m ; 22 m

13. $\pi r^2 = 254.34$
$r^2 = 254.34 \div 3.14$
$r^2 = 81$
$r = 9$
9 mm ; 18 mm

14. A: 2.5 cm ; 5 cm   B: 1.8 cm ; 3.6 cm
C: 2.2 cm ; 4.4 cm

15. 176.63   16. 30.96   17. 56.52
18. 123.84   19. 150.72   20. 6.22
21.

62.8 cm	314 cm²
75.36 cm	452.16 cm²
103.62 cm	854.865 cm²
122.46 cm	1193.985 cm²
138.16 cm	1519.76 cm²

5 Cylinders

Try It
2 ; 3 ; 37.68

1. $V = \pi \times 4^2 \times 1$
$= 50.24$ (cm³)

2. $V = \pi \times 1^2 \times 3$
$= 9.42$ (cm³)

3. $V = \pi \times 2^2 \times 5$
$= 62.8$ (cm³)

4. $V = \pi \times 1^2 \times 10$
$= 31.4$ (cm³)

5. $V = \pi \times 1.5^2 \times 0.5$
$= 3.5325$ (cm³)

6. $V = \pi \times 3^2 \times 3$
$= 84.78$ (cm³)

7. A: 1582.56 cm³   B: 508.68 cm³
C: 5425.92 m³   D: 226.08 m³
E: 17.6625 m³

8. $2 \times 3.14 \times 2^2$; $2 \times 3.14 \times 2 \times 5$
25.12 ; 62.8
87.92

9. $2 \times 3.14 \times 3^2 + 2 \times 3.14 \times 3 \times 10$
$= 56.52 + 188.4$
$= 244.92$ (cm²)

10. $2 \times 3.14 \times 8^2 + 2 \times 3.14 \times 8 \times 4$
$= 401.92 + 200.96$
$= 602.88$ (cm²)

11. 533.8 cm² ; 345.4 cm² ; 1055.04 cm² ;
1570 cm² ; 251.2 cm²

12. A: 200.96 m³ ; 200.96 m²
B: 100.48 m³ ; 125.6 m²
C: 100.48 m³ ; 150.72 m²
D: 175.84 m³ ; 200.96 m²

13. false   14. false   15. true   16. false

17. V: $3.14 \times 6.5^2 \times 8 = 1061.32$ (cm³)
S.A.: $2 \times 3.14 \times 6.5^2 + 2 \times 3.14 \times 6.5 \times 8$
$= 591.89$ (cm²)

18. V: $3.14 \times 2.5^2 \times 12 = 235.5$ (m³)
S.A.: $2 \times 3.14 \times 2.5^2 + 2 \times 3.14 \times 2.5 \times 12$
$= 227.65$ (m²)

19. V: $3.14 \times 4^2 \times 1.5 = 75.36$ (cm³)
S.A.: $2 \times 3.14 \times 4^2 + 3.14 \times 8 \times 1.5$
$= 138.16$ (cm²)

20. V: $3.14 \times 2.5^2 \times 7 = 137.375$ (m³)
S.A.: $2 \times 3.14 \times 2.5^2 + 3.14 \times 5 \times 7$
$= 149.15$ (m²)

21. V: $3.14 \times 2^2 \times 13.5 = 169.56$ (m³)
S.A.: $2 \times 3.14 \times 2^2 + 3.14 \times 4 \times 13.5$
$= 194.68$ (m²)

22. V: $3.14 \times 5.5^2 \times 13.2 = 1253.802$ (cm³)
S.A.: $2 \times 3.14 \times 5.5^2 + 3.14 \times 11 \times 13.2$
$= 645.898$ (cm²)

6 Volume and Surface Area

Try It
V: $3.14 \times 2^2 \times 5 = 62.8$ (cm³)
S.A.: $2 \times 3.14 \times 2^2 + 2 \times 3.14 \times 2 \times 5 = 87.92$ (cm²)

1. V: $4 \times 4 \times 10 = 160$ (cm³)
S.A.: $4 \times 4 \times 2 + 4 \times 10 \times 4 = 192$ (cm²)

2. V: $3 \times 4 \div 2 \times 6 = 36$ (cm³)
S.A.: $3 \times 4 \div 2 \times 2 + 3 \times 6 + 4 \times 6 + 5 \times 6 = 84$ (cm²)

3. V: $3.14 \times 3^2 \times 3 = 84.78$ (cm³)
S.A.: $2 \times 3.14 \times 3^2 + 2 \times 3.14 \times 3 \times 3 = 113.04$ (cm²)

4. V: $6 \times 6 \times 6 = 216$ (cm³)
S.A.: $6 \times 6 \times 6 = 216$ (cm²)

5. V: $(6.5 + 12) \times 8 \div 2 \times 7 = 518$ (cm³)
S.A.: $(6.5 + 12) \times 8 \div 2 \times 2 + 12 \times 7 + 8 \times 7 +$
$6.5 \times 7 + 9.7 \times 7 = 401.4$ (cm²)

6. V: $6 \times 3 \div 2 \times 2 = 18$ (cm³)
S.A.: $6 \times 3 \div 2 \times 2 + 6 \times 2 + 5 \times 2 + 4 \times 2 = 48$ (cm²)

7. A: 20.41 cm³ ; 47.1 cm²
B: 70 cm³ ; 120.5 cm²
C: 15.625 cm³ ; 37.5 cm²
D: 5.1 cm³ ; 21.4 cm²
E: 22 cm³ ; 103 cm²

8. A: 0.125 m³ ; 1.5 m²   B: 0.375 m³ ; 3.5 m²
   C: 0.125 m³ ; 1.8 m²
   a. 0.25 m³ ; 2.8 m²   b. 0.5 m³ ; 4.5 m²
   c. 0.5 m³ ; 4.5 m²   d. 0.625 m³ ; 4.8 m²
9. V: 6 x 4 x 3 – 3.14 x 1² x 6 = 53.16
   S.A.: 6 x 4 x 2 + 6 x 3 x 2 + 4 x 3 x 2 – 2 x 3.14 x
        1² + 2 x 3.14 x 1 x 6 = 139.4
   53.16 cm³ ; 139.4 cm²
10. V: 3.14 x 4² x 2 – 2 x 2 x 2 = 92.48
    S.A.: 2 x 3.14 x 4² + 2 x 3.14 x 4 x 2 – 2 x 2 x
         2 + 2 x 2 x 4 = 158.72
    92.48 cm³ ; 158.72 cm²
11. V: 3.14 x 6² x 3 + 10 x 3 x 3 – 3 x 3 x 3 = 402.12
    S.A.: 2 x 3.14 x 6² + 3.14 x 12 x 3 + 3 x 7 x 4
         = 423.12
    402.12 cm³ ; 423.12 cm²

7   2-D and 3-D Geometry

Try It

1.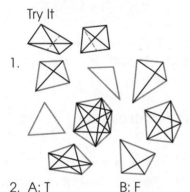

2. A: T   B: F   C: F
   D: T   E: F   F: T
   (Suggested drawings)

3.  A, B, D   4. A, D

5. A, B, D   6. A, C, D

7. A, B, C, D   8. A, D

9a. squares and rectangles
  b. squares, rectangles, parallelograms, and
     rhombuses
  c. squares, rhombuses, and kites
  d. squares and rhombuses

10. no ; (Suggested drawing)

11. A: hexagonal prism ; 8 ; 12 ; 18 ; 20 ; 20
    B: triangular pyramid ; 4 ; 4 ; 6 ; 8 ; 8
    C: pentagonal prism ; 7 ; 10 ; 15 ; 17 ; 17
    D: pentagonal pyramid ; 6 ; 6 ; 10 ; 12 ;12
    E: octagonal pyramid ; 9 ; 9 ; 16 ; 18 ; 18
    F: rectangular prism ; 6 ; 8 ; 12 ; 14 ; 14
    G: triangular prism ; 5 ; 6 ; 9 ; 11 ; 11
    H: heptagonal prism ; 9 ; 14 ; 21 ; 23 ; 23
  a. C   b. 30 edges   c. 10 faces

8   Lines, Angles, and Triangles

Try It

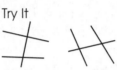

1. corresponding angles
2. consecutive interior angles
3. corresponding angles ;
   alternate interior angles
4. consecutive interior angles ;
   alternate interior angles
5. 120° ; 60°   6. 100° ; 80°
7. 125° ; 125°   8. 54° ; 126°
9. 135° ; 135°   10. 145° ; 35°
11. ∠c ; ∠d   12. ∠n, ∠p ; ∠m, ∠o
13. 48°   14. 118°
15. 84° ; 96°   16. ∠BOC ; ∠BOD
17. ∠QOR and ∠ROS ;
    ∠POR and ∠ROS, ∠POQ and ∠QOS
18. ∠WOX and ∠XOY ;
    ∠WOX and ∠XOZ, ∠WOY and ∠YOZ
19. 35°   20. 37°
21. 34°   22. 50° ; 40° ; 90°
23. 100° ; 100° ; 35° 24. 45° ; 55° ; 45°
25. 40° ; isosceles   26. 75° ; scalene
27. 60° ; equilateral 28. 112°
29. 64°   30. 35°
31. 61° ; 119°   32. 25° ; 45°
33. 40° ; 45°   34. 45° ; 80°
35. 30° ; 90°   36. 80° ; 42°

9   Cartesian Coordinate Plane

Try It
C(-2,3) ; D(1,-2)
1a. B(3,7), D(1,3)
    A(-1,7), F(-3,2)
    C(-4,-4), H(-1,-1)
    E(4,-4), G(1,-6)

b. I $(+,+)$; II $(-,+)$; III $(-,-)$; IV $(+,-)$
2. A   3. B   4. C
5. A   6. C   7. A
8.

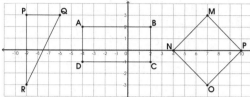

ABCD:
Perimeter: $(6 + 3) \times 2 = 18$ (units)
Area: $6 \times 3 = 18$ (square units)
PQR:
Perimeter: $3 + 6 + \sqrt{6^2 + 3^2} = 15.71$ (units)
Area: $6 \times 3 \div 2 = 9$ (square units)
MNOP:
Perimeter: $\sqrt{3^2 + 3^2} \times 4 = 16.97$ (units)
Area: $6 \times 3 \div 2 \times 2 = 18$ (square units)

9a.

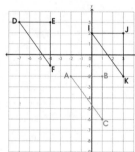

b. Translate it 5 units up and 5 units to the left.

Translate it 4 units up and 2 units to the right.

10a.

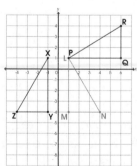

b. Rotate it 90° counterclockwise about $(1,1)$.

Reflect it in the y-axis.

11a.

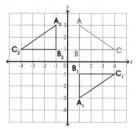

b. $A_1(1,-3)$
$B_1(1,-1)$
$C_1(4,-1)$
$A_2(-1,3)$
$B_2(-1,1)$
$C_2(-4,1)$

12a.

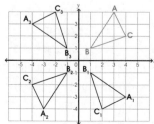

b. $A_1(4,-3)$ $A_2(-3,-4)$ $A_3(-4,3)$
$B_1(1,-1)$ $B_2(-1,-1)$ $B_3(-1,1)$
$C_1(2,-4)$ $C_2(-4,-2)$ $C_3(-2,4)$
13. $(a,-b)$; $(-a,b)$; $(b,-a)$; $(-a,-b)$; $(-b,a)$

10   Linear Patterns

Try It
B
1. 2 ; 6   2. 1 ; 3   3. 1 ; 2 ; 3 ; 4
3 ; 9   2 ; 5   6 ; 9 ; 12 ; 15
4 ; 12   3 ; 7   A
B   4 ; 9
             B
4. Pattern A: 10 ; 11 ; 6
Pattern B: 7 ; 9 ; $2n - 1$
Pattern C: 10 ; 13 ; $3n - 2$
5a. 14 ; 15 ; 22   b. 16 ; 19 ; 28
6. A: 1 ; 3 ; 13 ; 16 ; 19
B: 4 ; 5 ; 10 ; X ; 13
C: 3 ; X ; 7 ; 8 ; 9
7. Ann's Pattern: 3 ; 4 ; 5 ; 6 ; 7
Ben's Pattern: 0 ; 1 ; 2 ; 3 ; 4
Carl's Pattern: 4 ; 7 ; 10 ; 13 ; 16
Dan's Pattern: 0 ; 2 ; 4 ; 6 ; 8
8a. 12   b. 9
9a. 5   b. 9
10a. The term number is 3 for Ben and 2 for Dan.
b. The term number is 7 for Ann and 10 for Ben.
11. Carl ; Ben ; Dan ; Ann
12. Pattern A: 2 ; 3 ; 4 ; 5 ; 6
Pattern B: 8 ; 7 ; 6 ; 5 ; 4
Pattern C: 2 ; 4 ; 6 ; 8 ; 10

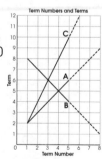

13a. 4 ; 5   b. 1 ; 2   c. 3 ; 6
14a. yes   b. no   c. Pattern B
15. no   16. no   17. no   18. Pattern C

11   Linear Equations

Try it
2 ; 2 ; 10 ; 2 ; 10 ; 2 ; 5
1. $2x + 5 - 5 = 11 - 5$ 2. $\frac{n}{5} - 1 + 1 = 4 + 1$
$\quad 2x = 6$ $\frac{n}{5} = 5$
$\quad 2x \div 2 = 6 \div 2$ $\frac{n}{5} \times 5 = 5 \times 5$
$\quad\quad x = 3$ $n = 25$

3. $3y + 2 - 2 = 8 - 2$
$3y = 6$
$3y \div 3 = 6 \div 3$
$y = 2$

4. $\frac{4}{9}k \times \frac{9}{4} = 8 \times \frac{9}{4}$
$k = 18$

5. $3 + \frac{m}{4} - 3 = 9 - 3$
$\frac{m}{4} = 6$
$\frac{m}{4} \times 4 = 6 \times 4$
$m = 24$

6. $12 - 2 = 2 + \frac{a}{3} - 2$
$10 = \frac{a}{3}$
$10 \times 3 = \frac{a}{3} \times 3$
$a = 30$

7. $13x = 52$
$13x \div 13 = 52 \div 13$
$x = 4$

8. $6 - 2 = k + k$
$2k = 4$
$2k \div 2 = 4 \div 2$
$k = 2$

9. $3y + 5y = 32$
$8y = 32$
$8y \div 8 = 32 \div 8$
$y = 4$

10. B
$5n - 10 = 20$
$5n = 30$
$n = 6$
$5 \times 6 - 10 = 20$

11. B
$9m - 10 = 8$
$9m = 18$
$m = 2$
$9 \times 2 - 10 = 8$

12. A
$x \div 6 + 4 = 7$
$x \div 6 = 3$
$x = 18$

$18 \div 6 + 4 = 7$

13. B
$\frac{3}{4}y - 5 = 4$
$\frac{3}{4}y = 9$
$y = 12$
$\frac{3}{4} \times 12 - 5 = 4$

14. A
$\frac{2}{5}q + 2 = 8$
$\frac{2}{5}q = 6$
$q = 15$
$\frac{2}{5} \times 15 + 2 = 8$

15. $y - 5 = 29$
$y = 34$
$34 - 5 = 29$

16. $z - 9 = -4$
$z = 5$
$5 - 9 = -4$

17. $p \times (-0.4) = 9$
$p = -22.5$
$-22.5 \times (-0.4) = 9$

18. $q + (-5) = 27$
$q = 32$
$32 + (-5) = 27$

19. $9y - y = 37 - 5$
$8y = 32$
$y = 4$
$9 \times 4 + 5 = 41$
$4 + 37 = 41$

20. $4p + 8p - 11p = -5$
$p = -5$
$4 \times (-5) + 5 + 8 \times (-5) = -55$
$11 \times (-5) = -55$

21. $i + 4i = 18 + 8 - 6$
$5i = 20$
$i = 4$
$4 + 6 + 4 \times 4 = 26$
$18 + 8 = 26$

22. 3
23. $2\frac{1}{3}$
24. $-3\frac{1}{2}$
25. 20
26. -3
27. $3\frac{3}{5}$
28. -11
29. 18
30. $4\frac{1}{2}$
31. 15

32. I like mathematics.

33a. $(9x + 4x) \times 2 = 234$
$26x = 234$
$x = 9$

b. $(9x + 4x) \times 2 = 65$
$26x = 65$
$x = 2.5$

34a. $4y \times 4y = 64$
$16y^2 = 64$
$y^2 = 4$
$y = 2$

b. $4y \times 4y = 256$
$16y^2 = 256$
$y^2 = 16$
$y = 4$

12 Graphs

Try It

B

1.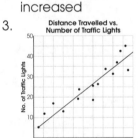

increasing
increased

2.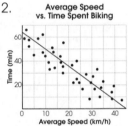

decreasing
decreased

3.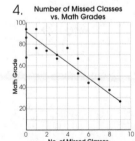

a. As the distance travelled increased, the number of traffic lights passed by increased.

b. He would pass by more traffic lights travelling 70 km because it is a longer distance.

c. He would pass by about 20 traffic lights.

4.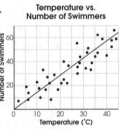

a. As the number of missed classes increased, the Math grade decreased.

b. Her grade is predicted to be about 75.

c. (Suggested answer)
A student's attendance in the Math class correlates with performance: the more classes a student misses, the lower the Math grade the student obtains.

5a. The intervals for the annual salary are smaller in Histogram A than in Histogram B. The intervals for the number of employees are greater in Histogram B than in Histogram A.
   b. Histogram A ; Histogram B ; Histogram B
   c. 14.28%
   d. It will affect the median salary.
6a. chocolate and mint   b. 17.5 ; 20 ; 25
   c. No, it is not suitable because there are no continuous intervals. The record of ice cream orders is a set of discrete data.
7a. More tickets were sold as the time got closer to 20:00.
   b. 24% ; 76%
   c. (Suggested answer)
   Most people were either sleeping or occupied with school or work between midnight and noon. Therefore, people tended to purchase tickets in the afternoon and the evening.

13   Theoretical and Experimental Probabilities

Try It
45% ; 25% ; 30%
1. TP   2. EP   3. EP   4. TP   5. EP   6. EP
7. TP: $\frac{1}{2}$; $\frac{1}{2}$ EP: $\frac{2}{5}$; $\frac{3}{5}$
8. TP: $\frac{1}{6}$; $\frac{1}{6}$; $\frac{1}{6}$; $\frac{1}{6}$; $\frac{1}{6}$; $\frac{1}{6}$
   EP: $\frac{1}{3}$; $\frac{2}{15}$; $\frac{2}{15}$; $\frac{2}{15}$; 0 ; $\frac{4}{15}$
9. TP: $\frac{1}{2}$; $\frac{1}{4}$; $\frac{1}{4}$ EP: $\frac{3}{5}$; $\frac{1}{4}$; $\frac{3}{20}$
10. TP: $\frac{2}{5}$; $\frac{2}{5}$; $\frac{1}{5}$ EP: $\frac{1}{3}$; $\frac{7}{15}$; $\frac{1}{5}$
11a. 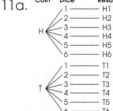 $\frac{1}{12}$; $\frac{1}{12}$; $\frac{1}{2}$; $\frac{1}{4}$; $\frac{1}{4}$
   b. (Individual experimental results)
12. TP: $\frac{1}{2}$; $\frac{1}{2}$
   EP: (Individual experimental results)
   a. (Suggested answer) C   b. B
13a. B   b. A   c. B   d. A

Level 3

1   Powers and Roots

Try It
9 ; 9 ; 3 ; 3

1. No. of blocks in one row of big square:
   $\sqrt{256}$ = 16
   No. of blocks in one row of medium square:
   $\sqrt{16}$ = 4
   No. of blocks in one row of small square:
   $\sqrt{4}$ = 2
   There are 2 blocks in one row.
2a. Alex's answer is better because it gives an exact answer without rounding.
   b. Doris found it in a more efficient way since it is easier to find the square roots of smaller numbers.
3a. $\sqrt{3}^2$ = 3 ; The answer is 3.
   b. $\sqrt{0.2137^2}$ = 0.2137 ; The answer is 0.2137.
4a. 36 = 2 x 2 x 3 x 3   81 = 3 x 3 x 3 x 3
   144 = 2 x 2 x 2 x 2 x 3 x 3
   210 = 2 x 3 x 5 x 7   500 = 2 x 2 x 5 x 5 x 5
   900 = 2 x 2 x 3 x 3 x 5 x 5
   b. 36, 81, 144, and 900 are perfect squares. Perfect squares have an even number of each prime factor.
5. 20 = 2 x 2 x 5
   The smallest possible integer is 5. Write 20 as a product of prime factors and see which prime factor there is an odd number of. The product of 20 and 5 is 100, which is a perfect square.
6. 2160 = 2 x 2 x 2 x 2 x 3 x 3 x 3 x 5
   Factors that are perfect squares:
   1
   2 x 2 = 4
   3 x 3 = 9
   2 x 2 x 2 x 2 = 16
   2 x 2 x 3 x 3 = 36
   2 x 2 x 2 x 2 x 3 x 3 = 144
   The factors are 1, 4, 9, 16, 36, and 144.
7. 25 x 80 = 2000
   44^2 = 1936 ← largest possible square
   45^2 = 2025
   2000 – 1936 = 64
   64 tiles will be left over.
8. 439 x 24 x 60 = 632 160 = 6.3216×10^5
   It is 6.3216×10^5 minutes.
9. 37 million x 1.26 = 46.62 million = 46 620 000
   = 4.662×10^7
   4.662×10^7 books are sold each year.
10. 755 billion = 755 000 million
   755 000 million ÷ 37 million = 20 405.41
   Each person would have to pay $20 405.41.

11a. $1.5 \times 10^8 \times 270\ 000 = 4.05 \times 10^{13}$
The distance is 4.05×10^{13} km.

b. $4.05 \times 10^{13} \div 4.28 = 9.46 \times 10^{12}$
1 light year is about 9.46×10^{12} km.

12. $(1.9 \times 10^{27}) \div (1.32 \times 10^{22}) = 143\ 939.39$
Jupiter is 143 939.39 times as heavy as Pluto.

13. $1.3 \times 10^9 \div 1000 = 1\ 300\ 000 = 1.3 \times 10^6$
1 300 000 or 1.3×10^6 times as many people live in India as in Vatican City.

14. 3.7 million $\times 2^2 = 14.8$ million $= 1.48 \times 10^7$
1.48×10^7 visitors are expected in 2026.

15. $600 \times 2^4 = 9600$
There will be 9600 mites.

16a. 1.21 m$^2 = 12\ 100$ cm^2
$12\ 100 \div 4.84 = 2500$
The area on the blueprint is 2500 times as small.

b. 9 m$^2 = 90\ 000$ cm^2
$90\ 000 \div 2500 = 36$
The area on the blueprint is 36 cm^2.

2   Fractions

Try It
$16 ; 5 ; 8\frac{1}{20} ; 8\frac{1}{20}$

1. $2\frac{1}{2} \times 5\frac{3}{5} = \frac{\cancel{5}^1}{\cancel{2}_1} \times \frac{\cancel{28}^{14}}{\cancel{5}_1} = 14$
She spent \$14.

2. $\frac{8}{25} (= \frac{32}{100}) < \frac{7}{20} (= \frac{35}{100})$
$\frac{35}{100} - \frac{32}{100} = \frac{3}{100}$
Conner has a better batting average by $\frac{3}{100}$.

3. $2\frac{3}{5} \div \frac{1}{4} = \frac{13}{5} \times \frac{4}{1} = 10\frac{2}{5}$
Her speed was $10\frac{2}{5}$ km/h.

4. $\frac{3}{7} \times 3\frac{1}{2} = \frac{3}{\cancel{7}_1} \times \frac{\cancel{7}^1}{2} = 1\frac{1}{2}$
There is $1\frac{1}{2}$ L of orange juice.

5a. $250 \times \frac{3}{10} = 75$
It takes him 75 minutes to plant 250 flowers.

b. $20 \div \frac{3}{10} = 66\frac{2}{3}$
He can plant 66 flowers.

c. Time saved when planting 1 flower:
$\frac{3}{10} - \frac{1}{4} = \frac{1}{20}$
Total time saved: $250 \times \frac{1}{20} = 12\frac{1}{2}$
He will save $12\frac{1}{2}$ minutes.

6. Half-pound: $\$3 \div \frac{1}{2}$ lb $= \$6$/lb
Three-eighth-pound: $\$2 \div \frac{3}{8}$ lb $= \$5\frac{1}{3}$/lb
The three-eighth-pound hamburger is a better deal.

7. Pizza Uno: $\$3 \div \frac{2}{3}$ pizza $= \$4\frac{1}{2}$/pizza
Pizza Duo: $\$4 \div \frac{3}{4}$ pizza $= \$5\frac{1}{3}$/pizza
Pizza Uno charges $\$4\frac{1}{2}$ for a whole pizza and Pizza Duo charges $\$5\frac{1}{3}$.

8. Gasoline consumed: $8 \div 100 \times 75 = 6$
Carbon dioxide: $6 \times 2\frac{1}{2} = 15$
The car produces 15 g of carbon dioxide.

9. $12 \times 8\frac{1}{2} + 12 \times 1\frac{1}{2} \times 3 = 156$
He earns \$156.

10a. $\$3300 \times (\frac{2}{15} + \frac{1}{12}) = \$715$
They donated \$715 altogether.

b. Administrative cost: $\$3300 \times \frac{1}{20} = \$165$
Seniors' home: $(\$3300 - \$165) \times \frac{10}{19} = \$1650$
The seniors' home will receive \$1650.

11a. $\$40\frac{19}{20} - \$1\frac{13}{20} = \$39\frac{3}{10}$
Each share increased in value by $\$39\frac{3}{10}$.

b. $\$39\frac{3}{10} \times 100 = \$3930$
He made \$3930 in profit.

c. $\$1\frac{13}{20} = \$1.65$ $\$40\frac{19}{20} = \$40.95$
1 Corel share was worth \$1.65 in September 2018 and \$40.95 in November 2019.

12a. $\frac{1}{2} \div 3 \times 5 = \frac{5}{6}$
The jug is $\frac{5}{6}$ full.

b. $1200 \times \frac{1}{2} \div 3 = 200$
One glass can hold 200 mL.

13a. $1\frac{1}{3} + 1\frac{1}{6} + \frac{5}{8} + 1\frac{1}{4} = 4\frac{3}{8}$
The total length is $4\frac{3}{8}$ km.

b. $1\frac{1}{4} \div 4\frac{3}{8} = \frac{2}{7}$
Section D takes up $\frac{2}{7}$ of the trail.

c. $(\frac{5}{8} + 1\frac{1}{4}) \times \frac{1}{2} = \frac{15}{16}$
Using the shortcut saves $\frac{15}{16}$ km.

14a. Eggs: $2 \div 4 = \frac{1}{2}$ Flour: $\frac{1}{2} \div 4 = \frac{1}{8}$
Milk: $\frac{1}{3} \div 4 = \frac{1}{12}$ Butter: $1\frac{1}{2} \div 4 = \frac{3}{8}$
Sugar: $\frac{3}{4} \div 4 = \frac{3}{16}$
$\frac{1}{2}$ egg, $\frac{1}{8}$ cup of flour, $\frac{1}{12}$ cup of milk, $\frac{3}{8}$ tbsp of butter, and $\frac{3}{16}$ tbsp of sugar are needed to make 1 crepe.

b. Eggs: $\frac{1}{2}$ x 6 = 3   Flour: $\frac{1}{8}$ x 6 = $\frac{3}{4}$

Milk: $\frac{1}{12}$ x 6 = $\frac{1}{2}$ Butter: $\frac{3}{8}$ x 6 = $2\frac{1}{4}$

Sugar: $\frac{3}{16}$ x 6 = $1\frac{1}{8}$

3 eggs, $\frac{3}{4}$ cup of flour, $\frac{1}{2}$ cup of milk, $2\frac{1}{4}$ tbsp of butter, and $1\frac{1}{8}$ tbsp of sugar are needed to make 6 crepes.

3 Decimals

Try It

$0.05 x 2469 = $123.45 ; 123.45

1. Line A: 2 + 0.05 + 0.017 = 2.067
   Line B: 3 + 0.2 + 0.02 = 3.22
   Difference: 3.22 − 2.067 = 1.153
   The difference is 1.153 m.

2. 0.00002 x 500 = 0.01
   Its length is 0.01 cm.

3a. $7.99 x 5 + $0.75 x 8 + $0.55 x 24 + $0.49 x 12
   = $65.03
   The total cost is $65.03.

b. $65.03 ÷ 25 = $2.6012
   Each student would pay $2.60.

4. $(2.4 \times 10^{19}) \div (9.46 \times 10^{12}) = 0.254 \times 10^7$
   = 2 540 000
   The distance is about 2 540 000 light years.

5a. $14.95 x 10 = $149.50
   The total cost is $149.50.

b. $14.95 x 7 + $14.95 ÷ 2 x 3 = $127.075
   The total cost is $127.08.

6. 14.25 x 3.5 + 16.50 x 4.5 = 124.125
   She earned $124.13.

7a. $60.50 + $15.25 x 45 = $746.75
   The total cost was $746.75.

b. $746.75 ÷ 45 = $16.59
   Each student had to pay $16.59.

8. Total cost: $30 x 3 + $0.1 x 1000 = $190
   Cost per person: $190 ÷ 4 = $47.50
   Each person would pay $47.50.

9a. ($0.15 − $0.12) x 75 = $2.25
   They will save $2.25 per month.

b. $2.25 x 12 = $27
   They will save $27 annually.

10a. Total: $0.25 x 5 + $0.10 x 7 + $0.05 x 8 = $2.35
   No. of candy bars: $2.35 ÷ $0.55 = 4.27
   He can buy 4 candy bars.

b. $2.35 ÷ $0.85 = 2.76
   He can buy 2 lollipops.

11. $125.50 − $35 − $32.95 − $19.95 − $18.50 = $19.10
   He spent $19.10 on that gift.

12. (0.141 + 0.098 + 0.118) ÷ 3 = 0.119
   The mean distance travelled each day was 0.119 km.

13a. 17.50 x 3.5 + 19.35 x 3.5 = 128.975
   Their employer will pay $128.98 in total.

b. (19.35 − 17.50) x 3.5 = 6.475
   Jacky will earn $6.48 more.

14a. (0.2 + 0.35) x 15 = 8.25
   He needs 8.25 kg of candy in all.

b. Red candy: 1.6 ÷ 0.2 = 8
   Green candy: 3.15 ÷ 0.35 = 9
   Yes, there will be enough for 8 party bags.

c. Red candy: 3 ÷ 0.2 = 15
   Green candy: 3 ÷ 0.35 = 8.57
   Red candy remaining: 3 − 0.2 x 8 = 1.4
   Green candy remaining: 3 − 0.35 x 8 = 0.2
   He can fill 8 party bags. 1.4 kg of red candy and 0.2 kg of green candy will be left over.

4 Percents

Try It

9.10 ; 9.10

1. $26 500 x 8% = $2120 ; 2120

2. $180 + $180 x 9% = $196.20 ; 196.20

3. $3600 + $3600 x 20% = $4320 ; 4320

4. $106 000 − $106 000 x 7% = $98 580
   $98 580 + $98 580 x 7% = $105 480.60
   $105 480.60

5a. $220   b. $8.80

6. 300 ÷ 50 000 = 0.6%
   0.6% of the units are defective.

7. 7200 x 27% = 1944
   1944 books are hardcover.

8. $700 x 35% = $245
   She spends $245 on utilities.

9. $110 ÷ $550 = 20%
   He withdrew 20% of his money.

10. $2000 x 2.4% x 3 + $1500 x 2.8% x 3 = $270
   He will receive $270.

11. 21 ÷ 60% = 35
   There are 35 students.

12. ($699.99 + $599.99) x 15% = $194.997
   They will save $195.

13. ($1 − $0.75) ÷ $1 = 25%
   The toy decreased by 25% in cost.

14a. ($10 − $7.50) ÷ $7.50 = 33.3%
   The cost increased by 33.3%.

b. $10 + $5.70 + $5.70 x 33.3% = $17.60
   He would pay $17.60.

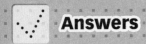

15a. $(12\,811\,000 - 10\,256\,000) \div 10\,256\,000 = 24.9\%$
The number of vehicles increased by 24.9%.

b. $12\,811\,000 + 12\,811\,000 \times 24.9\% = 16\,000\,939$
There were 16 000 939 vehicles.

c. $10\,256\,000 - 10\,256\,000 \times 75\% = 2\,564\,000$
2 564 000 vehicles would still be in service.

16. $\$5750 \div 5\% = \$115\,000$
He sold a total value of $115 000.

17. Percent increase: $(65¢ - 50¢) \div 50¢ = 30\%$
Price of milk: $\$3.29 + \$3.29 \times 30\% = \$4.277$
The price of a bag of milk would be $4.28.

18. Mr. Singh: $\$2520 \times 7\frac{1}{2}\% \times 2\frac{1}{2} = \$472.50$

Mrs. Brown: $\$2720 \times 7\% \times 2\frac{1}{2} = \$476$

Mrs. Brown earned more interest.

19. $\$70 \div 20\% = \$350$
His weekly pay was $350.

20a. $(5942 - 926) \div 5942 = 84.4\%$
It decreased by 84.4%.

b. $(197\,907 - 121\,679) \div 197\,907 = 38.5\%$
It decreased by 38.5%.

5 Ratios, Rates, and Proportions

Try It
15 ; 15 ; 3:4 ; 3:4

1a. 150:950 = 3:19
The ratio is 3:19.

b. $\dfrac{3}{19} = \dfrac{x}{2.85}$
$x = 0.45$
0.45 L of lemonade will be mixed.

2. $\dfrac{3}{2+3} = \dfrac{x}{1500}$
$5x = 1500 \times 3$
$x = 900$
Helen gets $900.

3. $\dfrac{5}{3+5} = \dfrac{45}{x}$
$5x = 45 \times 8$
$x = 72$
72 combos were sold.

4. $\dfrac{16}{100-16} = \dfrac{12.8}{x}$
$16x = 12.8 \times 84$
$x = 67.2$
The sale price is $67.20.

5. 45%:100% – 45%
= 45:55
= 9:11
The ratio is 9:11.

6. $4\frac{1}{2}$ h = 270 min
$\dfrac{20}{30} = \dfrac{x}{270}$
$x = 180$
180 letters can be delivered.

7. $\dfrac{6}{32} = \dfrac{x}{48}$
$x = 9$
9 L of honey can be collected.

8. Highway speed: $62 + 62 \times 50\% = 93$
Ratio: 62:93 = 2:3
The ratio is 2:3.

9. Bestmart: $\$4.41 \div 3$ kg = $1.47/kg
ABC Mart offers a better buy.

10. $\dfrac{1.2}{7.5} = \dfrac{x}{100}$
$x = 16$
16 m² of carpet can be purchased.

11. 20 gems: $\$5.99 \div 20$ gems = $0.2995/gem
50 gems: $\$12.99 \div 50$ gems = $0.2598/gem
50 gems is a better buy.

12a. $\dfrac{25}{2} = \dfrac{x}{3}$
$x = 37.5$
She can cycle 37.5 km.

b. $\dfrac{25}{2} = \dfrac{40}{x}$
$x = 3.2$
It takes 3.2 h.

13. $\dfrac{27}{15} = \dfrac{x}{60}$
$x = 108$
He would count 108 beats.

14. Barbara: $12 \div 9 = 1.33$ (calls/day)
Lydia: $7 \div 5 = 1.4$ (calls/day)
Lydia made more calls per day.

15. Team Tiger: $7 \div (7 + 5) = 58.3\%$
Team Wolf: $5 \div (3 + 5) = 62.5\%$
Team Wolf has a higher win percentage.

16a. $1460 \times 3.5 = 5110$
It travels 5110 m.

b. $292\,000 \div 1460 = 200$
It takes 200 s.

17. Speed (m/s): 13.3 ; 12.3 ; 19.5
Rank: 2 ; 3 ; 1

18. $\$37.50 \div 3 \times 5 = \$62.50$
He will earn $62.50.

19. Jo: 100 m $\div$ 13 s = 7.7 m/s
Ken: 500 m $\div$ 60 s = 8.3 m/s
Leo: 200 m $\div$ 25 s = 8 m/s
Ken is the fastest.

20a. $30 \div 12.5 = 2.4$
It takes 2.4 s.

b. $\dfrac{12}{16} = \dfrac{x}{50}$
$x = 37.5$
It appears to be 37.5 m tall.

c. $\dfrac{12}{16} = \dfrac{15}{x}$
$x = 20$
The model is 20 cm tall.

21. Amy: $2 \times 52 = 104$ (books/year)
Beth: $7 \times 12 = 84$ (books/year)
Connie: 90 (books/year)
Debbie: $\dfrac{1}{4} \times 365 = 91.25$ (books/year)
The girls who read the fewest books to the one who read the most are: Beth, Connie, Debbie, Amy.

22. $\dfrac{5}{20} = \dfrac{x}{56}$
$x = 14$
The lake should be 14 cm long.

23a. $\dfrac{2}{3} = \dfrac{x}{36}$ b. $\dfrac{2}{3} = \dfrac{12}{x}$

   $x = 24$ $x = 18$

   There are 24 fire   I have to walk
   hydrants.   18 city blocks.

6   Integers

Try It

-8 ; -8°C

1a. Townsville: -5 – (12) = -17
   The temperature change was -17°C.
   Pleasantville: -3 – (15) = -18
   The temperature change was -18°C.

  b. Day temperature: (12 + 15) ÷ 2 = 13.5
   The average day temperature was 13.5°C.
   Night temperature: (-5 + (-3)) ÷ 2 = -4
   The average night temperature was -4°C.

  c. Townsville to Pleasantville at night:
   -3 – (-5) = 2
   The temperature change was +2°C.
   Townsville during the day to Pleasantville
   at night: -3 – (12) = -15
   The temperature change was -15°C.

2. -5 – (-15) = 10
   The original temperature was 10°C.

3a. 7 – (-15) = 22
   The difference is 22°C.

  b. ((-15) + 7) ÷ 2 = -4
   The average temperature is -4°C.

4. ((-2) + 3 + 5 + (-1) + 7 + (-5) + 4) ÷ 7 = 1.6
   The average temperature was 1.6°C.

5. ((-3) x 5 + (-7) x 2) ÷ 7 = -4.1
   The average temperature was -4.1°C.

6. -5 + (-2) x 7 = -19
   The temperature was -19°C.

7. (-$30.90) + ($27.50) + (-$122.25) = -$125.65
   The overall change was -$125.65.

8a. Time difference: +8 – (-5) = +13
   Hong Kong: 6 + 13 = 19 = 7 p.m.
   It is 7 p.m. in Hong Kong.

  b. Time difference: -10 – 10 = -20
   Honolulu: 12 + (-20) = -8 = 4 p.m. Sunday
   It is 4 p.m. on Sunday.

9a. The Consumer Index showed the greatest
   increase.

  b. The Oil & Gas Index showed the greatest
   decrease.

  c. 7625.31 – (-21.35) = 7646.66
   The value was 7646.66.

  d. 8132.43 – (32.43) = 8100
   The value was 8100.

10a. The wind chill index is -22°C.

  b. An air temperature of -4°C and a wind
   speed of 24 km/h or an air temperature of
   -7°C and a wind speed of 16 km/h produce
   a wind chill index of -17°C.

  c. The air temperature is -9°C.

  d. The minimum wind speed is 40 km/h.

11. 4 x 2 – (-10) = 18
   The other integer is 18.

7   Circles

Try It

3.14 ; 3.14

1. Radius: 63 ÷ 2 ÷ 3.14 = 10.03
   Area: 3.14 x (10.03)^2 = 315.89
   The area is 315.89 cm^2.

2a. 10 x 6 = 60
   The perimeter is 60 cm.

  b. 2 x 3.14 x 10 = 62.8
   The circumference is 62.8 cm.

3a. 3.14 x (10 ÷ 2)^2 = 78.5
   The area is 78.5 cm^2.

  b. 3.14 x (30 ÷ 2)^2 – 78.5 = 628
   The area is 628 cm^2.

  c. 3.14 x (60 ÷ 2)^2 – 628 – 78.5 = 2119.5
   The area is 2119.5 cm^2.

  d. 60^2 – 2119.5 – 628 – 78.5 = 774
   The area is 774 cm^2.

4a. 3.14 x 10^2 = 314
   The area is 314 cm^2.

  b. 2 x 3.14 x 10 = 62.8
   62.8 cm of fringe is required.

5. 3.14 x 6^2 – 3.14 x 5^2 = 34.54
   The area is 34.54 m^2.

6. 8^2 – 3.14 x 3^2 = 35.74
   The area is 35.74 m^2.

7a. Dotted ring: 3.14 x 7.5^2 – 3.14 x 2.5^2 = 157
   Smallest circle: 3.14 x 2.5^2 = 19.625
   157 ÷ 19.625 = 8
   It is 8 times.

  b. Striped ring: 3.14 x 15^2 – 3.14 x 7.5^2 = 529.875
   529.875 ÷ 157 = 3.375
   It is 3.375 times.

8. Radius: $\sqrt{2 \div 3.14}$ = 0.8
   Circumference: 2 x 3.14 x 0.8 = 5.024
   She needs 5.024 m of trimming.

9. 3.14 x 4^2 – 2 x 3.14 x 2^2 = 25.12
   The area is 25.12 cm^2.

10. 6^2 – 3.14 x 3^2 ÷ 2 = 21.87
   The total area is 21.87 cm^2.

11. $2 \times 1 + 3.14 \times (1 \div 2)^2 \div 2 = 2.3925$
    The area is 2.3925 m².
12. Case A: $40^2 - 3.14 \times 5^2 \times 16 = 344$
    Case B: $40^2 - 3.14 \times 10^2 \times 4 = 344$
    Yes, the amount of waste is the same.
13. Triangular area: $2 \times 2 \div 2 = 2$
    Shaded area: $3.14 \times 2^2 \div 4 - 2 = 1.14$
    The shaded area is 1.14 m².
14. Rectangular pool: $6 \times 10 = 60$
    Radius of circular pool: $\sqrt{60 \div 3.14} = 4.37$
    Diameter of circular pool: $4.37 \times 2 = 8.74$
    The diameter of the circular pool is 8.74 m.
15. Radius: $\sqrt{36} = 6$
    Area of shaded quarter-circle: $\pi \times 6^2 \div 4 = 9\pi$
    The area is 9π cm².
16. $6\pi \div \pi \div 2 = 3$
    The radius is 3 units.
17. $100 \div \pi \div 2 = \dfrac{50}{\pi}$
    The radius is $\dfrac{50}{\pi}$ cm.
18. Radius of largest circle: $(5 + 5 + 3 + 3) \div 2 = 8$
    Area of largest circle: $\pi \times 8^2 = 64\pi$
    Area of Circles A and B: $\pi \times 5^2 + \pi \times 3^2 = 34\pi$
    Ratio: $64\pi : 34\pi = 32 : 17$
    The ratio is 32:17.
19. $2\pi(r + 10) - 2\pi r = 2\pi r + 20\pi - 2\pi r = 20\pi$
    The difference is 20π cm.
20. Upper path: $\dfrac{4\pi}{2} + \dfrac{4\pi}{2} = 4\pi$
    Lower path: $\dfrac{6\pi}{2} + \dfrac{2\pi}{2} = 4\pi$
    Ratio: $4\pi : 4\pi = 1 : 1$
    The ratio is 1:1.

8 Volume and Surface Area

Try It
4000 ; 200 ; 20 ; 20
1a. $10 \text{ L} = 10\,000 \text{ cm}^3$
    $10\,000 \div (20 \times 16) = 31.25$
    The height of the water is 31.25 cm.
 b. $1.5 \times 16 \times 20 = 480$
    The volume of the rock is 480 cm³.
2. $6 \div (3.14 \times 1^2) = 1.91 \text{ (m)} = 191 \text{ (cm)}$
    The depth of the water is 191 cm.
3. $2 \times 2.4 \div 2 \times 2 + 2 \times 3 + 2.6 \times 3 \times 2 = 26.4$
    26.4 m² of canvas is needed.
4a. $9.2 \times 8 \div 2 \times 2 + 9.2 \times 16 \times 3 = 515.2$
    The surface area is 515.2 cm².
 b. $9.2 \times 8 \div 2 \times 16 = 588.8$
    The volume is 588.8 cm³.

5a. Small bar: $3.6 \times 3.1 \div 2 \times 2 + 3.6 \times 20.7 \times 3 = 234.72$
    Large bar: $6 \times 5.2 \div 2 \times 2 + 6 \times 30 \times 3 = 571.2$
    234.72 cm² and 571.2 cm² of cardboard is needed.
 b. Small bar: $3.6 \times 3.1 \div 2 \times 20.7 = 115.506$
    Large bar: $6 \times 5.2 \div 2 \times 30 = 468$
    The volumes are 116 cm³ and 468 cm³.
 c. Small bar: $\$1.99 \div 116 = \$0.0172/\text{cm}^3$
    Large bar: $\$5.99 \div 468 = \$0.0128/\text{cm}^3$
    The large bar is a better buy.
6a. $6 \times 4 \times 2 + 8 \times 4 \times 2 + 8 \times 6 + 6 \times 4 \div 2 \times 2 + 5 \times 8 \times 2 = 264$
    264 m² of wood is needed.
 b. $6 \times 8 \times 4 + 6 \times 4 \div 2 \times 8 = 288$
    288 m³ of space is occupied by the shed.
7a. $2 \times 3.14 \times 3.4^2 + 2 \times 3.14 \times 3.4 \times 9.7 = 279.7$
    $2 \times 3.14 \times 5^2 + 2 \times 3.14 \times 5 \times 11.8 = 527.5$
    They are 279.7 cm² and 527.5 cm².
 b. $3.14 \times 3.4^2 \times 9.7 = 352.1$
    $3.14 \times 5^2 \times 11.8 = 926.3$
    The volumes are 352.1 cm³ and 926.3 cm³.
8a. A: $2 \times 3.14 \times 5^2 + 2 \times 3.14 \times 5 \times 15 = 628$
    B: $15 \times 10 \div 2 \times 2 + (10 + 15 + 18) \times 10 = 580$
    C: $9 \times 10 \div 2 \times 2 + (9 + 11 \times 2) \times 15 = 555$
    Container A has the largest surface area.
 b. A: $3.14 \times 5^2 \times 15 = 1177.5$
    B: $15 \times 10 \div 2 \times 10 = 750$
    C: $9 \times 10 \div 2 \times 15 = 675$
    Container A has the largest volume.
9. A: $3.14 \times 5^2 \div 2 \times 10 = 392.5$
    B: $(4^2 + 3.14 \times 2^2) \times 10 = 285.6$
    C: $(6 \times 2 + 2 \times 2) \times 10 = 160$
    The volumes are 392.5 cm³ for Container A, 285.6 cm³ for Container B, and 160 cm³ for Container C.
10. $3.14 \times 1.2^2 \times 1 = 4.5216 \text{ (m}^3) = 4521.6 \text{ (L)}$
    The volume of the water is 4521.6 L.
11. $5 \times 5 \times 1.5 - 3.14 \times 1.5^2 \times 1.5 = 26.9025$
    The volume is 26.9025 cm³.
12. V: $3.14 \times 3^2 \times 5 + 3.14 \times 3^2 \times 5 \div 2 = 211.95$
    S.A.: $3.14 \times 3^2 \times 2 + 2 \times 3.14 \times 3 \times 5 + 2 \times 3.14 \times 3 \times 5 \div 2 + 6 \times 5 = 227.82$
    The volume is 211.95 cm³ and the surface area is 227.82 cm².
13. $3.14 \times (12 - 1)^2 \times (30 - 1) = 11\,018.26$
    $11\,018.26 \text{ cm}^3 = 11.01826 \text{ L}$
    The capacity of the tank is 11.01826 L.

9 Angles

Try It

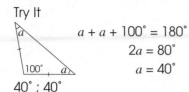

$$a + a + 100° = 180°$$
$$2a = 80°$$
$$a = 40°$$

40° ; 40°

1. $\angle EBC = \angle EBA + \angle ABC = 60° + 90° = 150°$
   $\angle EBC$ is 150°.

2. $\angle QPS + \angle TPR = 180° - \angle QPR = 180° - 60° = 120°$
   The sum is 120°.

3. $\triangle OAB$ is an isosceles triangle.
   $$2\angle OAB + 50° = 180°$$
   $$2\angle OAB = 130°$$
   $$\angle OAB = 65°$$
   $\angle OAB$ is 65°.

4. $A + C + E = 180°$
   $B + D + F = 180°$
   $A + B + C + D + E + F = 180° + 180° = 360°$
   The sum of the angles is 360°.

5. $a + 110° = 180°$ $b + 70° + 70° = 180°$
   $\quad\quad a = 70°$ $b = 40°$
   $c + c + 110° = 180°$
   $\quad\quad 2c = 70°$
   $\quad\quad c = 35°$
   a is 70°, b is 40°, and c is 35°.

6. $180° + 180° + 180° = 540°$
   The sum is 540°.

7. $180° \times 6 = 1080°$
   The sum is 1080°.

8a. A
  b. An isosceles triangle is created.
     $5.8 + 1.5 = 7.3$
     The height of the tree is 7.3 m.

9a. $a + 65° + 50° = 180°$
    $\quad\quad a = 65°$
    $b = a = 65°$
    $c + 65° + 55° = 180°$
    $\quad\quad c = 60°$
    a is 65°, b is 65°, and c is 60°.
  b. Since a is 65°, it is an isosceles triangle.
     d is 3 cm.

10. $\dfrac{x}{32} = \dfrac{10}{8}$
    $x = 40$
    The building is 40 m tall.

11. $x + 6x + x + 36° = 180°$
    $\quad\quad 8x = 144°$
    $\quad\quad x = 18°$
    $6x = 108°$
    $\angle R$ is 108°.

12. A and B are consecutive interior angles.
    $A + B = 180°$
    $\quad\quad B = 120°$
    $B \div 2 = 60°$
    $C = A = 60°$
    $D = B = 120°$
    $D \div 2 = 60°$

All triangles with three 60° angles are equilateral. So the field can be divided into 2 equilateral trangles – $\triangle ABD$ and $\triangle CBD$.

13. All quadrilaterals can be divided into 2 triangles by drawing a diagonal. The sum of the angles in 2 triangles is 360°.

14. Yes, it is possible. The angles at the centre can be found using the properties of opposite angles and supplementary angles. Diagonals of rectangles bisect each other so the remaining angles can be found through the properties of isosceles triangles.

15a. $\angle A + \angle B + \angle C = 180°$
       $\angle A + 2\angle A + 3\angle A = 180°$
       $\quad\quad\quad 6\angle A = 180°$
       $\quad\quad\quad \angle A = 30°$
     $\angle B = 60°$
     $\angle C = 90°$
  b. (Suggested drawing)

     AB is the longest side.
  c. The size of an angle corresponds to the length of its opposite side. The bigger the angle is, the longer the side is.

16. No, it is not possible. The last side would have to be 6 cm but $6 + 9 < 16$, meaning it would not connect to the other end of the 16-cm side.

10 Angles in Parallel Lines

Try It

175° ; No, the lines are not parallel because the sum of the interior angles is not 180°.

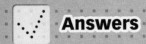

1. not parallel ; $60° + 130° = 190°$
   The sum of the interior angles is not 180°.
2. not parallel ; The corresponding angles are not equal.
3. parallel ; The alternate angles are equal.
4. parallel ; The corresponding angles are equal.
5. $x = y = 50°$ $x + y = 50° + 50° = 100°$
   The sum is 100°.
6. $a = 110°$ $60° + 110° = 170°$
   The lines are not parallel because the interior angles do not have a sum of 180°.
7. $a = f = 110°$
   $f + g = 180°$
   $g = 70°$
   a is 110°, f is 110°, and g is 70°.
8. Angles b, d, f, and h are the supplementary angles of Angle e.
9. $x = b$ by alternate angles
   $y = c$ by alternate angles
   $a + x + y = 180°$ by angles on a straight line
   So, $a + b + c = 180°$.
10a. $20° + 90° + a = 180°$
   $a = 70°$
   a is 70°.
   b. $\angle CDB = 10°$; No, they are not parallel. Their corresponding angles are not equal.
11a. PQ and SR are parallel lines because their interior angles have a sum of 180° (90° + 90°).
   b. "$\angle PQR$ and $\angle QRS$" and "$\angle SPQ$ and $\angle PSR$" are supplementary angles because they are the interior angles in parallel lines and the sum of each pair of angles is 180°.
   c. $\angle PQR + \angle QRS = 180°$
   $\angle SPQ + \angle PSR = 180°$
   Sum of the 4 angles: 180° + 180° = 360°
   The sum of the 4 angles is 360° because there are 2 pairs of supplementary angles.
12a. "$\angle ABD$ and $\angle BDC$" and "$\angle ADB$ and $\angle DBC$" are alternate angles.
   b. $\angle ABC$ and $\angle BCD$ are interior angles and have a sum of 180°.
   c. $\triangle ABD$ and $\triangle CDB$ are congruent because they share a side (BD) and have 2 pairs of equal sides (a property of parallelograms).
13. Draw Line BE to create 2 parallelograms.
   $\angle ABC = \angle ABE + \angle EBC$
   $\quad = \angle FEX + \angle XED$
   $\quad = \angle FED$

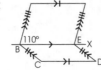

14. $\angle ABC = 60°$ by equilateral triangle
   $x + 90° + 60° = 180°$
   $x = 30°$
   x is 30°.
15. $70° + b = 180°$
   $b = 110°$
   b is 110°.
16a. $120° + d = 180°$ $100° + e = 180°$
   $d = 60°$ $e = 80°$
   d is 60° and e is 80°.
   b. $\angle EXD + e + d = 180°$
   $\angle EXD + 60° + 80° = 180°$
   $\angle EXD = 40°$
   $\angle EXD$ is 40°.
17. $\angle BCX + \angle XCD = \angle BCD$
   $\angle BCX + 90° = 140°$
   $\angle BCX = 50°$
   $\angle CBX + 50° + 90° = 180°$
   $\angle CBX = 40°$
   $\angle ABC = \angle CBX + 90° = 40° + 90° = 130°$
   $\angle ABC$ is 130°.
18a. $b = 85°$
   $a + 85° = 180°$
   $a = 95°$
   a is 95° and b is 85°.
   b. $100° + d = 180°$ $90° + 80° + g = 180°$
   $d = 80°$ $g = 10°$
   d is 80° and g is 10°.

11 Pythagorean Relationship

Try It
$4^2 + 5^2 = 41$ $6^2 = 36$
The sum of the squares of the two smaller sides does not equal the square of the longest side. It is not a right triangle.
1. A: $3^2 + 3.5^2 = 21.25$ $4^2 = 16$
   It is not a right triangle.
   B: $4^2 + 4^2 = 32$ $\sqrt{32}^2 = 32$
   It is a right triangle.
   C: $6^2 + 8^2 = 100$ $10^2 = 100$
   It is a right triangle.
   D: $3^2 + 5^2 = 34$ $6^2 = 36$
   It is not a right triangle.
2. Triangle B:
   Area: $4 \times 4 \div 2 = 8$ (cm²)
   Perimeter: $4 + 4 + \sqrt{32} = 13.66$ (cm)
   Triangle C:
   Area: $6 \times 8 \div 2 = 24$ (cm²)
   Perimeter: $6 + 8 + 10 = 24$ (cm)

3. $d^2 = 7^2 + 24^2$
   $d^2 = 625$
   $d = 25$
   The length of the diagonal is 25 m.

4. $c^2 = 3^2 + 3^2$ Perimeter:
   $c = \sqrt{18}$ $3 + 3 + \sqrt{18} = 10.24$
   The perimeter is 10.24 cm.

5. $32^2 + b^2 = 40^2$ Area: 32 x 24 = 768
   $b^2 = 576$
   $b = 24$
   The area is 768 m².

6. Side length: $\sqrt{36} = 6$
   $c^2 = 6^2 + 6^2$
   $c = 8.49$
   The length of the diagonal is 8.49 cm.

7. $a^2 + a^2 = 16^2$ Area: $\sqrt{128} \times \sqrt{128} = 128$
   $2a^2 = 256$ Perimeter: $4 \times \sqrt{128} = 45.25$
   $a^2 = 128$
   $a = \sqrt{128}$
   The area is 128 m² and the perimeter is 45.25 m.

8. $AC^2 = 8^2 + 8^2$ $AB^2 = \sqrt{128}^2 + \sqrt{128}^2$
   $AC = \sqrt{128}$ $AB = 16$
   The fence will be 16 m.

9. $AC^2 = 4^2 + 3^2$
   $AC = 5$
   Area of pad: $3.14 \times (5 \div 2)^2 - 4 \times 3 = 7.625$
   The area will be 7.625 m².

10. $h^2 + (4 \div 2)^2 = 4^2$ Area: $4 \times \sqrt{12} \div 2 = 6.93$
    $h = \sqrt{12}$
    The area is 6.93 m².

11. $AC^2 = 40^2 + 30^2$
    $AC = 50$
    Distance saved: 40 + 30 – 50 = 20
    He can save a distance of 20 m.

12a. $AC^2 = 3^2 + (4 + 4)^2$ $AB^2 + 2^2 = 4^2$
     $AC = \sqrt{73}$ $AB = \sqrt{12}$
     $BC = AC - AB = \sqrt{73} - \sqrt{12} = 5.08$
     The length of the window is 5.08 m.

   b. $3 \times (4 + 4) \div 2 - 2 \times \sqrt{12} \div 2 = 8.54$
      The area is 8.54 m².

13. Case 1 (if 9 cm is the longest side)
    $a^2 + 7^2 = 9^2$ Perimeter:
    $a = \sqrt{32}$ $\sqrt{32} + 7 + 9 = 21.66$
    Case 2 (if 9 cm is not the longest side)
    $c^2 = 7^2 + 9^2$ Perimeter:
    $c = \sqrt{130}$ $7 + 9 + \sqrt{130} = 27.4$
    The perimeter can be 21.66 cm or 27.4 cm.

14. $x^2 + 8^2 = 10^2$
    $x = 6$
    The distance is 6 m.

15. $AE^2 = 12^2 + 9^2$ $ED^2 = 3^2 + 4^2$
    $AE = 15$ $ED = 5$
    AD = AE + ED = 15 + 5 = 20
    AD is 20 cm.

16. $x^2 + 3^2 = 5^2$ Distance from top:
    $x = 4$ 10 – 4 = 6
    The distance from the top is 6 m.

17. $RP^2 = 3^2 + 4^2$
    $RP = 5$
    Area of shaded parts:
    $3.14 \times (5 \div 2)^2 \div 2 - 3 \times 4 \div 2 = 3.8125$
    The area is 3.8125 cm².

18. $AB^2 = 12^2 + (8 - 3)^2$
    $AB = 13$
    The distance is 13 m.

12 Coordinates and Transformations

Try It
17.21

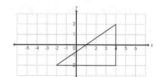

1.
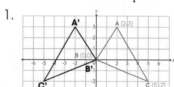

a. A'(-2,3), B'(0,0), C'(-5,-2)
b. $(5 \times 5 - 3 \times 2 \div 2 - 5 \times 2 \div 2 - 3 \times 5 \div 2) \times 2 = 19$
   The total area of the fields is 19 square units.

2.
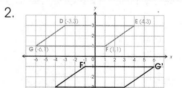

a. D'(3,-3), E'(-4,-3), F'(-1,-1), G'(6,-1)
b. 7 x 2 = 14
   The area of the rug is 14 square units.

3. (-1,0), (-2,-1), (-1,-3), (-3,-3), (-5,-2), (-5,0)

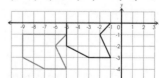

4. (Suggested answers)
a. translate 6 units to the left and 2 units down
b. rotate 180° about the origin
c. reflect in the x-axis

5a. The school's coordinates are (1,-2).

b. $\sqrt{4^2 + 5^2} = 6.4$

The school is 6.4 km from City Hall.

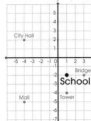

6a-b.

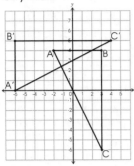

c. A(-4,7), B(1,7), C(1,-3)

d. AB = 20

BC = 20 ÷ 5 x 10 = 40

AC = $\sqrt{20^2 + 40^2}$ = 44.72

Total distance: 20 + 40 + 44.72 = 104.72

He has to travel 104.72 m.

e. 20 x 40 ÷ 2 = 400

The area is 400 m².

7. (Suggested answer)

Side length: 8 ÷ 4 = 2 (units)

The possible coordinates are (0,0), (0,2), (0,4), (2,0), (2,4), (4,0), (4,2), and (4,4).

8. The other possible coordinates are (0,0), (5,0), (5,-2), (-5,0), and (-5,-2).

9. (Suggested answers)

Way 1: Rotate 180° about the origin.

Way 2: Reflect in the x-axis and then reflect in the y-axis.

10a. The x-coordinate is one less than the y-coordinate in each point.

b. 3 x 4 = 12

The area is 12 square units.

13 Patterning

Try It

7 ; 10

3 ; 2 ; 28

1a. 1, 3, 6, 10, 15   b. 3, 6, 10, 15, 21

c. Frame 7 ; Frame 7

d. 9 ; 16 ; B

2a. 9 ; 16   b. $s = d^2$

c. 25 squares ; 49 squares

d. Diagram 6 ; Diagram 8

3a. 1, 3, 5, 7 ; A   b. 17 numbers

1, 3, 7, 13 ; B   c. 211

4. Yes, she will say the number 203.

5a. 25, 225, 625, 1225...

b. The next 4 numbers are 2025, 3025, 4225, 5625.

c. Start at 25. Add 200. Then add 200 more than the previous term each time.

6a. Each term is the sum of the two previous terms.

b. 21, 34, 55, 89, 144, 233, 377, 610

c. 6765 – 4181 = 2584

The term is 2584.

d. ①, ①, 2, ③, ⑤, 8, ⑬, ㉑, 34, ⑤⑤, ⑧⑨, 144, ㉝㉝, ㉝㉞, 610

Two odd numbers are followed by an even number in a repeating pattern.

7a. 2, 4, 8, 16, 32   b. There are 2^n layers.

c. 2^{10} = 1024

She will get 1024 layers.

d. 2^7 = 128

She will get 128 layers after 7 folds.

8.

4	5	6	7	n
1	2	3	4	$n - 3$
2	3	4	5	$n - 2$

9. 3, 5, 7, 9 ... → $2n + 1$ 2(51) + 1 = 103

4, 7, 10, 13 ... → $3n + 1$ 3(34) + 1 = 103

Yes, 103 will be the 51st term in Pattern A and the 34th term in Pattern B.

10. 0, 2, 2, 4, 6, 10, 16, 26, 42, 68, 110

The 2nd term is 2.

11. 3^7 has 8 (or 7 + 1) factors.

14 Linear Equations

Try It

$n - 5 + 7 = -20$

$n + 2 = -20$

$n = -22$

-22

1a. Let x be the third side.

$x + 3 + 6 = 13$

$x = 4$

The third side is 4 cm long.

b. Let x be the length of the other two sides.

$x + x + 7 = 13$

$x = 3$

The other two sides are 3 cm long each.

2a. $x + x + 2 + 10 = 24$

$2x = 12$

$x = 6$

$x + 2 = 8$

The sides are 6 cm, 8 cm, and 10 cm long.

b. $10 \times h \div 2 = 24$
$h = 4.8$
The height is 4.8 cm.

3. Let e be how long an elephant sleeps.
$2e - 1 = 8$
$2e = 9$
$e = 4.5$
An elephant sleeps for 4.5 hours.

4. Let k be how much Kate has.
$\frac{1}{2}k + 5 = 30$
$\frac{1}{2}k = 25$
$k = 50$
She has $50.

5. Let n be the cost of Nadine's gift.
$\frac{1}{2}n + 3.5 = 12$
$\frac{1}{2}n = 8.5$
$n = 17$
Her gift cost $17.

6. Let j be Jane's age.
$2j - 4 = 10$
$2j = 14$
$j = 7$
She is 7 years old.

7a. Let p be the number of pups in the first litter.
$1 + 2(p - 1) = 9$
$2(p - 1) = 8$
$p - 1 = 4$
$p = 5$
There were 5 pups in her dog's first litter.

b. $5 + 4 + 9 = 18$
Her dog had 18 pups altogether.

8a. Let c be the total cost.
$c = 4000 + 0.2 \times 40\ 000 = 12\ 000$
The total cost is $12 000.

b. Let d be the distance travelled.
$4000 + 0.2d = 8200$
$0.2d = 4200$
$d = 21\ 000$
He travelled 21 000 km.

9a. Let s be the number of tea bags in the smaller box.
$8s + 16 = 144$
$8s = 128$
$s = 16$
There are 16 tea bags in the smaller box.

b. Smaller box:
$0.75 \div 16$ tea bags = $0.0469/tea bag
Larger box:
$5.99 \div 144$ tea bags = $0.0416/tea bag
The larger box is a better buy.

10a. Let b be Bonnie's earnings.
$b = 225 \times 2 + 25 = 475$
Bonnie earns $475.

b. Let b be Betty's earnings.
$2b + 25 = 225$
$2b = 200$
$b = 100$
Betty earns $100.

c. $2n + 25$

11. Let r be the number of guests at Ron's party.
$2r + 10 = 48$
$2r = 38$
$r = 19$
19 guests attended Ron's party.

12. Let n be the original number.
$(n - 10) \div 2 = -11$
$n - 10 = -22$
$n = -12$
The original number was -12.

13. Let p be the world population in the year 1 CE (in billions).
$20p + 1.33 = 7.33$
$20p = 6$
$p = 0.3$
The population in the year 1 CE was 0.3 billion.

14. Let w be the width.
$2(w + w + 5) = 70$
$2w + 5 = 35$
$w = 15$
Length: $w + 5 = 20$
Area: $15 \times 20 = 300$
The area is 300 cm².

15a. Let t be the length of the rental time.
$25 + 5.25t = 40.75$
$5.25t = 15.75$
$t = 3$
The canoe rental is 3 hours long.

b. Let t be the length of the rental time.
$25 + 5.25t = 50$
$5.25t = 25$
$t = 4.76$
He can rent a canoe for 4 hours.

15 Graphs

Try It
The data is a census, and is a set of secondary and continuous data. A line graph is the most appropriate.

1a.

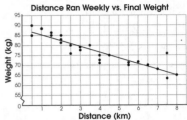

Distance Ran Weekly vs. Final Weight

b. As the distance ran each week increased, the final weight decreased.

c. The person would weigh about 70 kg.

2.

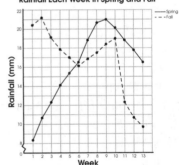

Votes for Each Candidate

a. The data is a census, and is a set of secondary and discrete data. A double bar group is used to compare boys' and girls' votes for each candidate.

b. Jane received almost twice as many votes from boys than girls.

c. Sarah received the most votes from girls. Alvis received the most votes from boys.

d. Alvis won with 73 votes.

3.

Rainfall Each Week in Spring and Fall

a. There are 2 sets of continuous data to be represented and compared, so a double line graph is the most appropriate.

b. There was about the same amount of rainfall in Week 6 of the seasons.

c. She would have enjoyed Week 9 in the spring or Week 2 in the fall most.

d. (Suggested answer)
There was about 15 mm of rain in the first week of summer and about 8 mm in the first week of winter.

4.

Weight (kg)	Frequency
30 – 39.9	5
40 – 49.9	4
50 – 59.9	5
60 – 69.9	3
70 – 79.9	3
80 – 89.9	3
90 – 99.9	2
100 – 109.9	2
110 – 119.9	3

Weights of Sheep

a. The data is a sample, and is a set of primary and continuous data.

b. Yes, it is appropriate to use a histogram because the data is continuous.

c. $5 \div 30 \times 800 = 133.3$
There are about 133 lambs.
$(2 + 3) \div 30 \times 800 = 133.3$
There are about 133 mature male sheep.

16 Probability

Try It
A ; $\frac{1}{4}$; $\frac{1}{4}$; $\frac{1}{4}$; $\frac{1}{4}$

1. C ; $P(A) = \frac{1}{8}$; $P(B) = \frac{1}{8}$; $P(C) = \frac{3}{8}$; $P(D) = \frac{3}{8}$

B ; $P(A) = \frac{1}{4}$; $P(B) = \frac{1}{4}$; $P(C) = \frac{1}{4}$; $P(D) = \frac{1}{4}$

A ; $P(A) = \frac{2}{5}$; $P(B) = \frac{1}{5}$; $P(C) = \frac{1}{5}$; $P(D) = \frac{1}{5}$

2. ✔ ; ✔ ; ✘ ; ✘ ; ✘ ; ✘

3a. The probability is $\frac{1}{2}$.

The probability is $\frac{1}{12}$.

The probability is $\frac{1}{6}$.

The probability is $\frac{1}{6}$.

Coin Dice Outcome
H: 1 — H,1; 2 — H,2; 3 — H,3; 4 — H,4; 5 — H,5; 6 — H,6
T: 1 — T,1; 2 — T,2; 3 — T,3; 4 — T,4; 5 — T,5; 6 — T,6

b. (Suggested answers)
Coin: flipping heads and flipping tails
Dice: rolling an odd number and rolling an even number

4a.

+	1	2	3	4	5	6
1	2	3	4	5	6	7
2	3	4	5	6	7	8
3	4	5	6	7	8	9
4	5	6	7	8	9	10
5	6	7	8	9	10	11
6	7	8	9	10	11	12

b. The probability is $\frac{5}{36}$.

The probability is $\frac{1}{6}$.

The probability is $\frac{11}{36}$.

5. The probability is $\frac{1}{2}$.

6a.

b.

c. Spinner A: $120 \times \frac{1}{5} = 24$

Spinner B: $120 \times \frac{1}{3} = 40$
$40 - 24 = 16$
She should expect it to stop on red 16 more times.

ASSESSMENT TESTS 1 AND 2

Test-taking Tips

Writing tests can be stressful for many students. The best way to prepare for a test is by practising! In addition to practising, the test-taking tips below will also help you prepare for tests.

Multiple-choice Questions

- Read the question twice before finding the answer.
- Skip the difficult questions and do the easy ones first.
- Come up with an answer before looking at the choices.
- Read all four choices before deciding which is the correct answer.
- Eliminate the choices that you know are incorrect.
- Read and follow the instructions carefully:
  - Use a pencil only.
  - Fill one circle only for each question.
  - Fill the circle completely.
  - Cleanly erase any answer you wish to change.

    e.g.

    ●   ⊗   ☑   ◉   ⊖
    correct   incorrect

Open-response Questions

- Read the question carefully.
- Highlight (i.e. underline/circle) important information in the question.
- Use drawings to help you better understand the question if needed.
- Find out what needs to be included in the solution.
- Estimate the answer.
- Organize your thoughts before writing the solution.
- Write in the space provided.
- Always write a concluding sentence for your solution.
- Check if your answer is reasonable.
- Never leave a question blank. Show your work or write down your reasoning. Even if you do not get the correct answer, you might get some marks for showing your work.

Multiple-choice Questions

① Which of the following is equal to 360?

- ○ $2^2 \times 3^2 \times 5^2$
- ○ $2^3 \times 3^2 \times 5^1$
- ○ $2^4 \times 3^1 \times 5^2$
- ○ $2^2 \times 3^3 \times 5^0$

② What is the correct way to put the following in scientific notation?

$276 million spent over 12 years

- ○ $\$2.3 \times 10^6$/year
- ○ $\$23 \times 10^6$/year
- ○ $23 million/year
- ○ $\$2.3 \times 10^7$/year

③ What are the GCF and LCM of 30 and 45?

- ○ GCF: 15
  LCM: 90
- ○ GCF: 15
  LCM: 30
- ○ GCF: 5
  LCM: 1350
- ○ GCF: 45
  LCM: 90

④ Which of the following can be expressed as a rational number?

- ○ $\sqrt{300} \div \sqrt{3}^2$
- ○ $\sqrt{2^2 + 3^2}$
- ○ $(\sqrt{4} \times \sqrt{8})^2$
- ○ $\sqrt{7^2 \times 41}$

⑤ What is the answer?

$$1\frac{1}{4} \times (\frac{4}{5} - \frac{1}{3}) \div (\frac{2}{3} + \frac{1}{2}) = ?$$

○ $8\frac{1}{2}$

○ $\frac{1}{2}$

○ $\frac{7}{36}$

○ $\frac{49}{72}$

⑥ What is the missing number?

$$(-4) + (-3) \times \boxed{} = 11$$

○ -5

○ -2

○ +2

○ +5

⑦ Kelly buys a video game at a discount of 15%. If the sales tax is 13%, how much does she pay?

$79.99

○ $76.83

○ $80.03

○ $102.39

○ $155.98

⑧ Which has the greatest answer?

○ $0.5 \times \frac{7}{10} + 1.2$

○ $(\frac{1}{2})^2 + (1.2)^2$

○ $2.8 \div 2\frac{1}{3} - 0.2$

○ $20 - 3\frac{1}{4} \times 5.6$

⑨ Which of the following does not describe the same circle as the rest?

○ radius = 1.5 cm

○ diameter = 4 cm

○ circumference = 12.56 cm

○ area = 12.56 cm²

⑩ What is the surface area of the cylinder?

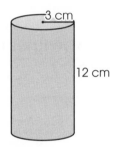

○ 56.52 cm²

○ 226.08 cm²

○ 254.34 cm²

○ 282.6 cm²

⑪ Which type of quadrilateral has diagonals that are always perpendicular bisectors?

○ trapezoids

○ rectangles

○ parallelograms

○ rhombuses

⑫ What is the missing side length? (Round to the nearest hundredth.)

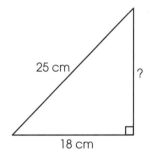

○ 17.35 cm

○ 24.64 cm

○ 25.46 cm

○ 30.81 cm

⑬ What are the values of x and y?

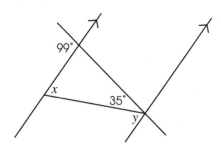

○ $x = 81°$
 $y = 35°$

○ $x = 64°$
 $y = 64°$

○ $x = 35°$
 $y = 99°$

○ $x = 81°$
 $y = 64°$

⑭ Below is a formula for a pattern in which t is the term and n is the term number.

$t = 3n + 1$

Which of the following is not a term in the pattern?

○ 7

○ 19

○ 26

○ 31

⑮ Which experimental probability is incorrect?

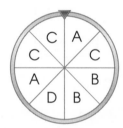

Frank spun the wheel 24 times and got 4 As, 8 Bs, 10 Cs, and 2 Ds.

○ $P(A) = \frac{1}{6}$

○ $P(B) = \frac{1}{3}$

○ $P(C) = \frac{5}{12}$

○ $P(D) = \frac{1}{8}$

Open-response Questions

⑯ Find the sum of the shaded angles. Show your work.

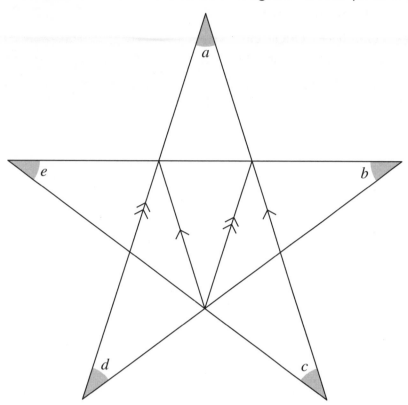

⑰ Taylor cut a triangular prism out of a cylinder. The volume of the triangular prism is a quarter of the original cylinder. Including the newly created inner surfaces, what is the surface area of the remaining cylinder?

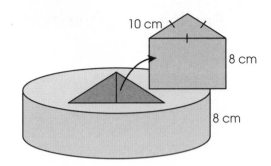

⑱ Mr. Lee recorded the cost of each meal sold in his restaurant last Friday and displayed the results in a histogram.

What range of the cost accounted for 50% of the meals sold last Friday?

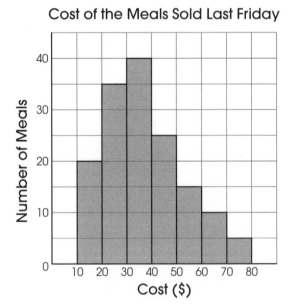

Cost of the Meals Sold Last Friday

Multiple-choice Questions

① Which is the correct way to arrange the following numbers from smallest to greatest?

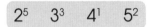

$$2^5 \quad 3^3 \quad 4^1 \quad 5^2$$

○ $2^5 > 3^3 > 4^1 > 5^2$

○ $4^1 > 5^2 > 3^3 > 2^5$

○ $4^1 < 5^2 < 3^3 < 2^5$

○ $2^5 < 3^3 < 4^1 < 5^2$

② Which is not a rational number?

○ $4.\overline{6}$

○ -8×10^{-2}

○ $\sqrt{12} \times \sqrt{3}$

○ $\sqrt{50}$

③ Which number is not written in scientific notation?

○ 0.98×10^4

○ 4.23×10^{-5}

○ 1.09×10^3

○ 8×10^{-2}

④ Which is equal to $0.8\overline{4}$?

○ $\dfrac{84}{100}$

○ $0.848484...$

○ $\dfrac{38}{45}$

○ $\dfrac{76}{84}$

⑤ What is the answer?

2.835 ÷ 0.42 x 3.52 = ?

○ 20.24

○ 23.76

○ 25.45

○ 67.50

⑥ What is the simple interest earned from $5000 at 2% per year for 4 years?

○ $40

○ $300

○ $400

○ $500

⑦ What is the cost of 9 plants?

5 plants for $15.95

○ $25.95

○ $28.71

○ $31.90

○ $35.44

⑧ What are the missing signs in order?

(☐ 3) ☐ (☐ 5) = ☐ 8

○ +, +, −, −

○ +, −, +, −

○ −, +, −, −

○ −, −, +, +

⑨ What is the total area of the shaded parts?

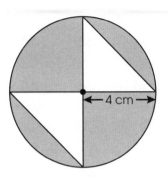

- ○ 16 cm²
- ○ 25.12 cm²
- ○ 34.24 cm²
- ○ 50.24 cm²

⑩ Which cylinder has the smallest volume?

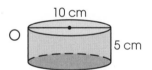

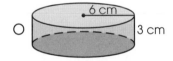

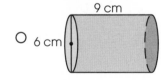

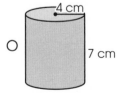

⑪ A pyramid has 9 faces and 16 edges. How many vertices does it have?

- ○ 8 vertices
- ○ 9 vertices
- ○ 11 vertices
- ○ 16 vertices

⑫ What is the simplified form of this expression?

$$\frac{48a^4b^4}{12a^2b^3} - (3a)(ab)$$

- ○ ab
- ○ a^2b
- ○ $7ab^2$
- ○ $\frac{4a}{b}$

⑬ Which quadrant on a Cartesian coordinate plane has negative *x*-coordinates and positive *y*-coordinates?

○ Quadrant I

○ Quadrant II

○ Quadrant III

○ Quadrant IV

⑭ What is *x*?

$$\frac{2}{3}x + 3 = 1.5x - 7$$

○ $\frac{5}{6}$

○ $8\frac{1}{3}$

○ 10

○ 12

⑮ What are the missing data values?

32	34	38	44
32	34	38	44
?	?	?	?
42	49	46	39

mean: 40   mode: 32
median: 40   range: 18

○ 41, 43, 43, 52

○ 32, 36, 50, 50

○ 32, 41, 45, 50

○ 40, 44, 46, 58

Open-response Questions

⑯ Prove that △ABC and △DEF are similar. Show your work.

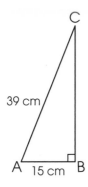 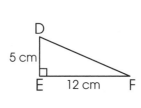

⑰ Joel and Billy are 50 m apart. If Joel moves 5 units to the right and 1 unit down and Billy moves 6 units to the left and 2 units up, what will the distance between Joel and Billy be?

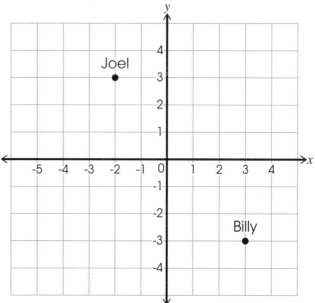

⑱ A vending machine sells water, pop, and juice. Drink sales are recorded every 2 hours. Plot the line for the juice sold on the graph.

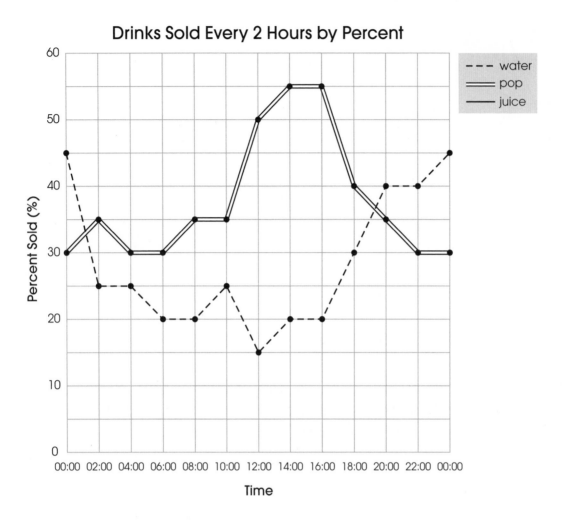

Drinks Sold Every 2 Hours by Percent

What time did each type of drink sell most?

Assessment Test 1

1. $2^3 \times 3^2 \times 5^1$
2. $\$2.3 \times 10^7$/year
3. GCF: 15
   LCM: 90
4. $(\sqrt{4} \times \sqrt{8})^2$
5. $\dfrac{1}{2}$
6. -5
7. $76.83
8. $20 - 3\dfrac{1}{4} \times 5.6$
9. radius = 1.5 cm
10. 282.6 cm²
11. rhombuses
12. 17.35 cm
13. $x = 64°$
    $y = 64°$
14. 26
15. $P(D) = \dfrac{1}{8}$
16.

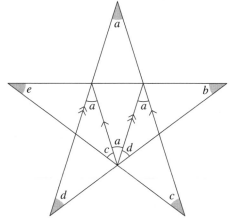

First find the equivalent angles of $\angle a$, $\angle c$, and $\angle d$ by corresponding angles. Then find the equivalent angle of $\angle a$ by alternate angles.

Finally, the angles $\angle b$, $\angle e$, and ($\angle c + \angle a + \angle d$) are the angles of a triangle, and thus have a sum of 180°.

So the sum of the shaded angles is 180°.

17. Height of the base of the triangular prism:
    $\sqrt{10^2 - (10 \div 2)^2} = \sqrt{75}$
    Volume of the triangular prism:
    $10 \times \sqrt{75} \div 2 \times 8 = 346.41$
    Volume of the original cylinder:
    $346.41 \times 4 = 1385.64$
    Radius of the cylinder:
    $\sqrt{1385.64 \div 8 \div 3.14} = 7.43$
    Surface area of the remaining cylinder:
    $2 \times 3.14 \times 7.43^2 + 2 \times 3.14 \times 7.43 \times 8 - 10 \times \sqrt{75} \div 2 \times 2 + 10 \times 8 \times 3 = 873.37$
    The surface area is 873.37 cm².

18. There was a total of 150 meals. 50% of the meals is 75 meals.
    The range of $20 to $40 accounted for 50% of the meals sold last Friday.

Assessment Test 2

1. $4^1 < 5^2 < 3^3 < 2^5$
2. $\sqrt{50}$
3. 0.98×10^4
4. $\dfrac{38}{45}$
5. 23.76
6. $400
7. $28.71
8. $-, +, -, -$
9. 34.24 cm²
10.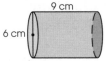
11. 9 vertices
12. a^2b
13. Quadrant II
14. 12
15. 32, 41, 45, 50
16. $BC^2 + 15^2 = 39^2$ $\qquad$ $DF^2 = 5^2 + 12^2$
    $\qquad$ $BC^2 = 1296$ $\qquad$ $DF^2 = 169$
    $\qquad\quad$ $BC = 36$ $\qquad\quad$ $DF = 13$

    $\dfrac{AB}{DE} = \dfrac{15}{5} = 3$

    $\dfrac{BC}{EF} = \dfrac{36}{12} = 3$

    $\dfrac{AC}{DF} = \dfrac{39}{13} = 3$

    The ratio of the three sides are the same, so $\triangle ABC$ and $\triangle DEF$ are similar.

17.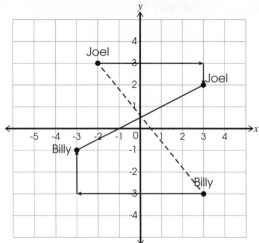

Current distance in units: $\sqrt{6^2 + 5^2} = \sqrt{61}$
New distance in units: $\sqrt{3^2 + 6^2} = \sqrt{45}$
Let x be the new distance in metres.

$\dfrac{x}{50} = \dfrac{\sqrt{45}}{\sqrt{61}}$

$\quad x = 50 \times \dfrac{\sqrt{45}}{\sqrt{61}}$

$\quad x = 42.94$

The distance will be 42.94 m.

18.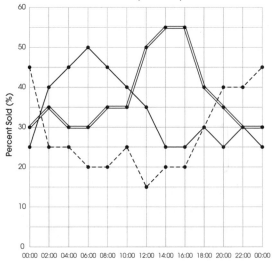

Water was sold most at 00:00, pop was sold most between 14:00 and 16:00, and juice was sold most at 6:00.